Cache la Poudre

Fall Mountain, in the Mummy Range, is one of the major sources of the Poudre's South Fork. *Courtesy of the U.S. Forest Service.*

CACHE LA POUDRE

The Natural History of a Rocky Mountain River

Howard Ensign Evans
and
Mary Alice Evans

UNIVERSITY PRESS OF COLORADO

Second Edition

The University Press of Colorado is a cooperative publishing enterprise supported, in part, by Adams State College, Colorado State University, Fort Lewis College, Mesa State College, Metropolitan State College, University of Colorado, University of Northern Colorado, University of Southern Colorado, and Western State College of Colorado.

The paper used in this publication meets the minimum requirements of the American National Standard for Information Sciences—Permanence of Paper for Printed Library Materials. ANSI Z39.48–1984

Library of Congress Cataloging-in-Publication Data

Evans, Howard Ensign.
Cache la Poudre: the natural history of a Rocky Mountain river / Howard Ensign Evans and Mary Alice Evans. — 1st ed.
p. cm.
Includes bibliographical references (p.) and index.
ISBN 0-87081-188-6 (alk. paper); ISBN 0-87081-301-3 (pbk., alk. paper)
1. Natural history — Colorado — Cache la Poudre River Region. 2. Stream ecology — Colorado — Cache la Poudre River. 3. Cache la Poudre River (Colo.) I. Evans, Mary Alice. II. Title.
QH105.C6E94 1991
508.788'68—dc20 90-13076
CIP

CONTENTS

PREFACE

On a map of North America, the Cache la Poudre River is but a wisp of a line running from the mountains of northern Colorado to the South Platte River. Even close up, it passes as a river only by the standards of the semiarid West. Yet it is the lifeline of the cities of Fort Collins and Greeley and of several other settlements within its watershed. And it is a perennial joy to those who like to fish, hunt, raft, hike, or simply seek in nature something they have lost in the mad scramble of the times.

As teachers of biology, we have long been attracted by the incredible diversity of the West, where so many remarkable plants and animals thrive in settings that defy description. To move to a home overlooking the canyon of the Cache la Poudre, as we did upon retirement a few years ago, was in a sense a homecoming (for we had dreamed of such a country) and in a sense a rebirth — finally we were free to become involved in the lives of plants and animals we had spent so many years talking about. But, being teachers, we still cannot resist communicating our enthusiasms. This book is the result.

Our major source of information has been the river itself and the country it drains, for we have spent many days wandering its banks and those of many of its tributaries, rafting a bit of the canyon during spring runoff, and now and then hauling trout from its pools. However, it would have been impossible to put our impressions into book form without the help of several people who were generous with ideas and references or who read part or all of the manuscript critically. We especially wish to thank John Barber, James E. Hansen, Barbara Mattingly, Paul Opler, Robert and Esther Swan, Robert and Dorothy Udall, J. V. Ward, Dieter Wilken, and the late David Harris. Many neighbors and friends who live in and enjoy the Poudre country have also been encouraging and helpful.

We have made much use of the libraries of Colorado State University, the Fort Collins City Library, the City Library and Museum of Greeley, and the Fort Collins libraries of the U.S. Forest Service and the Colorado Division of Wildlife. Marian Hershcopf, librarian of the Fort Collins offices of the Division of Wildlife, and Karen McWilliams, local history coordinator of the Fort Collins Library, have been especially helpful. Senator Timothy Wirth kindly copied for us certain congressional documents pertaining to the naming of the river.

For the use of photographs, we are indebted to Stephen Corn, David Leatherman, David Palmer, and Jack and Iola Revis. John Heaton and Cindy Rivera of the U.S. Forest Service gave us access to photographs in their files.

The drawings were made by Susan Strawn, a member of the Guild of Natural Science Illustrators, formerly an illustrator for the U.S. Fish and Wildlife Service and now curator of exhibits for the Loveland (Colorado) Museum and Gallery.

Parts of the text appeared in somewhat different form in *Colorado Outdoors*, in *Antaeus*, and in the book *On Nature*, edited by David Halpern and published by North Point Press. They are used here with permission.

HOWARD AND MARY ALICE EVANS
LIVERMORE, COLORADO

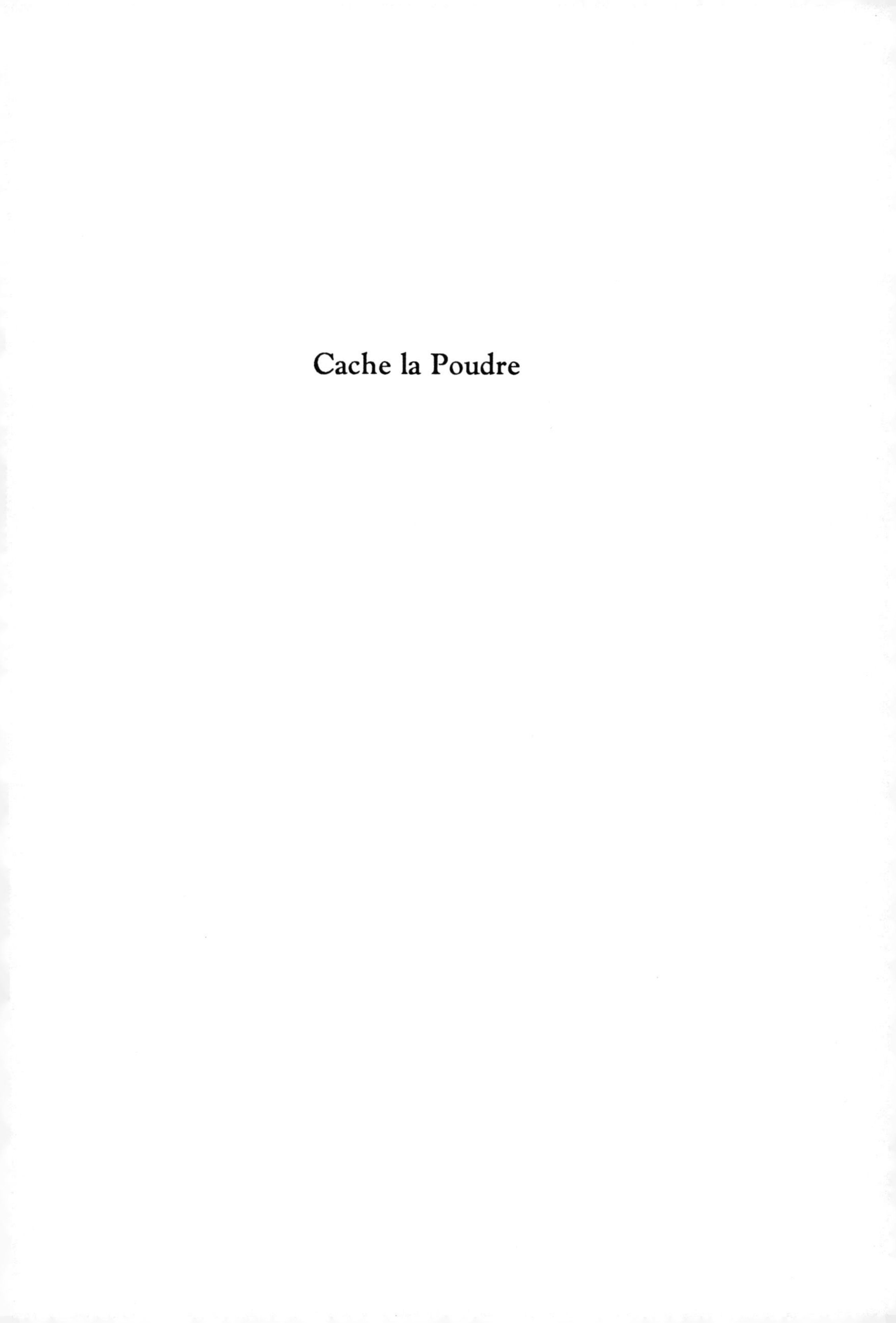

Cache la Poudre

1
THE SETTING

Approaching the foothills of the Rocky Mountains on July 12, 1842, in search of a new trail to the Far West, John C. Frémont, with Kit Carson as a guide and twenty-four others, mostly Canadian voyageurs, reached "a very beautiful mountain stream . . . flowing with a full swift current over a rocky bed. . . . In the upper part of its course, it runs amid the wildest mountain scenery." Frémont and his party headed north to Fort Laramie and saw little of the canyon of the Cache la Poudre, but in the following year, on their second expedition, they were back in what Frémont called an "uncertain and dangerous region . . . seldom visited, and little known." On July 29 the expedition "was compelled by the nature of the ground to cross the river eight or nine times," a laborious procedure, since they were carrying a howitzer as well as supplies for a long trip through unknown country.

"It was a mountain valley of the narrowest kind — almost a chasm," Frémont went on,

> and the scenery was very wild and beautiful. Towering mountains rose about; their sides sometimes dark with forests of pine, and sometimes with lofty precipices, washed by the river; while below, as if they indemnified themselves in luxuriance for the scanty space, the green river bottom was covered with a wilderness of flowers, their tall spikes sometimes rising above our heads as we rode among them. A profusion of blossoms on a white flowering vine [*Clematis*, or virgin's bower], which was abundant along the river, contrasted handsomely with the green foliage of the trees.
>
> The stream was wooded with cottonwood, boxelder, and cherry, with currant and serviceberry bushes. After a somewhat laborious day, during which it had rained incessantly, we encamped near the end of the pass at the mouth of a small creek, in sight of the great Laramie Plains.

It is clear from Frémont's description, and from his sighting of the Laramie Plains, that after entering the canyon, he had followed not the main stem of the Cache la Poudre but some distance of the North Fork, before continuing to the north. Frémont called the stream Cache à la Poudre and was the first to provide a description of a portion of it, but he was not the first to visit it. William Ashley had led a contingent of fur traders across the lower reaches of the river in February 1825, on his way to a rendezvous on the Green River, and in July 1835, Colonel Henry Dodge crossed the river with a company of dragoons. Undoubtedly trappers had roamed the area for beaver for some years earlier, but they left no records.

Ashley did not name the river in the journals of his 1825 expedition, but one of the men who accompanied him, Albert Gallatin Boone, a grandson of Daniel, reported that some of Ashley's supplies (including gunpowder) were hidden in a cache along the river while the party made short trading excursions in the area. The group included several French-Canadian guides and trappers, who evidently supplied the name for the river. Ashley's journals suggest that his camp lay further south, perhaps on the Little or Big Thompson River. So he either cached his supplies on a different river than that on which he camped, or the Cache la Poudre was misnamed by later arrivals.

One of the earliest settlers in the Poudre Valley, Antoine Janis, had a different story. According to the younger Janis, his father had helped dig the cache during November 1836, during an expedition of the American Fur Company that was delayed here because of a heavy snowstorm. It is this story that was picked up by the *Fort Collins Courier*, February 8, 1883, and later included in Ansel Watrous's widely cited *History of Larimer County, Colorado* (1911).

There are several reasons for questioning this story. The younger Janis was only twelve years old in 1836, and he admitted to seeing Colorado for the first time in the mid-1840s. Furthermore, the name of the river was known to Colonel Dodge a year before that. The Dodge Expedition's report to Congress states that on July 18, 1835, they "passed the mouth of the Cache-de-la-Poudre." It is probable that Frémont had read this report, and perhaps Boone's, before he planned his own expeditions. In her article on Janis in Leroy R. Hafen's series of books on the mountain men of the West, Janet Lecompte speaks of the "absurdities" of Janis's story, and Jeff Rennicke (in *The Rivers of Colorado*) remarks that Janis's story "is best told around a campfire far from a library or after a few rounds at the bar."

In 1910 the Daughters of the American Revolution erected a monument concerning the naming of the Cache la Poudre. It still stands along a road in Bellvue, just west of Fort Collins. The site was selected by a committee on the basis of available evidence, some early residents claiming to have remembered the hole left when the cache was removed. In any case the monument says "near this spot" and attributes the cache simply to "trappers," wisely leaving out specifics. The date given, 1836, is surely incorrect, since Dodge knew the name of the river a year before that.

In any case the exotic name suits the river well; no commonplace name would do for so fine a stream. Nowadays the river is usually called simply "the Poudre" (*poo*-der); but then, we live in a frenetic and unromantic age.

The Cache la Poudre is no longer the wild and rugged torrent of Frémont's time. Much of it is accessible by paved roads, and even its deepest recesses are not far from well-used trails. But still it is a river of great charm, small enough to be the object of very special attachment to those who know it well, large enough to embrace, with its many tributaries, a vast area of country — 1,900 square miles — that is home to a great many plants and animals and to ranchers and to people who simply like to live in or by the mountains, seeking inspiration in the snowy peaks and the limpid waters that drain them. And it was still sufficiently pristine that a major part of the river was designated a National Wild and Scenic River in 1986, the first in Colorado to be so named. It is by most standards a minor river — no more than a stream, really — but it is easy to love.

The mature Cache la Poudre, as it flows through Fort Collins and Greeley, the major cities of north central Colorado, represents a gathering of waters from hundreds of sources: from shallow gulleys that carry only occasional runoff from melting snow or summer cloudbursts to deep, wooded ravines loud with torrents racing to the plains. East of Greeley the Poudre joins the South Platte, a river that has already drained a major part of the Front Range of the Rockies via such tributaries as the Big Thompson, St. Vrain, Boulder Creek, Clear Creek, and its own major branches. It was at the junction of the South Platte with another tributary, Cherry Creek, that gold was discovered in 1858, beginning an immigration that, only 132 years later, has produced sprawling metropolitan Denver, where water to quench the thirst and grow the lawns of millions is now a more relevant quest than that for gold.

The Platte is a much maligned river, appropriately named the "flat river" by French-Canadian explorers. Loren Eiseley described it as "a curious stream . . . a rambling, dispersed series of streamlets flowing erratically over great sand and gravel fans." Eiseley nevertheless could not resist shedding his clothes and floating on the river for a time, "sliding down the vast tilted face of the continent [feeling] the cold needles of the alpine springs at my fingertips, and the warmth of the Gulf pulling me southward."

James Michener, whose novel *Centennial* is based on this part of Colorado, called the South Platte "a nothing river . . . a mile wide and an inch deep." When *Centennial* was filmed for television, production crews were headquartered in Greeley; the village of Orchard, east of Greeley, became "Centennial"; and mountain scenes were filmed in Poudre Canyon. The Blue Valley of Michener's novel was presumably inspired by the Cache la Poudre.

The South Platte valley provided a major route for immigrants, for it provided water, trees for shade and fuel, and a sure track to the mountains. To travelers weary of the endless plains, the mountains spoke of a different world. From a distance, in the morning light, they were the shining mountains, filled with promise. Close up, they were an apparition novel to eastern eyes, forested across the middle altitudes, bare and often snow-covered above, bare and arid below — both a lower and an upper treeline. Forests filled with game, streams with fish. Meadow-filled spaces in the forests here and there — mountain "parks," among the sweetest places to linger. The streams that poured onto the plains proved the keys to travel in the mountains; harnessed, they proved the keys to making the plains a place of ranches, gardens, and cities.

The Poudre, it was soon discovered, is a three-headed stream, with two major forks joining the main stem many miles from its source. The Poudre, including its South Fork, begins in what is now Rocky Mountain National Park and drains some of the high peaks that are the glory of that park. Natives tend to call the South Fork the "Little South," in

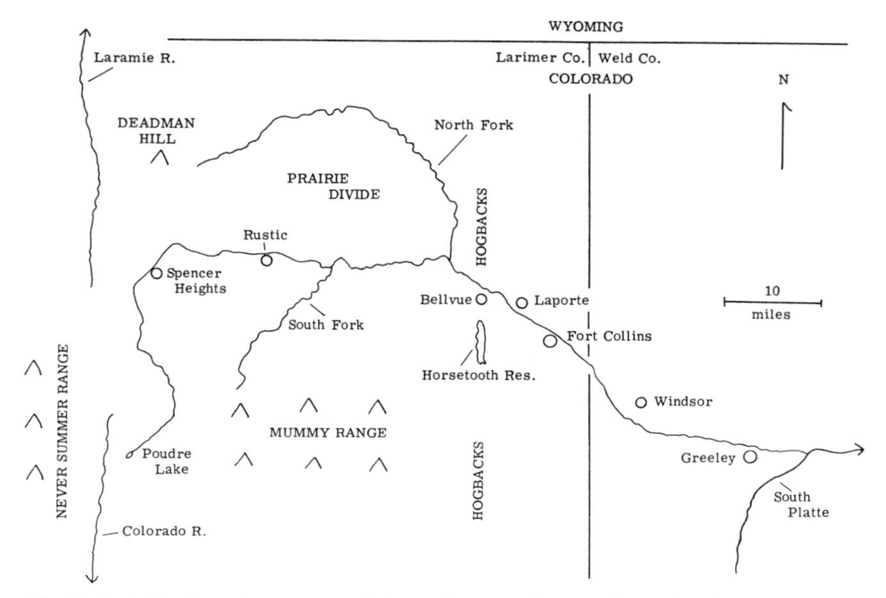

The Cache la Poudre and its two major forks, with cities, villages, and other landmarks indicated.

contrast to the upper parts of the Poudre itself, the "Big South." Many of the waters of the Poudre and its South Fork rise in the Mummy Range, which separates the Poudre and Big Thompson drainages. The highest point in the Mummy Range is Hague's Peak; at 13,560 feet it falls a bit short of the highest peaks in the Front Range.

The name "Mummy" seems singularly inappropriate for that imposing range, visible as it is for many miles to the east and to the north and south. Early visitors apparently saw a resemblance to a reclining Egyptian mummy (perhaps they were affected by the altitude!). There seems nothing dead or Egyptian about these mountains; they are very much alive and very Colorado.

The Arapahoes called them the White Owls, a name much more descriptive of their brooding, snowcapped crests. It is not certain who first called them the Mummies — it may have been Albert Bierstadt, who visited the area in 1876. Despite our admiration for Bierstadt's romanticized paintings of the Rockies, clearly the Arapahoes had better rapport with these mountains.

In contrast to the Poudre proper and its South Fork, both born in the tundra of the high peaks, the North Fork begins in forested country

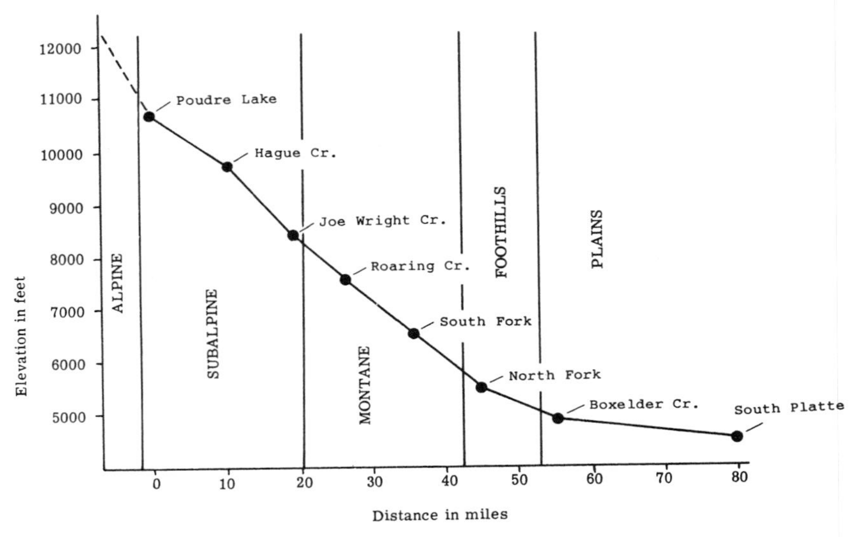

Profile of the Cache la Poudre River.

near Deadman Hill, at 10,700 feet elevation not quite breaking treeline. The North Fork follows a gentle gradient through rolling hills, finally entering the Poudre not far from its exit onto the plains. Although the North Fork drains a vast area, this is not an area of permanent snows or substantial rainfall, and many of its tributaries are small or intermittent. It is a leisurely stream, seemingly content to take its time before joining the more impetuous main stem of the Cache la Poudre, already augmented by the equally impetuous South Fork.

For the past fifteen years, we have lived near the Poudre and have spent many days exploring the river and its surroundings. Our house stands on a small granite cliff at 7,800 feet elevation, overlooking several of the valleys the Poudre and its tributaries have carved. From our deck we can look down on some of the headwaters of Gordon Creek and beyond them to the deep ravine of Elkhorn Creek. Farther still we can see the canyon the Poudre itself has sliced through the mountains; and yet farther the complex system of valleys in the drainage of the South Fork, beginning in the rugged terrain and ice fields of the Mummy Range. From our aerie we watch the seasons follow one another. Yet each day is different: today a storm on the distant peaks, a golden eagle coursing the valley below, the first tint of green in the aspens; tomorrow — we'll see.

Strata in the ancient metamorphic rocks along Poudre Canyon are often twisted in odd ways.

A Geological Perspective

Persons of European extraction have lived in the Poudre basin for less that two hundred years, native Americans (whom through a misunderstanding we call Indians) for perhaps eleven thousand years. Native plants and animals have lived here very much longer than that, and before them other kinds, long since extinct. The Rockies themselves are very old indeed. Their oldest rocks are believed to be about 1.8 billion years old, more than a third as old as the earth itself. These ancient metamorphic rocks have been greatly altered from their original form by the action of pressure and heat over long periods of time. They frequently have a layered appearance, but the layers are often upright or twisted and irregular. The original rocks were mainly sedimentary, chiefly shales and sandstones, but they have been transformed into schists of several kinds, with here and there veins formed by later intrusions of lighter colored granite or of very dark basalt. Schists are brittle rocks in which some layers are more resistant to erosion than others. So they often erode to form jagged cliffs and pinnacles with crumbled rock at the base. They can be seen in many parts of the Rockies and are especially conspicuous along the Narrows of Poudre

Canyon. Some of the most striking formations occur in the canyon just west of the highway tunnel at the mouth of Cedar Creek.

From time to time, there were great underswellings of magmas that cooled to produce the igneous rocks (granites) so common in other parts of the Poudre drainage — Horsetooth Rock, overlooking Fort Collins, is a good example, as is Greyrock, a monolith reached by a popular trail a short distance up Poudre Canyon. These are more solid, massive rocks, though often fissured in diverse patterns; when they erode, they form large, heavy boulders. The overall color is grayish, though in places the high proportion of feldspar gives the rocks a pinkish cast. Almost all are covered with lichens, giving them a blotchy appearance. The granites and schists together form the ancient "basement rocks" of the mountains.

Geologists believe that around 300 million years ago, there was a mountain range just west of the present location of the Front Range. These "ancestral Rockies" were completely eroded away over a long period of time. They were, in John McPhee's words, scarcely more related to the present Rockies "than two families who happen at different times to live in the same house." But their erosion produced vast amounts of sediment that eventually formed sandstones, shales, and limestones. Some of these sedimentary rocks were laid down in shallow seas that once covered the area, as evidenced by the presence of fossils of marine animals in them (for example, at Fossil Creek just south of Fort Collins). Others were laid down in freshwater floodplains of the eroding ancestral Rockies. These contain fossils of land animals, including dinosaurs. (Strata bearing dinosaur bones are poorly formed in the Poudre drainage, but near Morrison, Colorado, only about seventy miles away, school teacher Arthur Lakes first found the remains of "superdinosaurs" in 1877. Quite recently, in 1988, a team led by Robert Bakker of the University of Colorado Museum discovered the bones of a huge dinosaur, the "Masonville monster," just south of the Poudre drainage. This was a fast-moving carnivore, with jaws that would have enabled it to swallow an animal the size of a Hereford cow. Footprints of dinosaurs do occur near Park Creek, a tributary of the Poudre just north of Fort Collins.)

The mountains we now call the Rockies began to rise about 70 million years ago as a result of forces from below. This has often been called the Laramide Revolution. It is a revolution only in terms of the geological time clock — it went on for millions of years. The origin of

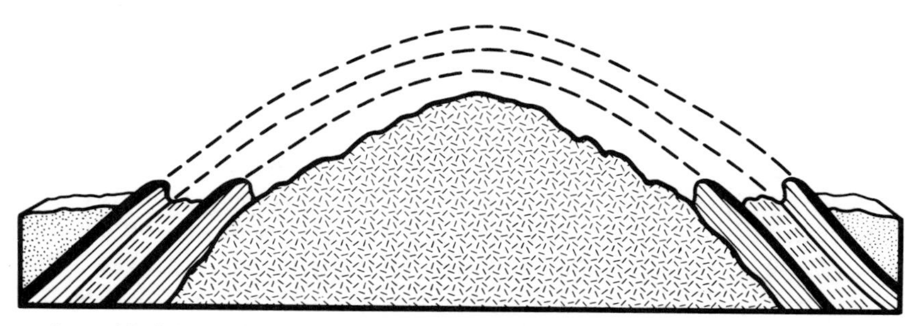

A simplified sketch showing the formation of the hogbacks as the Rockies were elevated.

the word "Laramide" is a story in itself. Jacques LaRamie was a French-Canadian trapper who roamed the North Platte basin for beaver with a group of other trappers in about 1820. He left his companions to explore a branch of the North Platte that flowed in from the south, but he never returned. His comrades found his cabin, but they found no trace of LaRamie. The stream came to be called Laramie's River, the plains it entered the Laramie Plains, and the mountains to the east and north the Laramie Mountains. Fort Laramie later became a major post on the Oregon Trail, and the city that grew on the plains was called Laramie. Geologists eventually seized on the word to designate an event of fantastic proportions — the elevation of a great mountain range — all because an obscure trapper lost his life in a time when life was decidedly precarious in unknown wilds that were the home of unpredictable Indians.

As the basement rocks pushed upward during the "revolution," they collected moisture from the clouds and gave birth to streams that carried sediments — bits of the mountains themselves — and so began the dissection of the mountains even as they were rising. Perhaps none of these streams would have been recognizable as the ancestor of our Cache la Poudre. As the mountains rose, the hundreds of feet of sedimentary rock that overlay the basement rocks were pushed up as a great dome. Being softer, they were subject to relatively faster erosion. Now they are gone from the high country but survive along the rim of the uplift as strata tilted strongly toward the mountains, leaving, as Jeff Rennicke says in *The Rivers of Colorado,* the basement in the attic. These are the "hogbacks" that fringe the eastern side of the Front Range for many miles — hogbacks because their crests, maintained by layers of more resistant rocks, suggest the hoary back of a wild hog (at least to people with good imaginations). Since the older sediments were beneath the younger, they are closest to the mountains, with progressively younger ridges toward the east.

During uplifts beginning about 28 million years ago, and again five to seven million years ago, not only the mountains but much of Colorado, Wyoming, and neighboring states were raised by several thousand feet, bringing these areas to roughly their present levels. The effect on the mountains was to greatly increase stream gradients, which began to cut deep canyons and to breach the hogbacks. Sometime during these millennia, the course and basin of the Cache la Poudre began to assume their present forms. The vast deposits of gravel along its course through the plains attest to the many tons of soil and rock the stream has torn from the mountains. It is, of course, still at work. The flood of July 31, 1976, tore great chunks from the channels of some of the Poudre's tributaries, and in the neighboring Big Thompson River, 200-ton boulders roared down the canyon, destroying homes and bridges. One hundred and forty-five people lost their lives. Such is the force of erosion, always at work but fortunately usually with much less violence.

The story would not be complete without adding two more elements: fire and ice. At various times during the evolution of the mountains, hot magmas pushed up through cracks in the igneous and metamorphic rocks, forming veins and dikes of intrusive material. The magmas cooled quickly and crystals of various minerals formed: quartz (usually white or milky), feldspar (usually pinkish), mica (flat, transparent or black sheets), and other minerals, on some of which we place considerable value. Today the walls of the canyon and its tributaries contain tailings from many small mines, though nowhere in the Poudre drainage were there mines as productive as those south of the area, for example in Central City or Cripple Creek. Nonetheless, there was a famous though short-lived gold mining town, Manhattan, and some nearby silver mining areas. There were also copper, zinc, lead, uranium, commercial diamond, and coal mines, none containing high-grade ores. We'll discuss some of these later.

In addition to these mineral intrusions, there were volcanic eruptions in parts of the mountains. The Never Summer Range, mainly west of the Poudre drainage, is primarily volcanic in origin. Poudre Lake, the river's main source, is guarded by pillars of volcanic tuff, and

Specimen Mountain, just to the north, was once thought to be an old volcanic cone, though many geologists now believe it consists solely of outpourings of volcanos once active to the northwest. These outpourings probably came as a dense cloud that collapsed to form rock while still hot. The color of this mountain, a pinkish, yellow-gray, is typical of the volcanic ash in the area. The canyon northwest of Specimen Mountain, where the Colorado River rises, is often called "Little Yellowstone" because of the pink-and-yellow bands on its walls. Although the western slopes of the mountain drain into the Colorado, the eastern slopes drain into the Poudre, mainly via Willow Creek. Specimen Mountain may have received its name because it once provided students with many geological specimens. A popular trail leads up to the mountain from Poudre Lake and is a good place to spot mountain sheep.

Over the past two million years, glaciers have played a major role in sculpting the Rockies. As snows of the Ice Age accumulated and became compacted, they formed great masses of ice that moved down from the peaks, gathering rock and scooping out broad, U-shaped valleys. Glaciers formed and receded several times, and during the coldest periods built up layers over 1,500 feet thick. The largest glacier in what is now Rocky Mountain National Park was formed in the valley of the Colorado River. This huge river of ice, twenty miles long from its head at La Poudre Pass to the area west of the park where Shadow Mountain Reservoir is now located, overflowed eastward across Milner Pass into the valley of the Poudre. Thus the pass was flattened, a lake bed gouged out, and the highest valley of the Poudre, at its headwaters, is wide and flat, in contrast to most alpine valleys, which are deep and V-shaped.

A further, lower section of the valley of the Poudre was also scoured out by glacial action. Beginning near the community of Spencer Heights and extending downstream for about seven miles to where the old Home Post Office stood, the valley is again U-shaped. A terminal moraine, an accumulation of rocks and soil formed when the glacier melted back, partially blocks the canyon. A highway turnoff at the Home Moraine is supplied with signs describing the glaciation in this part of the valley.

There are no longer any glaciers in the Poudre drainage, discounting a few small ones high in the Mummy Range, and the steep, gravel-laden torrents that once raced to the plains have been replaced by streams usually more gentle. Living our minuscule lives as we do, we find it hard to imagine the vast expanses of time and the powerful forces that shaped this now benign landscape. But to imagine it, with the help of the findings of geologists, is to value all the more the land that is home to so many plants and animals — and to us. There is grandeur and beauty in a granite cliff stained with lichens, in a cirque lake fringed by slopes streaked with ice and snow, in a clear stream racing over pebbles gathered from diverse sources. And there is personal satisfaction in knowing, at least in general terms, how these forms of land and water had their origin.

There are a few more mind-stretching panoramas than can be found among the hogbacks that parallel the eastern edge of the mountains. These, as we have said, are remnants of the sedimentary rocks that once overlay the much more ancient rocks that were thrust up to form the mountains. They are therefore tilted up toward the mountains, with more resistant strata forming the crests of the hogbacks, the more easily eroded strata forming the valleys between them. The ridges closest to the mountains date from what paleontologists call the Paleozoic era (literally, the age of ancient animals — before there were mammals, birds, or even dinosaurs). Proceeding eastward, successive hogbacks are composed of younger rock and span the Mesozoic era; altogether they represent some 250 million years of geologic time.

One of the best places to view the hogbacks is in Lory State Park, just west of Fort Collins and a few miles south of the point where the Poudre leaves its canyon. It is on the west side of Horsetooth Reservoir, which was completed in the early 1950s, and occupies a valley between parallel hogbacks. The trail up Arthur's Rock climbs 1,200 feet over ancient basement rocks, and from lookouts along the way and from the top one can look eastward across successive tiers of hogbacks. The closest (westernmost), of reddish sandstone and limestone, is the Ingleside Formation of the Paleozoic era. Beyond it are the first Mesozoic hogbacks, the grayish Lyons sandstone, and the reddish Lykins Formation, the latter forming the shores and much of the floor of the reservoir. On the east side, the Morrison Formation (where dinosaur bones occur in some places, though not here) slopes up to the blocky ridges of the Dakota sandstone, dating from the Cretaceous, the last period of the Mesozoic, about 100 million years ago. Along much of the Front Range, the Dakota Formation forms the outermost hogback fringing the mountains.

In places where streams have cut through the hogbacks, their strata, tilted upward toward the mountains, lie revealed. This is the Ingleside Formation, of late Paleozoic time, about 250 million years old.

At other places along the base of the mountains, the hogbacks appear rather different, depending upon the thickness of the beds, nature of the erosion, and other factors. Colors of the rocks range all the way from whitish through grays and browns, pinks, brick-red, and other colors not easily described. The roadcut on U.S. Highway 287 through Owl Canyon, some fifteen miles north of Fort Collins, displays a startling range of colors. Red Mountain and Steamboat Rock, a few miles further north, are scenic remnants of colorful rock. A valley to the east of these, in which Park Creek Reservoir is located, is bordered on the west by intensely deep red strata and on the east by a broad band of pale rocks showing the cross-bedding characteristic of ancient sand dunes. It is indeed a wonderland of geologic history laid bare.

The tilting of the sedimentary rocks toward the mountains, forming hogbacks separated by narrow valleys of more easily eroded rocks, is almost universal along Colorado's Front Range. There is a notable exception near the village of Livermore, about twenty miles northwest of Fort Collins. Although Livermore is framed on the east by a colorful hogback, for several miles to the west the deep reddish, Paleozoic sandstones are horizontal, grading almost imperceptibly into the igneous rocks of the foothills. The late David Harris, former head of the geology department at Colorado State University, who knew the geology of the Front Range like no one else, told us that a pair of major faults bordered this area on the north and on the south and converged at the western end. The block between the faults was dropped, leaving the rocks in the horizontal position in which they were formed. In places the North Fork of the Poudre has carved a channel through these rocks, forming steep cliffs over some of which the Indians used to drive bison to their deaths.

One of the more spectacular structures in the sedimentary rocks is the Bellvue Dome — really a half dome, rounded on the east side (facing Laporte) and abruptly precipitous on the west side (facing Pleasant Valley, where Bellvue is located). The Poudre, only a mile or so from the canyon's mouth, flows along the west side of the dome, where Watson Lake and a fish hatchery are now located. The dome is not a typical hogback in appearance or in its believed origin. According to some geologists, during mountain building times two large blocks of basement, metamorphic rock, broken along fault lines, were pushed up above surrounding rocks. The sedimentary layers that had been formed over the basement rock draped themselves like layers of blankets around the protruding blocks. When further mountain building occurred and the sedimentary layers were tilted, the dome protruded above the rest. A layer of very hard sandstone capped the top and east side of the dome, protecting the less resistant, reddish layers beneath; but on the west side these were exposed and subjected to extensive erosion. West of the river and Watson Lake, there are remnants of these same reddish sandstones, but here they lacked the resistant cap rock and have been seriously eroded. The result is a great arc of colorful cliffs that loom above the river and the lake, making fishing there a special delight even when "they aren't biting."

Quarries, Mines, and Disappointments

As early as the 1870s, some of the sandstones in the hogbacks were found to be useful for building. Much of the quarrying occurred in the area now occupied by Horsetooth Reservoir, and rocks were first hauled out by wagon and used for early building in Fort Collins. The restored Avery House on Mountain Avenue in Fort Collins was built of sandstone from this area, and this sandstone was also used for buildings on the campus of the agricultural college (later Colorado State University). Then in 1881 the Greeley, Salt Lake and Pacific Railroad Company was formed, and its spokesmen announced that tracks would be laid through Fort Collins, up Poudre Canyon, and over the divide to Salt Lake City; eventually it would be extended to the Pacific Coast. This ambitious scheme did not materialize, but a spur was built from Bellvue to the quarries at what was then called Petra.

The quarries were leased by the Union Pacific Railroad in 1882, and William H. B. Stout from Nebraska was put in charge. Stout supplanted Petra as the post office name, and the settlement even acquired a school. The quarry business flourished, and long trains carried away the sandstone. Nebraska's capitol and state penitentiary were built from some of it, and stone was also sent to Denver, Cheyenne, and Omaha. Quarrying continued steadily until the panic of 1893 but never completely recovered from that stoppage. The Stout Post Office was closed in 1906, but the school continued serving the valley until 1946, when it was bought by the Bureau of Reclamation. The bureau's engineers used it as an office to oversee the building of the dams needed to form Horsetooth Reservoir. The reservoir, named for the huge tooth-shaped rock on the skyline above it, was part of the Colorado-Big Thompson Project, a major scheme for bringing Western Slope water to the eastern plains. The remains of Stout are now home to the fish that have been stocked in the reservoir.

There are no longer major rock quarries in the Poudre drainage, but gravel deposits along the river's floodplain are being quarried at various points all the way to Greeley and beyond. The deposits consist of sand and of cobbles that have been rounded by stream action. Sorted to size, they are used for road building and for decorative and other purposes. The holes produced by the quarries are often filled with water, and some of the ponds have been stocked with warmwater fish such as bass and catfish.

Ever since humans have lived in the Poudre basin, they have also plumbed the rocks for whatever useful or financially rewarding minerals they might conceal. Indians used flint, chalcedony, and similar hard substances for making projectile points, scrapers, knives, and other tools. White settlers quarried limestone for making cement (as they still do). A source of alabaster was found in some of the hogbacks, and for a time the sculpting of alabaster vases, candleholders, and other

Manhattan, a gold boomtown that thrived for a few years in the 1880s on a small tributary of the Poudre. *Courtesy of Jack and Iola Revis*.

ornamental objects was a small cottage industry in and around Fort Collins.

Coal was discovered in the 1860s about twenty-five miles north of Fort Collins, not far from the Wyoming border, and for a time it was used for heating homes in Cheyenne. Several small mines used primitive equipment and relied on mules to haul the carts from the mines. Local people often collected their own coal, particularly during the depression years of the 1930s. The coal was of low quality, with a high sulfur content, and the mines have been abandoned for many years. On the plains east of the hogbacks are a number of oil fields, and the town of Wellington, on Boxelder Creek northeast of Fort Collins, was once an oil boomtown.

All of this activity involved the exploitation of sedimentary deposits in the hogbacks and adjacent plains. But it was the search for gold and other precious metals among the igneous and metamorphic rocks that lured people to the mountains once the rage for beaver fur had subsided. It was some years before it was realized that local ores were usually not rich enough to justify the cost and labor of extracting them.

The best known of the gold-mining towns was Manhattan, which we mentioned earlier, but prospectors also often traveled up the Poudre Valley to two other mining towns just to the west. These were Lulu City (in the upper Colorado River drainage) and Teller City (in the upper reaches of the North Platte drainage). Manhattan had its beginnings shortly after gold was discovered in 1886 in a small, high valley a few miles north of Rustic. Approximately four thousand prospectors arrived, and the town grew rapidly, even for a time having a newspaper, the *Manhattan Prospector*. Like most mining towns, it had a hanging tree. There is no evidence that it was ever used, but it was always there if needed. The gold rush faded rapidly, and all that remains today of Manhattan is the grass-covered townsite, a few more recent diggings, and a small cemetery.

Rustic itself was briefly a center of mining activity, both copper and gold being found nearby. One promising area was on Sevenmile Creek, which flows into the Poudre from the northwest. Another mining settlement was at Maysville in Crown Point Gulch to the south and above Rustic. When we visited Maysville a few years ago, the few tumbledown cabins were overgrown with brush.

Copper King Mine, established in 1910 on Prairie Divide, a broad expanse of meadow at 8,000 feet elevation between two tributaries of the North Fork of the Poudre, was a source of copper and zinc for several years before it was closed down. In 1949, however, pitchblende was found in the mine tailings, so it was reopened as a uranium mine. It operated for about four years and was again closed when this ore dwindled. For a time local promoters reopened it as a "Radon Mine," allowing people, for a price, to come and sit in the mine to receive radiation for treatment of whatever ailed them. How many took advantage of the opportunity, or how much they paid, we do not know.

At Chicken Park, an open area a short distance west of Prairie Divide, tiny commercial diamonds were found in igneous intrusions. They were found because geologists working in the area had realized that they were finding formations and minerals often associated with diamonds elsewhere. Mining these diamonds, however, proved to be less than worthwhile financially.

But far more important than these limited and often illusory sources of minerals and precious stones was the soil itself, soil resulting from the erosion of the rocks and enriched by a succession of plant life

Cache la Poudre, one of Colorado's most popular trout streams. *Photograph by W. A. Parsons, U.S. Forest Service.*

over the centuries. The plants in turn provided the staff of life for herbivores — deer, elk, bison, bighorn sheep, diverse rodents and insects — and for the animals that preyed upon them. All were adapted for life in a semiarid climate, where snowfall and rains were often less that generous and rivers unpredictable. The Indians, too, became adjusted to the constraints of the land; they were mobile enough to take advantage of available resources, and their numbers were never high. When people of European origin entered this country, they were often shocked by what they found. Major Stephen Long, after his expedition to the Rockies in 1820, proclaimed this the "Great American Desert." In *Centennial,* his fictional account of the settling of north central Colorado, James Michener remarked: "It lacks water — my God, how it lacks water." A reporter for the Geneseo, Illinois, *Republic,* after visiting the newly founded city of Greeley, had these unflattering words: "Greeley is located . . . on a barren, sandy plain . . . midway between a poverty stricken ranch and a prairie-dog village. . . . It is bounded chiefly by prickly pears."

But people came, lured by furs, by gold, and by the Homestead Act of 1862 and the desire to have a piece of the continent as their own to develop and to leave to their children. Many realized that, with enough water, the "desert" could be converted to a pleasant and productive human habitat. The Cache la Poudre, as well as other streams in the South Platte drainage, became the key to solving most of the problems of settlement in north central Colorado — as they still are. "It is the proper destiny of every considerable stream in the West to become an irrigating ditch," wrote Mary Austin in *The Land of Little Rain*.

Soon after settlers first occupied the Poudre basin, they began to find ways to divert, augment, store, and distribute the available water. The continuing struggle to achieve a balance between the necessary exploitation of the Poudre's waters and the need to preserve parts of the basin for recreation and as an investment in the future is a theme to which we will return in a later chapter. First we wish to salute the Cache la Poudre not for its uses, actual and potential, but for its intrinsic values, its native plants and animals, its unsung tarns and gullies, the many permutations of the stream as it travels from the high mountains to well out on the plains. Gathering its waters from the high forests and the tundra, sometimes well over 12,000 feet in elevation, it eventually disgorges itself, murky and sluggish, into the South Platte at 4,600 feet elevation. Though canoeists sometimes try sections of the river on the plains and intrepid rafters and kayakers enjoy challenging the canyon when the river is high from snowmelt, this will not be a typical river journey, for the Poudre is not truly navigable. Rather it will be a leisurely hike along the river and some of its tributaries, stopping to watch a mountain bluebird, to examine a pasque flower, or simply to muse about the relationship between nature and humankind.

We shall begin in chapter 2 with the tundra, then in the following four chapters trace the river through mountain forests and meadows, down the main stem of its canyon, and finally through the foothills and across the plains. In chapter 7 we shall explore the two major tributaries: the North Fork, beginning in rolling, forested country on Deadman Hill; and the South Fork, beginning in the tundra and ice fields of the Mummy Range. In chapter 8 we shall explore a few lesser tributaries of our choosing. The final two chapters will be concerned with the impact of humans on the Poudre basin. We hope you will join us, not for a grand adventure, but for a quiet meandering through some very beautiful country.

2
THE HIGH COUNTRY

Who can say where a river begins? It begins in melting snowdrifts, in drippings from mossy banks, in springs seeping from hillsides, in wet meadows, in innumerable tiny rivulets that search downward to join others and still others — a gathering of waters from thousands of unguessable sources, blended into a torrent that is now and then, here and there placid and reflective, here and there and now and then turbulent and boisterous. Always in song, a faint tinkling in the rocks, the varied medley of a robust stream, the roar of a cataract. And lucky is the person who spreads his bedroll beside such a stream, knowing he will be rewarded all night long by the sounds of water over rocks, the hymn of the mountains.

The Cache la Poudre gathers its waters from a vast area of north central Colorado — an area nearly as large as the state of Delaware — and even accepts a few trickles from across the Wyoming border. The acknowledged source is Poudre Lake, just a few feet east of the Continental Divide at Milner Pass, in Rocky Mountain National Park. To have a lake essentially on the Continental Divide is unusual — the Poudre is individualistic right from its start. It is also one of the few rivers of the world whose source is accessible by a well-traveled, paved thoroughfare, Trail Ridge Road (U.S. Highway 34), open each year from late May into September, depending on the timing of spring and autumn snowstorms.

Rocky Mountain National Park was carved out of national forest lands in 1915, the realization of a dream of naturalist Enos Mills. Mills had written innumerable letters and articles supporting park status for the high country around Estes Park, and he had lectured widely on the esthetic and spiritual values of the mountains. He was supported by the then recently formed Colorado Mountain Club, by Estes Park's "grand old man," F. O. Stanley, the inventor of the Stanley Steamer and builder of Estes Park's most prominent structure, the Stanley Hotel, and by many others. There was, of course, opposition, especially from those who had used the area to run cattle and to hunt, fish, and log freely. In 1913 Robert Marshall, an employee of the U.S. Geological Survey, submitted a report to Congress recommending that the area be preserved as a park, and shortly thereafter a bill was passed and signed by President Woodrow Wilson, creating the thirty-second addition to the national park system. Trail Ridge Road, completed in 1933, roughly follows an old Indian trail across the mountains.

The road crosses the Poudre — an easily jumpable little stream — just as it leaves Poudre Lake. There is a place to park at the divide. Beyond this point waters drain into Beaver Creek, which descends rapidly to the Colorado River only two or three miles away as the raven flies. From here they flow to the Gulf of California (in theory, for in fact the Colorado no longer reaches the gulf). The east-flowing waters of the nascent Cache la Poudre have a much more devious route to follow — to the Platte, the Missouri, and the Mississippi — before reaching the Gulf of Mexico.

A continental divide is by definition the crest of the continent. Since Poudre Lake lies essentially on the divide, where do its waters come from? In fact Milner Pass is a relatively low pass, a mere 10,758 feet above sea level, with mountains of 12,000 feet or more on either side. It is these mountains and the melting of snow that accumulates in the pass that maintain the lake at a level that overflows to form the Cache la Poudre. No sooner does the stream leave the lake than it is joined by other streams entering the valley from either side. The forests extend upward along the valley slopes for only about half a mile, terminating at treeline, about 11,300 feet elevation. Above this is alpine tundra, the ultimate source of much of the Poudre's water, a land without trees and tall bushes, subject to freezing temperatures and snow for eight or nine months of the year and still containing melting snowbanks by the time of the first snows of September. The tundra, writes Ann Zwinger, "is like a great sponge, hoarding snow and melt water and releasing it throughout the summer." U.S. Forest Service researchers tell us that only 3.5 percent of Colorado's surface area is covered by tundra, yet tundra initiates 20 percent of Colorado's stream flow.

"Among the unfinished parts of the globe," Thoreau said of the tundra. But there is much to be seen. The low bushes in the foreground are willow "trees." *Courtesy of the U.S. Forest Service.*

THE TUNDRA

There is no better place to study the land above the trees than along Trail Ridge Road, where the National Park Service has provided turnoffs, guided walks, and hiking trails with informative signs. From the Medicine Bow Curve Turnoff, one can look down on the long, meadowed valley of the upper Cache la Poudre and gain an impression of the many sources of water that gradually broaden and deepen it.

The tundra itself at first seems bleak and unrewarding, an impression perhaps reinforced by the nearly constant winds and the exertion of moving about in the thin air. "The tops of mountains are among the unfinished parts of the globe," wrote Thoreau of the summit of Katahdin. Yet this is a unique and fascinating place. "The alpine tundra," notes Ann Zwinger, "is a land of contrast and incredible intensity, where the sky is the size of forever and the flowers the size of a millisecond."

Much of the high country of Rocky Mountain National Park consists of gently rolling surfaces, interrupted here and there by cliffs sometimes hundreds of feet high. Boulders litter the surface, often forming ridges or diverse patters resulting from repeated freezing and thawing of the ground. The vegetation, however diminutive, is never monotonous, varying from place to place depending upon exposure to the wind, soil characteristics, or how recently the snowbanks have melted from that area. In places where the soil is moist and stable, there may be meadows of grasses and sedges. In windswept areas the soil may be mostly bare and covered with pebbles; such fell-fields, as they are called, are often sparsely covered with cushion-like plants that hug the ground closely. Some depressions may contain patches of dwarf clovers, while others may be splashed with the gold of alpine buttercups. In places there are willow "trees" only a few inches high and bearing catkins an inch or two long. "No other plant of high altitudes knows its business so well," wrote Mary Austin of the willows of the high Sierras. "It hugs the ground, grows roots from stem joints where no roots should be, grows a slender leaf or two and twice as many erect full catkins that rarely, even in that short growing season, fail of fruit."

According to Ann Zwinger and Beatrice Willard, whose book *Land Above the Trees* is indispensable to anyone exploring the tundra, Colorado has more than 300 species of alpine plants, twice that of West Coast tundras and three times that of the mountains of the eastern states. Many of the very same species occur in the Alps and in northern Eurasia, having spread throughout the nearly continuous tundra of the Far North and down the spine of the Rockies. During periods of continental glaciation many thousands of years ago, sea levels were lower, permitting plants and animals to spread across a land bridge that is now the Bering Strait between Siberia and Alaska. Cold-adapted plants spread south and then, as the glaciers receded and the climate warmed, either perished or survived only at high altitudes. There are far more similarities among the alpine floras of the world than among plants inhabiting forests or prairies.

There may be no more than forty-five frost-free days in the alpine meadows of the Rockies, and plants must grow, flower, and seed quickly, even though most are able to grow at quite cool temperatures. Almost all are perennials, growing each season from a rootstock containing food reserves. There would often not be time for seeds to germinate and plants to become established. While stems are short, flowers are often as large as those of lower altitudes. Alpine sunflowers, perhaps the showiest flowers of the tundra, have blossoms two to three inches across, though the stems rarely exceed six to eight inches. Perhaps

Alpine buttercups spring from the bare, rocky soil of the tundra.

because of their rather ragged blossoms, they are often called "old-men-of-the-mountains." Still another name for them is Rydbergia, after their discoverer, Per Axel Rydberg, a Swedish emigré who spent many years roaming the Rockies and in 1906 wrote the pioneering *Flora of Colorado*.

The small size of alpine plants not only makes them more wind resistent but requires less expenditure of food reserves than would the production of tall stems. As a further adaptation, many contain red pigments called anthocyanins, especially evident in the spring and in late summer, when the green of chlorophyll does not obscure them. Anthocyanins are produced from carbohydrates stored in the roots and are able to use sunlight to produce warmth, enabling plants to get a head start as soon as the snows have melted. Many alpine plants spread by vegetative growth, and those that set seed are often wind pollinated (grasses, sedges, and willows, for example). Others are pollinated by small flies that are common on the tundra, or by bumblebees. Bumblebees not only maintain heat because of their fuzzy bodies but are able to take flight on cool mornings by "shivering" their flight muscles until they reach a temperature sufficient for flight, well above that of the surrounding air. Several kinds of small butterflies occur on the tundra, visiting flowers for nectar when the sun shines but clinging to low plants when the winds threaten to blow them from the mountains.

Perhaps the most riveting of the alpine plants are the cushion plants that hug the ground in the coarse soil of fell-fields. Moss campion, a plant of circumpolar distribution, is one of the most showy of these; an individual plant may bear hundreds of pink flowers for a short time in the summer. According to Zwinger and Willard, a mature plant may be as much as twenty years old; its earlier years are spent growing slowly, establishing a deep taproot that probes for water, anchors it against the wind, and serves for food storage. Sometimes moss campion grows close beside two other cushion plants, white phlox and the nearly stemless alpine forget-me-not. In their *Field Guide to Rocky Mountain Wildflowers*, John and Frank Craighead and Ray Davis comment with their usual élan: "Growing thus together, they appear to be a single cushion of varicolored flowers — the red, white, and blue symbolizing the complete freedom that comes to all outdoor lovers in the vastness of the mts."

Despite the short summer season on the tundra, there is a sequence of bloom, beginning with the buttercups, which according to the Craigheads and Davis "seem to spring up as if by magic, blooming almost as soon as snow melts. In fact, they can be found growing under the edges of snowdrifts, sometimes pushing up through 2–3 in. of snow and ice. Heat given off during respiration of a growing plant is sufficient to melt a hole 1 in. or so in diameter." Much depends upon the meltback of drifts. Moss campion may bloom in June and as late as August, depending upon the timing of meltback.

We confess to a special liking for mid- to late August on the tundra. Some of the flowers are gone, and reddish colors are showing in some of the leaves. It is then that the arctic gentians are in bloom, their oversized, fluted blossoms capping stems no more than a few inches high. There is something glacial about them, portending the snows soon to come. Perhaps it is the green-blue tints in the off-white blossoms, rather like the colors of icebergs.

Pocket gophers abound on the tundra, working through the ground like small bulldozers and leaving piles of freshly worked soil here and there. Plants often become established in these mounds, forming "gopher gardens." Alpine sunflowers, bluebells, and candytuft are especially likely to be clumped there. These gopher gardens tend to succumb to wind erosion, to be replaced by others. Even though gophers have an enduring appetite for plants, they do tend to improve the diversity by their earth-moving activities.

It comes as a surprise to lowlanders to discover pocket gophers on mountaintops, as they are used to them as pests of lawns and gardens. In fact they thrive in the mountains, living in tunnels from a few inches to a foot or two beneath the surface or, in winter, beneath the snow. In the winter they often line snow tunnels with soil, and when the snow melts, the earthen shells remain on the surface. If it were not for these shells and the piles of earth the gophers periodically clear from below, their presence would scarcely be noticed.

Not so the marmots, much larger rodents that spend much of their time above ground, though maintaining deep burrows under rocks where they hibernate in winter. Although known to biologists as yellow-bellied marmots, they are more reddish-brown than yellow, especially the bushy tail. A dash of white across the snout gives them a snobbish appearance as they perch on piles of rocks as if they were kings of the hill. Marmots live in family groups, usually a male and several females along with a few yearlings. They mate in the spring, and after the young are born a month later, the offspring of the previous year are gradually driven from the nest. Each family has a home territory, and adults signal their property rights to neighboring families. It is said that the whistles can be varied to form six different calls, and there are also grunts and tooth chatter. Marmots range all the way from the foothills to well above timberline. If the Rockies can be said to have a voice, it is surely the whistle of the marmot.

One other mammal that is a regular inhabitant of the alpine tundra is a small, round-eared relative of the rabbit, the pika. Pikas live in rock piles and talus slopes, mostly above 10,000 feet elevation. They usually attract attention by their alarm calls, which are more nasal than those of marmots, rather like a Bronx cheer. They are remarkable ventriloquists, their calls seeming to come from one spot while they are actually sitting on a rock some distance away. Pikas do not hibernate, but spend much of the summer harvesting plants, some of which they eat and some of which they pile under rocks and cure as hay for the winter. If a person sits quietly, he or she can often see them dashing about the rocks, usually with a mouthful of plant material. Although pikas tend to trim down the meadows around their homes, it is difficult to bear a grudge against these hardy and entertaining denizens of the high country.

Edwin James, a member of the Long Expedition of 1820, may have been the first to see a pika. He believed it to be a rodent, but it is kin of the rabbit. *Photo by David Leatherman.*

For most of the year, pikas are unsociable animals, each maintaining a territory that is marked off by rubbing the secretions of cheek glands onto rocks and defended by chasing away intruders. In the breeding season, the males briefly enlarge their territories to include those of one or more females, and following mating the females share their territories with their offspring for a few weeks. Since territories tend to be crowded together in good habitats, usually about five to an acre, the young must grow rapidly and be able to compete for a territory and to harvest food for the winter in only a few weeks. There are usually two litters a year, so talus slopes may become very crowded, and the intense competition for space sometimes results in much mortality among the young. The diverse interactions among pikas involve a complex vocal repertory with at least nine different sounds, each conveying a different message. This contrasts with their cousins, the rabbits and hares, which go about their business without much to say to one another.

One of the best ways to spot the favorite perch of a pika or a marmot is to look for vertical streaks of orange lichen on the sides of boulders. These brightly colored lichens thrive in the presence of ammonia from mammal urine. There are many other kinds of lichens embellishing the rocks, often forming complex patterns of black, brown, gray, and diverse shades of green. Indeed throughout the Rockies, lichens add color to the somber granites and gneisses. Lichens have been used as sources of natural dyes in many parts of the world; they also serve as food for many animals. Each kind of lichen is a cooperative association between one species of alga and one of fungus, the fungus supplying the supporting structures and the alga manufacturing food through photosynthesis. Over time, lichens produce acids that erode rock surfaces, permitting other plants to take root in soil that accumulates and allowing water to enter crevices and freeze, assisting in the eventual breakdown of the rocks. Not all lichens live on rocks; some form a crust on the soil, protecting it from erosion by wind and water. Though sometimes frowned on as the "trash" of the plant world, lichens play subtle roles that are seldom appreciated.

Despite the short summer season on the tundra, several kinds of birds call it home. They arrive and begin nesting as soon as there are snow-free areas in June and produce fully fledged young only a few weeks later. Water pipits are brownish-gray birds without prominent color markings, while horned larks have black "horns" and some yellow on the throat, though it is not always easy to see. The two species are about the same size and both have a streak of white on each side of their tails; both have rather soft, tinkling songs that they often produce on the wing. When they walk, pipits bob their tails up and down, perhaps the best way to tell the two birds apart from a distance. In late summer they depart, pipits to the south and horned larks to the nearby plains.

Pipits and larks have slender bills and are primarily insect eaters. Another characteristic tundra bird, the rosy finch, has a thick bill and like other finches feeds primarily on buds and seeds, though not passing up an occasional insect. These are the most alpine of all birds, usually nesting in rocky cliffs above 12,000 feet, even as high as 13,500 feet. The nests are built of grasses and mosses in cavities among the rocks, where they are sheltered from the wind. Rosy finches sometimes remain in the high country until fall, finally being driven to lower altitudes by fierce winter storms. Even so, they remain in cold, snowy country through the winter, feeding in flocks on whatever seeds they can find on windswept slopes.

Rosy finches present an enigma to bird watchers. In Colorado's tundra, they are "brown-capped," but persons living on the eastern

This white-tailed ptarmigan, being held by a research biologist, is in plumage intermediate between the white of winter and the mottled colors of summer. *Courtesy of the U.S. Forest Service.*

slopes of the Front Range, as we do, find their feeders visited in winter by "gray-crowned" rosy finches. Evidently members of the brown-capped race migrate down the western slopes of the Rockies, while gray-crowns, which winter along eastern slopes, breed further north, from Montana into Canada. There are still other races, and in some places flocks contain more than one race, as well as intergrades.

Through the colder parts of winter, gray-crowned rosies provide much of our entertainment. Great flocks of them descend on our feeders, consuming huge quantities of birdseed but paying for their keep by brightening our winter days. Their patterns of delicate pastel colors are something special, a rich brown body suffused with rose on the breast and rump, wing tips flecked with white, a black spot above the bill, and a gray bonnet on the back on the head like that of a Victorian matron. There are no other North American birds with anything like this color pattern, and one wonders how it may have evolved. At least bird lovers can be thankful that rosies are so easy to identify, in contrast to the "little brown birds" that make up so much of the finch and sparrow clan.

Remarkably there is one bird that remains on or near the tundra year-round, the white-tailed ptarmigan. The scientific name is particularly fitting: *Lagopus leucurus* (Greek for "hare-footed with a white tail"). These are plump, partridge-like birds that spend most of their time on the ground, and their feet are indeed thickly padded like those of snowshoe hares, a useful adaptation in this snowy environment. In winter ptarmigan are nearly pure white, but in summer the feathers of the back are brown, blending with the soil. When approached they squat motionless, and they must be difficult indeed for predators to spot. But with patience, visitors to the tundra along Trail Ridge Road can often see them feeding on seeds and berries in the low vegetation.

At mating time, in the spring, male ptarmigan establish territories and defend them with hoots and clucks as well as by inflating a red comb above each eye. When a male is joined by a female — usually his mate from the previous season — mating follows and several eggs are soon laid in a simple nest hidden among plants. Care of the young is left to the mother, who herds the chicks into places where there are buds and seeds to be found.

Outside the breeding season, ptarmigan, like other kinds of grouse, form unisexual flocks. Males form groups of up to fifteen individuals and spend the colder months of the year in places where there are plenty of willows, either above or near treeline. Females form larger flocks, sometimes forty or more, and range into meadows and thickets below treeline. In both cases willow buds and twigs make up about 90 percent of the winter diet. During storms they roost in deep, soft snow, surviving even the severest of winter extremes.

Learning about the winter diet and movements of ptarmigan must have been a challenging experience for researchers such as Clait Braun, Terry May, and Richard Hoffman, then graduate students at Colorado State University who traversed the high country by foot or on snowshoes or skis, watching for birds or their tracks or droppings. As necessary, they captured birds with a fish pole fitted with a noose, then weighed, aged, sexed, and banded them before release. It was surely hard and finger-chilling work, but to be alone on the high mountains in midwinter must have been an experience not soon forgotten. Incidentally, the proliferation of ski resorts in Colorado, as well as the widespread use of snowmobiles, does not augur well for ptarmigan populations. Fortunately those in Rocky Mountain National Park are largely immune to those threats.

In the winter the tundra is a bitterly cold and windy place, with scarcely any signs of life, though pikas, pocket gophers, and male ptarmigan are still active. In spring, which does not arrive until June, the migrants are returning, the marmots are out sunning themselves, and flowers are following the meltback of snowdrifts. The drifts bleed in the warming sun, forming thousands of streamlets that trickle down the slopes to join others and rush into the canyons. Leaving the tundra, they first pass through a zone of stunted, twisted trees before reaching the forest. This zone of dwarf trees struggling to survive at timberline is the krummholz, a German term meaning "crooked wood." It is a unique place, a lesson on life's tenacity in adversity.

The Krummholz

To be sure, there may be more moisture here than in the tundra, since some of the tundra's snow tends to be swept down the slopes. And temperatures average a degree or two higher and the winds are less severe (though severe enough!). Conditions here are barely sufficient for trees to become established. Being trees they try to grow upward, only to be battered by the winds and cased in ice and snow wherever their tops extend above the protecting drifts. So the trees that succeed in taking root are short, twisted, and bent away from the direction of the prevailing winds, that is, generally toward the east or southeast. The krummholz above the sources of the Cache la Poudre consists of Engelmann spruce, with a smattering of subalpine fir and limber pine. Some of the trees, though small, are hundreds of years old.

Often the trees in the krummholz are clumped in "tree islands," since grouping enhances resistance to the wind. Trees that emerge from deep snow often have their lower branches matted and covered with a black growth. This is the result of infection with snow-mold fungus, which thrives in a mixture of snow and ice close to the freezing point. The nature of these dwarf forests varies greatly from place to place, depending particularly upon the steepness and direction of the slope. In winter, areas close to treeline are subject to avalanches, since the trees are too small and scattered to retard slippage of the snow.

The krummholz is well within the altitudinal range of one of the Rockies' most spectacular birds, Clark's nutcracker. Nutcrackers are especially attracted to the seeds of limber pines. These are members of the "white pine" group, that is, they have five needles in a cluster rather than two or three like other pines of the Poudre drainage. They are

Along Trail Ridge Road, Clark's nutcrackers sometimes become quite tame and will accept food from passers-by. *Photo by David Leatherman.*

especially well adapted to rough, rocky exposed terrain and tend to occur in isolated groves rather than broad stands like other pines.

Clark's nutcrackers are large, pale gray birds with black wings and tail broadly trimmed with white. Their powerful bills are used for hammering apart pinecones to get at the seeds. They breed very early in the season, often laying their eggs in March. Females have been seen incubating their eggs in snowstorms, with the temperature close to zero.

When pine seeds are ripe in the fall, nutcrackers collect them in great quantities and cache them for recovery during the winter and spring. The seeds are buried an inch or two deep, usually on cliff ledges or south-facing slopes. A single nutcracker may store as many as fifty thousand seeds. Since they put only a few seeds in a cache, each bird must remember several thousand hiding places. Evidently they memorize large landmarks in the area as well as small landmarks close to the caches. They have even been seen uncovering caches under several feet of snow. It is estimated that it takes about ten thousand seeds to support a nutcracker from October to April. Even so, they bury many more seeds than they need in order to compensate for a considerable loss to rodents. When recovering seeds, they land at a selected spot, probe with their bill, then dig with sidesweeping motions of the bill. When seeds are found, they are cracked open at the site or carried back to the nest in a pouch beneath the tongue.

These unusual birds were fittingly named for a remarkable man, William Clark. Although Clark had little formal education, in the course of his expedition with Meriwether Lewis, he learned to be a superb geographer as well as an accurate observer of the environment through which they passed. It was on August 22, 1804, while crossing what is now Idaho, that Clark noted "a bird of the woodpecker kind which fed on Pine burs . . . about the size of a robin." That he called it a woodpecker is not surprising, since its flight is undulating and its huge bill suggestive of a woodpecker's. Specimens were collected and eventually found their way to pioneer ornithologist Alexander Wilson, who figured the bird in his *American Ornithology* of 1811, appropriately on the same plate with Lewis's woodpecker. Wilson called it "Clark's crow," a suitable name since it is a member of the crow family.

Several mammals occur sporadically close to treeline. Pikas live in the talus slopes and marmots in rocky outcrops. Snowshoe hares sometimes occur here, though preferring more heavily forested country a bit lower down. Like the ptarmigan, they are clothed in white during the cold months and are active all through the year, in winter sometimes seen bounding along like a bundle of wind-blown snow. Bighorn sheep and elk sometimes roam the krummholz in summer. (In Europe the name "elk" is applied to what we call the moose, so Americans should use the Indian name "wapiti," though they usually don't. Moose have been introduced into north central Colorado, where they once occurred naturally, but so far they have only occasionally entered the Poudre watershed and never at this high an altitude).

High talus slopes are the only home of a small, coal-black butterfly called the rockslide alpine (*Erebia magdalena*). In their book *Butterflies of the Rocky Mountain States*, Clifford Ferris and F. Martin Brown remark that "collecting under such conditions is an unforgettable experience; the effects of high altitude and the uncertain footing on the talus combine to make the capture of *magdalena* a feat to be long remembered and cherished." Those of us who are not ardent lepidopterists are content to watch them flutter over the rocks like dead leaves tossed in the wind.

Mountain weather is notoriously changeable. Visitors to the high country pick sunny days when they can, but even so, afternoon clouds sometimes build up, and rain, hail, or even snow may begin suddenly. Enos Mills roamed these mountains in all kinds of weather and tells of some of his encounters with storms, floods, and avalanches in his book *The Spell of the Rockies*. Sometimes electrically charged clouds settle on the mountains, producing eery buzzing sounds and causing one's hair to stand on end. Winds can be severe at any time of year, but especially so in winter. One winter day Mills set up a wind meter on Long's Peak and recorded a wind speed of 170 miles an hour before the meter blew to pieces.

A late spring snowstorm can wipe out an entire population of a butterfly, and a heavy frost in August can kill back many plants before they have finished blooming. Observing the twisted trees of the krummholz, one can only admire the persistence of life under seemingly impossible conditions.

As one descends the slopes, the forests of dwarf, weather-worn trees give way to taller and straighter ones; mountain chickadees, kinglets, and other small birds chipper overhead, and the ground is covered with broom huckleberry. But now we are in a very different world altogether, one deserving of its own chapter.

3
THROUGH MOUNTAIN MEADOWS AND FORESTS

Origins

On a bright morning in mid-July, we drove to Milner Pass, traversing Trail Ridge Road before it had acquired its usual bumper-to-bumper summer traffic. We parked at the pass and stepped out into meadows awash with color: the white crowns of bistort, like minuscule snowballs; the rose-pink of Indian paintbrushes; the yellow of buttercup-like potentillas. Poudre Lake was barely ruffled by a light breeze, embraced by dark green meadows, and guarded by breccia pinnacles and by steepled spruces. Surprisingly several dragonflies patrolled the lake. Dragonfly larvae surely cannot live in waters so cold and so briefly free of ice. These were ten-spotted skimmers, among the most wide-ranging of dragonflies. Probably they had strayed up from the basin of the Colorado River, only a few miles to the west.

It was hard to believe that the tiny stream that left the east side of the lake was really the Cache la Poudre River, a river that, with the help of many tributaries as well as long-extinct glaciers, would in time produce a valley that is in some places a thousand feet or more below the surrounding mountains. Here it was only a foot or two wide and an inch or two deep, nearly hidden by the grasses and wildflowers. Poudre River Trail begins at the lake, and we followed it for several miles. Here was a river fresh from the womb, a river we knew so well and in so many moods as a major stream far below. It is not every day that one can observe, firsthand, the birth and early days of something he has loved in its maturity.

The valley of the Poudre is nearly straight for several miles and has the typical U-shaped profile of a once-glaciated valley. The stream itself winds a crooked course flanked by meadows on either side and framed by forests on the slopes. In places the meadows are filled with bushes,

Poudre Lake is unique in being almost on the Continental Divide, at Milner Pass in Rocky Mountain National Park.

knee to waist high, willows and bog birches. Within a mile or two, the stream has broadened and can be jumped with difficulty, but it is still shallow and reveals the varicolored stones over which it flows. In this straight, northeast-flowing part of the valley, before the Poudre joins Chapin Creek and turns north, there is a descent of only 600 feet in about five miles. So it is a gentle stream, though doubtless boisterous enough at the peak of snowmelt in May and June.

Even in mid-July there were lingering snowdrifts in protected places. Rivulets poured into the valley from both sides, and parts of the meadows were decidedly boggy. It was the height of bloom for the wildflowers, and in the course of the morning we recorded fifty-four kinds, not all of which we could identify with certainty in our field guides. Some were unmistakable: the pink, stalked blossoms of elephant head, each blossom suggesting the ears and trunk of a tiny elephant; bluebells and harebells; marsh marigolds; a modest member of the orchid family, lady's tresses. Most were not like the miniplants of the tundra; indeed the curious blue-purple blossoms of monkshood sometimes met us at eye height.

We wondered if the Indians, the trappers, and the early explorers reveled in the display of colors as we did. Doubtless they were preoc-

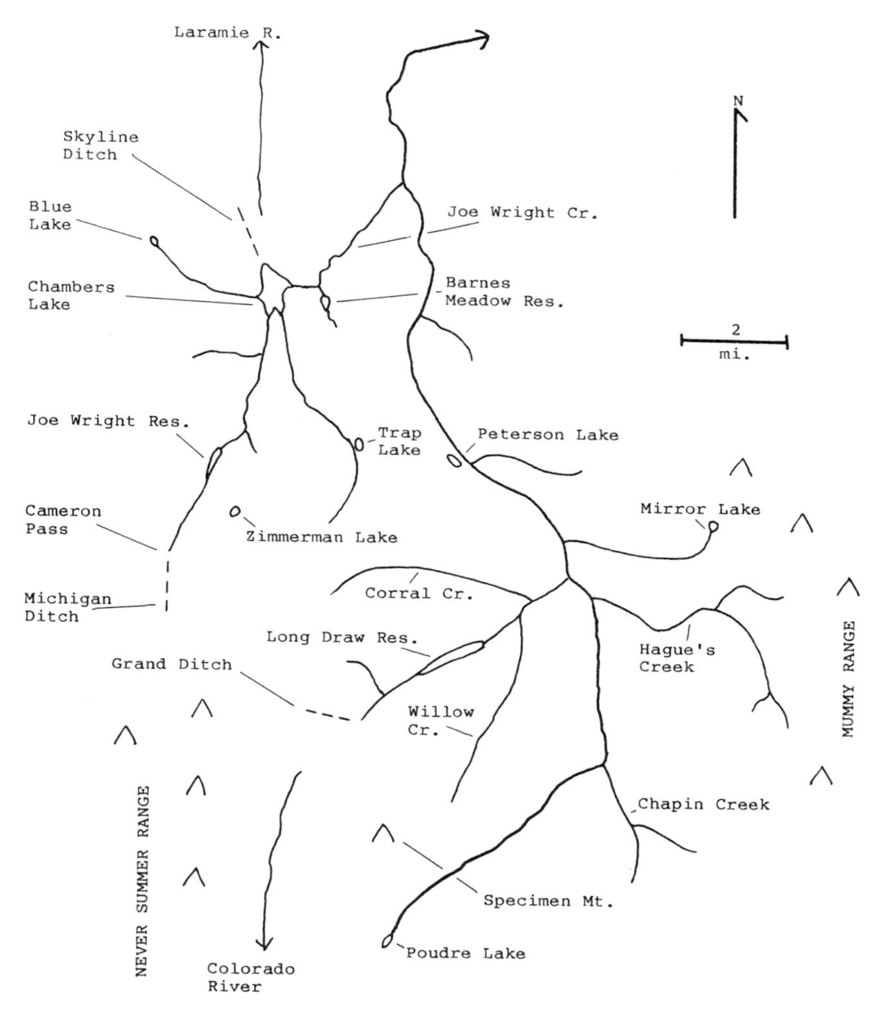

The upper Cache la Poudre basin.

cupied with mere survival and learned to evaluate plants for their usefulness. Yampa, a carrot-like plant abundant in these meadows, was found to have tubers that are palatable and filling, tasting a bit like parsnips. It was an important food for the Indians, who taught some of the early mountain men how to find and prepare it. The rootstocks of bistort were cherished by the Cheyenne Indians, who used them in stews. Early explorers and settlers used willow bark either in tea, for fevers, or in a poultice for wounds. Willows (*Salix*) contain a glycoside called salicin, closely related to acetylsalicylic acid, better known as aspirin. By no means are all alpine plants beneficial. One that we saw in abundance that July morning was death camas, an attractive member of the lily family that contains alkaloids reputed to be more toxic than strychnine.

Butterflies of several kinds were taking advantage of all this flowering. There were fritillaries, orange-winged and spangled with dark spots; sulphurs, bright yellow with dark-bordered wings; and satyrs in delicate patterns of brown. Parnassians, the most elegant of Rocky Mountain butterflies, flitted moth-like over the meadows. These are medium-sized butterflies with white wings spotted with black and red. Our species is *Parnassius phoebus*, named for Mt. Parnassus in Greece, fabled home of Phoebus (Apollo), as classical a name as one can imagine. It is a common alpine butterfly throughout the Rockies and ranges north to Alaska and also throughout cooler parts of Eurasia. The caterpillars feed on stonecrop (*Sedum*); we have often looked for them but have never found them.

Bushy, high-altitude meadows are prime habitat for several elusive birds, and we were lucky to see Wilson's warblers, named for pioneer ornithologist Alexander Wilson, and Lincoln's sparrows, named not for Abraham but for Thomas Lincoln, a young companion of Audubon's. White-crowned sparrows were less elusive; they seemed to trill from every copse. These are favorites of students of birdsong, since local populations develop their own variations on a basically simple song. In their laboratory at Colorado State University, Myron Baker and his students tutored nestling and fledgling white-crowned sparrows with recordings of their home dialect. After a few months, they exposed them to appropriate day length and artificially elevated their hormone levels. Females responded consistently to their own dialect but almost never to alien dialects.

In further experiments the songs were dissected and resynthesized in an effort to learn which part of the song was important to the females. Each song has four parts: an introduction, a complex trill, a simple trill, and a coda (a classical sonata in miniature!). To oversimplify, it turned out that the simple trill seemed more important than other parts of the song in producing a response by the females.

Baker and his students believe that females, returning to their natal sites in the mountains in the spring, will tend to mate with males singing in the dialect they learned as fledglings. This will tend to accentuate the behavioral isolation of each population, perhaps, in time, permitting them to undergo obvious evolutionary changes. Since such dialects are widespread among birds, this may help to explain why there are so many species and subspecies of sparrows that are often confusing to the nonspecialist. Since our offices at Colorado State University were adjacent to Dr. Baker's bird-rearing facilities, we were often treated to the cheerful songs of white-crowns in the dead of winter.

The forests that fringe the valley of the upper Poudre have their own company of birds: mountain chickadees, ruby-crowned kinglets, hermit thrushes, red crossbills, and others. On our hike we saw a gray jay being pursued by a robin (yes, robins nest all the way up to timberline). Like other jays these birds often rob the nests of other birds. Nevertheless, hikers in the high country have a special feeling for these handsome, white-capped birds. The jay, says Arthur Cleveland Bent in his classic series of books on bird life histories, "greets the camper, when he first pitches camp, with demonstrations of welcome, and shares his meals with him; it follows the trapper on his long trails through the dark and lonesome woods, where any companionship must be welcome; it may be a thief, and at times a nuisance, but its jovial company is worth more than the price of its board." It will eat most anything the woodlands (or the camper) have to offer, from soap to plug tobacco, according to Bent. One camper found them inordinately fond of baked beans, of which "they regularly took four in one load, three in the throat and one held in the bill." Little wonder that the jays are often called "camp robbers," "meat hawks," or other names describing their eagerness to partake of anything remotely edible. Another name, "whiskey jack," does not, however, denote a fondness for hard liquor; it is said to be a corruption of an Indian name for the jay, "wiss-ka-chon."

Gray jays live year-round in the high forests, building their nests in spruces or pines in March or April, when there is still plenty of snow in the woods. The young are born when the first insects are flying, and these are their preferred food. In the fall the jays gather berries and whatever other edibles they can find and store them in caches that serve them in the winter. We always look forward to meeting them when hiking in the high country, and they always seem genuinely pleased to see us, if only to inquire into the contents of our backpacks.

The forests along the upper valleys of the Cache la Poudre consist almost entirely of Engelmann spruce and subalpine fir. These are slender, towering trees, fragrant as only such trees can be. They grow remarkably close together, so that the interior of the forest is dark even on a sunny day. These forests have been stable over long periods of time. Engelmann spruce are one of the few trees that can germinate and grow in the dense shade of mature trees. When old trees die, there are young ones ready to shoot up and take their places. In the words of John W. Marr, in his study of the ecosystems of the Front Range, "Many generations of trees have lived, died, and fallen over in these long-persisting stands, and wind-throw of both living and dead trees is common. The resulting tangle of stumps and fallen logs in all stages of decay, often with no systematic orientation, makes passage through these stands a tedious and tiresome activity." Even the birds seem scarce, now and then twittering from branches far above and out of sight. Wildflowers are sparse except in clearings and forest edges. In many places the ground is uniformly covered with broom huckleberry, its tiny berries serving as food for various birds and mammals. Rotting logs support lichens, mosses, and fungi. It is as close to a primeval setting as one is likely to find on our now thoroughly tamed continent.

George Engelmann, for whom these stately trees were named, was a well-to-do St. Louis physician whose life spanned much of the nineteenth century. He was an ardent botanist and built up a large private herbarium that later became part of the collections of the Missouri Botanical Gardens. He visited Colorado several times and studied the coniferous trees; a mountain was later named for him. It was Charles Parry who in 1863 named *Picea engelmanni*, Engelmann spruce, after him. Parry, an Iowa physician, was also an ardent botanist much attracted to the Rocky Mountains. According to Joseph Ewan, in his book *Rocky Mountain Naturalists*, Parry, "surely did more than any other single person to make known the plant life of the central Rocky Mountains." Parry's clover is an important plant of the tundra, Parry's primrose is one of the more spectacular wildflowers of alpine meadows and streamsides, and Parry's harebell one of the more delicate. All three were named for Parry by Harvard botanist Asa Gray, to whom Parry sent many of his specimens. Gray himself visited Colorado in 1872 and with Parry climbed what are now known as Gray's and Parry's peaks. All three peaks — Gray's, Parry's, and Engelmann's — are well over 13,000 feet in elevation and thus extend far above timberline; the

Blue columbine, Colorado's state flower, graces rocky outcrops on the upper Cache la Poudre.

three are not in the Poudre drainage, but west of Denver. It is good to remember these pioneers as we roam the high country and respond to the beauties around us.

The first major tributary of the Poudre is Chapin Creek, which drains the west sides of Mount Chapin, Mount Chiquita, and Ypsilon Peak, all part of the Mummy Range. The creek and mountain were named for Frederick Chapin, an easterner who came to Colorado in the 1880s and climbed several peaks; he later wrote a book entitled *Mountaineering in Colorado*. The valley of Chapin Creek also has a U-shaped profile, meadowed along the stream and forested along the slopes, as does the Cache la Poudre for several miles beyond the junction. So it seems probable that glacial tongues once shaped these valleys, too.

To wildflower lovers — and who is not? — these are breathtaking meadows. Columbine abound, each blossom tricolored: a center of yellow stamens, five white petals, and an outer circlet of five petal-like sepals that vary in color from deep to pale blue (rarely white). Five spurs, well over an inch long, extend below each blossom. These unusual members of the buttercup family are specialized for pollination by hawkmoths, which hover in front of the blossoms and uncoil their long tongues to probe for nectar deep within the spurs.

Aside from columbine the most eye-catching flowers of these meadows are the Indian paintbrushes, although these are not quite what they seem. The "flowers" are actually garishly colored bracts that enclose inconspicuous tubular, yellowish flowers. Furthermore, paintbrushes are semiparasites, with seedlings sending out rootlets to penetrate those of neighboring plants, from which they derive water and perhaps some of their food. Older plants usually survive on their own. They range all the way from tundra to plains, and the numerous species sometimes hybridize, producing a bewildering array of colors and forms. Yellow and rose paintbrushes tend to be short plants with compact inflorescences, while orange and red species are taller, with more ragged bracts of color. It is the scarlet paintbrush that so vividly adorns these valleys, the state flower of Wyoming competing for attention with the blue columbine, the state flower of Colorado.

Not all the wildflowers here are as brilliantly colored. In damp places there are patches of succulent green plants, often as high as a person's head, bearing large, pleated leaves. Yet the most they can provide is a terminal cluster of small, greenish-white flowers. This is false hellebore, an offbeat member of the lily family. There seems nothing false about these plants — they assert themselves boldly among the more delicate plants of these meadows. Presumably they bear some resemblance to "true" hellebore, a Eurasian plant of the buttercup family that is sometimes cultivated in North America. The roots and young shoots of false hellebore contain alkaloids that have proved valuable as a sedative and for slowing heartbeat and lowering blood pressure. In high concentrations, however, they are poisonous. Livestock have sometimes been killed by eating the young plants, and there are reports of honeybees being poisoned by taking nectar from the blossoms. Clearly these plants are not ones to be used as emergency rations by persons lost in the mountains. On the other hand, elk thistles, spiny and much less appetizing-looking tall plants in these mountains, have roots and stems that are filling and tasty. Truman Everts, lost for a month in Yellowstone National Park in 1870, is said to have survived until rescued by eating the roots of these thistles. Clearly the appearance of a plant provides no clues to its desirability as food.

With luck the cautious hiker may see a herd of elk feeding among the bushes along the stream. In summer the herds consist mainly of cows accompanied by their calves and young from the previous year. The bulls are off in the forest, alone or in small groups, their great antlers hardening for the autumn rut. Then their bugling will echo through the valleys. Elk hunting is a major sport in Colorado, but here in Rocky Mountain National Park all wildlife is protected. However, those in the upper Poudre Valley are close to the edge of the park, and elk cannot read signs! At one time, about 1900, the elk in Colorado had been reduced to a few bands, perhaps not over one thousand in all. Repeated introductions from more northern localities restored the population to many thousands, and game management, largely funded by hunting and fishing licenses, has resulted in continuing good population levels.

Elk feed primarily on grasses and sedges, though not turning down an occasional wildflower. In winter they wander into lower valleys where the snow is not as deep. Here they may browse on sagebrush, rabbitbrush, or even junipers. In early days elk ranged throughout much of North America, even in the plains and eastern forests. To see them today is to recapture a bit of the America of the pioneers.

Between three and five miles downstream from the junction of Chapin Creek with the Poudre, several changes, both natural and political, occur in the valley. Forests begin to encroach on a narrowing, more steep-sided valley. Hague's Creek flows in from the east, a major stream that drains a considerable area of the Mummies, including the west slopes of Hague's Peak. The creek and the peak were named for Arnold Hague, a Yale graduate in geology who in 1871 climbed Long's Peak with author and historian Henry Adams and with Clarence King, another Yale graduate who was director of the U.S. Geological Survey of the fortieth parallel. Hague is said to have used the top of Hague's Peak as a triangulation point.

A bit further downstream, Cascade Creek joins the Poudre, also from the east. Its origin is Mirror Lake, a beautiful cirque lake accessible by trail from the Poudre. One July day we hiked this trail, camping on a windy bluff among bluebells and bistort overlooking the lake. Cliffs a thousand feet high on the west side of the lake were still streaked with snow, and we were thankful that we had a sturdy tent and reliable down sleeping bags. A spectacular sunset gave us hope for a warm day ahead, but in fact when we returned to the Poudre that evening, we had to

Mirror Lake is a typical glacier-formed cirque lake, nestled deep in the Mummy Range. *Courtesy of the U.S. Forest Service.*

make camp in a bitter hailstorm. Such are the vicissitudes of mountain weather.

Between Hague's and Cascade creeks, La Poudre Pass Creek enters from the west from Long Draw Reservoir, greatly augmented by Grand Ditch, which takes water from the upper reaches of the Colorado River drainage — one of several points at which the Poudre, through human intervention, "steals" water from other river systems. La Poudre Pass is on the Continental Divide, but it is a relatively low pass, a mere 10,200 feet. Hiking the trail above the reservoir, it is difficult to realize one is at the pass, so gentle is the climb. But beyond to the west, the slopes descend steeply to the upper valley of the Colorado. Specimen Mountain is to the south and the eroded yellow volcanic rock of "Little Yellowstone" is visible.

Grand Ditch was begun in 1890, and its fourteen miles plus Long Draw Reservoir were finally finished in the 1930s. The Ditch winds around the eastern slopes of the Never Summer Range, intercepting sixteen tributaries of the Colorado River; its scar is visible from Trail Ridge Road. It was dug largely with picks and shovels manned primarily by Chinese laborers who were paid no more than a dollar a day. They lived mostly on rice that was brought up the Poudre Valley by burros.

Grand Ditch, started in the 1890s, intercepts several of the tributaries of the Colorado River and diverts the water to the Cache la Poudre.

The name Grand Ditch does not imply anything "grand" about the ditch, though it is impressive enough; it was named when the Colorado still was called the Grand River. It was begun before the area was part of the national park, and in 1923, when it was decided that a storage reservoir was necessary, an act of Congress was needed to remove land from the park holdings for the reservoir, and another to extend the upper end of the ditch so that the reservoir could be filled to capacity. Grand Ditch is listed now in the National Register of Historic Places.

Before it joins the Poudre, La Poudre Pass Creek is augmented by Willow Creek from the south, draining the eastern slopes of Specimen Mountain, and by Corral Creek from the north. Before descending to the junction, Corral Creek flows through broad meadows over two miles long (Corral Park) paralleling in part Long Draw Road and providing spectacular views of snowcapped mountains to the west. The remains of an old corral provided the name for the creek and the park. The corral may have been built by lumbermen cutting railroad ties as a place to contain their horses, then later used by ranchers when they grazed their cattle here in the summer.

THE BIG SOUTH

At La Poudre Pass Creek, we leave Rocky Mountain National Park and enter Roosevelt National Forest. This is a forest of 782,000 acres that was established in 1910 and, in 1932, named for Theodore Roosevelt, father of the national forests. At this point the Poudre River Trail becomes the Big South Trail, "south" because most hikers enter it from State Highway 14 to the north and head south along the trail, "big" to distinguish it from trails along the smaller South Fork of the Poudre, often called the "Little South." Here the river enters the Comanche Peak Wilderness, which includes about ten miles of the river as well as a large area to the east, including the crest of Comanche Peak. This is one of four wilderness areas in the Poudre drainage; another, the Neota Wilderness, can be entered via a trail from La Poudre Pass.

After entering the national forest, the river assumes a very different character. With all this new water, it is robust, difficult to cross, plunging over boulders or racing through narrow defiles. In places there are granite walls or large boulders beside the river, so that the trail is routed a short distance up the valley slope. Where there are flat places close to the river, there is often evidence of past campsites, but U.S. Forest Service regulations now restrict camping within a hundred feet of the river.

Hiking along the Big South Trail one July day, we came upon one of the most precious of the forest's gems, twinflower (*Linnaea borealis*), said to be a favorite of the great Swedish naturalist Carl Linnaeus, for whom it was named. These fragile members of the honeysuckle family range throughout the cooler parts of the Northern Hemisphere. To find a blanket of these paired, pink, bell-like flowers is a sufficient reward for a long day's hike.

These are cold, crystal-clear waters, but the hiker must be wary about drinking from the river or from small streams or springs that enter from the sides. Even here the waters may be contaminated by a microscopic one-celled organism called *Giardia lamblia*. Under high magnification this is an attractive little animal with whip-like locomotor appendages and a pair of nuclei that resemble eyes. If ingested in numbers, these organisms can produce fever, cramps, and severe diarrhea, a condition called giardiasis.

The source of the contamination is fecal material that is washed into the stream. Until recently few people had heard of *Giardia,* and streams and springs in the high country were perfectly safe to drink. Apparently the greater use of the forests by hikers, hunters, and fishermen has produced the contamination, for people are often careless as to where they leave their wastes. It is possible that wild animals, particularly beavers, become infected by way of human wastes and thereby increase the contamination. In any case hikers should carry enough water to meet their needs.

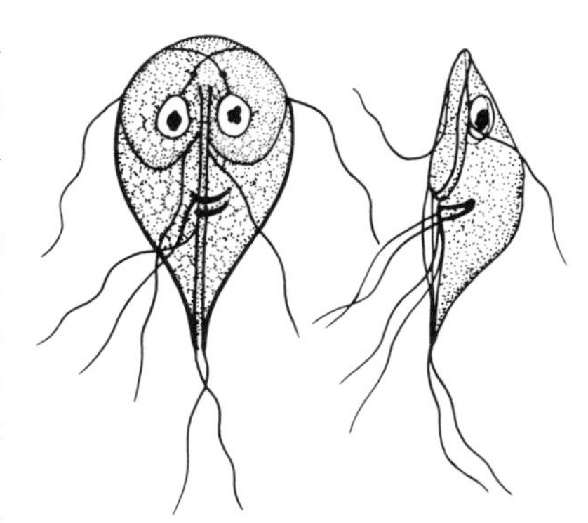

Giardia as it appears under the microscope, on the left "face on," on the right from the side.

This part of the valley is a favorite haunt of an incredible bird, the dipper, or water ouzel. Dippers belong to a unique group of birds; there are only five species of dippers in the world, and only one in North America, confined to mountain streams of the West. These are stocky, sooty-gray birds that can often be seen doing "push-ups" on the rocks in the stream. Periodically they dive beneath the water and emerge with a stonefly or mayfly larva in their bills. They are able to walk or swim underwater, even in the swiftest currents, and they may remain submerged for a minute or more. Dippers do not migrate, at least not very far; in winter they seek places where there is open water where they may still dive for food.

We have found the nests of dippers on several occasions, always attached to rock walls overlooking the stream. They are built of grasses and mosses, with the entrance on one side. Dippers produce a sharp, liquid chirp as they fly from rock to rock and now and then can be heard to sing above the noise of the stream. It is a complex and rather wonderful song for so demure a bird. John Muir, in his well-known essay "The Water-Ouzel," describes it in this way:

> The more striking strains are perfect arabesques of melody, composed of a few full, round, mellow notes, embroidered with delicate trills which fade and melt in long slender cadences. In a general way his music is that of the streams refined and spiritualized. The deep booming notes of the falls are in it, the trills of rapids, the gurgling of margin eddies, the low whispering of level reaches, and the sweet

Dippers never stray far from the mountain streams where they find their food and nesting sites. *Photo by David Leatherman.*

> tinkle of separate drops oozing from the ends of mosses and falling into tranquil pools.

As one descends the Big South Trail, lodgepole pines become dominant trees on the slopes, although spruces are still plentiful in the valley bottom, with willows and alders hugging the stream. Lodgepoles are straight and slender trees that grow remarkably close together. They usually occur in pure stands of about the same age, a result of having replaced forests once destroyed by fire. The cones of these pines usually remain on the trees and closed for long periods; following a fire they open and release the seeds, reforesting devastated areas.

As a result of the growth habit of the trees, the trunks are of nearly uniform diameter for a considerable height. The Indians used smaller trees for making poles for their teepees and for making drag-sleds with which the squaws carried their belongings from one camp to another. Early settlers found the trees ideal for building log fences before the advent of barbed wire, and they were (and still are) perfect for building log cabins. Builders of the early railroads esteemed their straight boles for ties. "Tie boys" had camps in many higher parts of the valley, cutting

Nokhu Crags rise above Cameron Pass to a height of 12,485 feet.

trees through the winter and using the spring runoff to send them down to the plains. By the late 1880s, the readily available trees had all been cut. Most of the lodgepole pines now seen in the upper Poudre system represent the following generation, most being about one hundred years old.

Joe Wright Creek

At the lower end of the Big South Trail, on State Highway 14 at 8,450 feet elevation, the Poudre is joined by another significant tributary, Joe Wright Creek, named for an early trapper in the area. Since the highway more or less follows this creek to its source at Cameron Pass, it lacks the pristine atmosphere of most other tributaries in the high country. But it is good to have a bit of the upper Poudre system accessible to those who cannot or will not hike. The highway over Cameron Pass was not completed until 1926 and not improved and paved until the 1970s. Much earlier, in 1881, S. B. Stewart had completed a toll road over the pass and on to Teller City, west of the Never Summer Range. Although Stewart and his associates had invested $20,000 in the road, it lasted only six years, and as miners rushed

Lake Agnes, though not part of the Poudre drainage, nevertheless provides water to the Poudre via Michigan Ditch.

to Cripple Creek's more productive ores Teller City became a ghost town.

Cameron Pass, at 10,320 feet elevation, is a great place to stop and admire the wildflowers in spring and summer and in winter to ski cross-country. The Nokhu Crags, just to the southwest, are among the most rugged peaks in the Rockies. Although some of the surrounding mountains are volcanic in origin, the Crags are composed of metamorphic rocks, vertical layers of flint-like rocks eroded between the layers to form a jagged profile. Old-timers called the Crags "Old Sawtooth," but the Colorado Geographic Board adopted the name Nokhu, based on an Arapahoe word meaning "where the eagles nest."

Just west of the Crags, nestled among towering cliffs, is a small lake with an island near the center. It was once called Island Lake, but John Zimmerman renamed it for his infant daughter Agnes. (We'll have more to say about the Zimmermans in a later chapter.) Zimmerman believed the lake occupied a volcanic crater, but in fact it is a typical cirque lake, formed by glacial action. The lake can be reached by a fairly short hike from the trailhead, an easy way to gain an intimate view of some glorious alpine country without backpacking deep into the wilds.

Cameron Pass is not on the Continental Divide. If one empties a canteen at the pass, half will theoretically reach the North Platte and half the South Platte, and the waters will be reunited in Nebraska. Since the Nokhu Crags and Lake Agnes are west of the pass, they are not truly part of the Poudre drainage. However, as early as the 1890s a seven-mile ditch was dug from the outlet of Lake Agnes, along the slopes of the Crags, all the way to Cameron Pass, where it adds its flow to the nascent Joe Wright Creek. The tributaries it intercepts are those of the Michigan River (flowing into the North Platte), so it is called the Michigan Ditch. It is the second of seven intermountain diversions we'll have occasion to mention.

Cross-country skiers at the pass are sometimes astonished to see a strange insect living on top of the snow. This is the snow fly, *Chionea nivicola*, *chion* being Greek for "snow" and *nivicola* Latin for "living on snow." Although less than an inch long, its black body and long, spreading legs make it conspicuous on the white background. These are true flies, though they have no wings at all. They have been seen to be active on the snow at an air temperature of 15º F, and when picked up they are repelled by the heat of the hand. In the summer they live under vegetation or in rodent nests. Hardly anything is known about their sex lives or what they eat.

The forests around Cameron Pass are prime habitat for a fascinating but secretive bird of prey called the boreal owl. These owls range throughout the far north of both North America and Eurasia and rarely venture south of the Canadian border. Only recently have ornithologists come to realize that there are breeding populations in parts of the Colorado Rockies. These are small owls that are more often heard than seen. In the early spring breeding season, they produce a series of sharp whistles that sometimes can be heard a mile away. David Palmer, while a graduate student at Colorado State University, located several near Cameron Pass by driving slowly along roads and listening for their calls. He was able to capture several with mist nets baited with live mice and with tape-recorded songs. Three of the owls were fitted with radio transmitters and followed for several months to determine their home ranges and hunting behavior. In the breeding season, he found, males stay within a home range about a mile in diameter, but at other seasons they range more widely. They prey mainly on voles (small rodents with blunt noses and short tails), but also take an occasional bird.

One of David Palmer's objectives was to learn how these owls

A boreal owl has been fitted with a radio transmitter so that its movements can be followed by researchers. *Photo by David Palmer.*

coexist with another owl of similar size, the saw-whet owl. Saw-whets occur widely in more temperate parts of the continent and receive their name from their metallic, "saw-filing" calls. In the Poudre system, Palmer found that saw-whets occur up to about 9,000 feet elevation, primarily in mixed forest, while boreal owls occur above 9,000 feet in dense spruce-fir forests. Since saw-whets prey primarily on deer mice, these two very similar owls effectively do not compete either in preferred habitat or in type of prey.

We have had no experience with boreal owls, but saw-whets once nested in an old flicker hole in one of the pine trees near our home. When the young owls left the nest, they obligingly perched for a day on limbs overlooking our picnic table, peering at us but sitting like statues before flying off during the night. David Palmer climbed the tree and extracted several pellets from the abandoned nest. To our knowledge the owls have never returned to this site.

There are three reservoirs on or just off Joe Wright Creek — Joe Wright, Barnes Meadow, and Chambers Lake — all of them popular with anglers. Unimproved side roads provide access to Peterson Lake, Trap Lake, Long Draw Reservoir, and to the valley of the upper Laramie River. Two beautiful natural lakes are accessible by short hikes,

This immature saw-whet owl perched, with three others, only a few feet from our picnic table, watching us while we lunched.

Zimmerman and Blue, the latter within the Rawah Wilderness. Though natural, Zimmerman has a small dam built by the Colorado Division of Wildlife to enhance its value for fishing.

Hiking from Chambers Lake up the Blue Lake Trail early one summer, we came upon a place where snowbanks were just melting back and avalanche lilies were springing up to follow the meltback. These are the gayest of mountain flowers, each plant having a pair of succulent leaves and a single nodding yellow blossom. According to the Craigheads and Davis in their *Field Guide,* Indians collected the bulbs and ate them boiled, or dried them for winter use. The bulbs are also relished by bears and are stored for winter use by various rodents; the green pods that follow the flowers are eaten by elk, deer, and bighorn sheep. H. D. Harrington, in his book on edible plants of the Rockies, says that the bulbs are pleasant eaten raw but even better when boiled. But, he adds, this "lovely plant is certainly too beautiful to gather indiscriminately as food." We concur.

Many of these lakes and reservoirs have stories connected with them, but we cannot interrupt our narrative for all of them. The depression in which Chambers Lake rests at one time formed the headwaters of the Laramie River, but a landslide closed off the valley

Avalanche lilies follow the meltback of the snows in the high country.

and caused a small lake to form and drain into Joe Wright Creek. The landslide scar can still be seen on the side of nearby Cameron Peak. The slide is believed to have occurred between 8,000 and 12,000 years ago and may have taken only a few minutes to happen.

The lake is named for Robert Chambers, who camped there in 1858 while trapping beaver and hunting bears. One day his ammunition ran low, so the story goes, and he sent his son (also Robert) to Laporte for a fresh supply. When the lad returned, he found that his father had been killed and scalped by the Indians, who also burned the cabin and took the furs. Robert, Jr., left the area but later spread the word that good timber was to be found there. Soon the area became a camp for cutting railroad ties, which were floated down Joe Wright Creek and the Poudre during the spring runoff.

Somewhat later, in 1891, the waters of the West Branch of the Laramie River were partially diverted to Chambers Lake via Skyline Ditch, which has since been improved and is still in use. About the same time, a dam was built to enlarge the lake. When it was completed and the lake full, William Rist, an engineer for the Larimer County Ditch Company, examined the dam and found it safe. But it was raining heavily, and he had trouble getting back to town to file his report. There was a flood and the bridges were out — the dam had already broken! "Huge spruce trees seventy feet high just keeled over as the flood hit them. . . . The Larimer County Ditch Company had all kinds of damage suits on their hands after the flood," so recalls Norman Walter Fry, who lived on the Poudre for many years. The dam was rebuilt more substantially in 1910.

The vicinity of Chambers Lake is one of the few places in the Rockies south of Canada where wood frogs occur. Wood frogs are well known to easterners and to Canadians — in fact, they are the only frogs known to occur north of the Arctic Circle. In the Rockies they occur in only a few isolated pockets where there are shallow, sedge-filled "pot-hole" ponds with little water flowing in or out. Evidently they moved south into the Rockies during the ice ages, then, when the glaciers retreated, remained as small populations here and there. The few scattered breeding colonies in north central Colorado and adjacent parts of Wyoming are separated from the continuous part of the range in Canada by 450 miles (except for another isolated population in the Big Horns of Wyoming). The Colorado wood frogs have been isolated for so long that they have evolved differences in color and body-limb proportions, so that they have sometimes been considered a different species or subspecies. In Colorado, wood frogs have been classified as a threatened species, one of several in the Poudre drainage.

Wood frogs are small, brownish frogs with a black mask. In May they gather in ponds and the males produce a hoarse call, rather as if they had a "frog in their throat" (we suppose that is how that expression came about). At mating time the female lays one to two thousand eggs that within three weeks produce a lively batch of tadpoles. Trout and frogs do not usually occur together, since trout are voracious predators on tadpoles; but in any case trout do not thrive in the kinds of ponds preferred by wood frogs. Since these ponds have little value to people other than their esthetic qualities, they have often been needlessly destroyed. For example, when the highway to Cameron Pass was rerouted and paved, several breeding sites were destroyed, and when Lost Lake (adjacent to Chambers Lake) was deepened to make it more suitable for trout, the frogs vanished. But now that these obscure amphibians have been declared threatened, perhaps there is hope for them.

Spruces, firs, and lodgepole pines dominate the landscape in the vicinity of Cameron Pass and Chambers Lake, but as one descends the valley he or she becomes aware of a very different tree, one especially beloved by westerners — trembling aspen. Like lodgepole pines, these are pioneer trees, filling in empty spaces and taking over when more long-lived trees have been destroyed by fire, insects, or logging. Although aspens occur from coast to coast, they are especially precious in the West, where they are the only tall, broad-leafed deciduous trees of the high mountains. Their ability to carry out photosynthesis in their bark may account for their ability to thrive in country otherwise dominated by coniferous trees. In the fall the leaves turn gold — a gold spiritually far more rewarding than any that can be grubbed from the rocks. In October, State Highway 14 becomes a gateway to one of the finest displays in the Rockies.

Aspens occur in groves that are the result of a system of underground runners established by a tree that began as a seed. Since all the trees in the grove are the vegetative offspring of a parent tree, all are genetically identical, forming a clone (from the Greek word for a twig or slip). Members of one clone may differ from others in such things as leaf size, time of leafing or leaf fall, or color of the autumn foliage. In that lies the fascination of aspen watching; on a valley slope on a day in early autumn, some patches may be yellow, others copper or bronze, while others may still be green or already leafless. Clones also differ in their susceptibility to damage by insects or frost.

Aspen trees have flowers of one sex only, and since clones contain genetically identical trees each clone is all male or all female. Two researchers at the University of Colorado, Michael Grant and Jeffry Mitton, found that close to the foothills of the Rockies clones are more than 50 percent female, while in the high country (over 9,000 feet elevation) male clones exceed female in a ratio of nearly two to one. Female growth rates are also lower than those of males at higher altitudes. It appears that females are less well adapted to the high country, perhaps because females require more nutrients to set seeds, and these are less plentifully acquired when growing seasons are short.

As every hiker knows, these are talking trees. The leaf blades are longer than the leaves and are flattened at right angles to the leaves, so that the leaves do indeed tremble with every passing breeze. Because of the open canopy and the silver-gray, light-reflecting trunks, aspen groves are sunny places, with an understory of grasses, lupines, larkspurs, wild strawberries, and many other plants. There is a no more delicious place to pitch a tent than among aspens.

Very often the bark of aspens is scarred, the result of feeding by elk, bighorn sheep, or porcupines, usually in winter. Where beavers occur, they depend heavily on aspen for winter food, cutting the trees and dragging their branches under the water; branches may also make up part of their dams. In winter aspen buds are fed upon by rabbits, grouse, and songbirds, and in summer so many kinds of insects feed on the leaves that one wonders that so many remain to brighten the forests.

Although foresters tend to think of aspens as weed trees, the wood is tough and the grain often twisted. Early settlers used aspen for horse stables and corrals, since the wood is resistant to kicking and stomping. Nowadays it is sometimes used as firewood or for pulp. But most of all, aspens are cherished for their individuality and for the diversity they introduce into mountain forests that are sometimes dark and seemingly endless. In her book *Beyond the Aspen Grove*, Ann Zwinger has, as usual, just the right words: "Conifers have a majestic monotony, like someone who is always right. They are too timeless to mark the seasons. But aspen has eclat, a glorious brashness in defiance of the rules, the flapper who does the Charleston in the midst of the grand waltz. The landscape would be dull indeed without them."

Although we have discussed aspens as trees of the high country, they in fact occur well down the canyon and its tributaries, at least as low as 6,000 feet elevation, and they are planted as ornamentals in Front Range cities. But Engelmann spruce, subalpine firs, and lodgepole pines will be left behind as we descend the river.

The main stem of the Cache la Poudre, from Big South trailhead to the plains, is well traveled and provided with numerous national forest picnic areas and campgrounds that are mostly full on summer weekends. People from cities of the Front Range and plains, indeed from many parts of the country, find the canyon a respite from smog, noise, and the fatigue of travel, as well as a place to inhale the sweet odors of the forest, to treat the eyes to the variety of wildflowers, and to listen to the chorusing of the waters. In the next chapter, we resume our trip down the river, from the confluence of Joe Wright Creek and the Poudre to the foothills and plains, a drop of about 3,500 feet over about forty-five miles. We have so far followed the river for about twenty miles from its source at Poudre Lake, with a drop of about 2,260 feet. So we are still a good bit less than halfway on our journey.

4

A CANYON FOR EVERYONE

The country we have traversed so far is in the public domain — national park or national forest. Even Joe Wright Creek, though paralleled by a paved road, is in national forest except for one small area. Below the junction of Joe Wright with the Poudre, it is a different story. Although most of the country away from the river is part of Roosevelt National Forest, there are numerous private inholdings along the river, some occupied by homes, others by stores, cafes, motels, or trailer parks. Fortunately there are fewer than along many Colorado rivers, and most are small and blend reasonably well with the surrounding terrain. There is still plenty of public access, but it is no longer easy to "hike the valley" unless one is willing to walk along the highway.

Another major change occurs at this junction. Here at about 8,500 feet, we leave the alpine and subalpine regions of the ecologists and enter the montane region. These roughly defined regions are characterized by differences in temperature and moisture and by plants and animals that are adapted for these differences. For example, as we descend we shall see no limber pines or pikas except on mountains that tower above the valley, and flowers such as avalanche lilies and twinflowers will have been left well behind. In the alpine and subalpine, the average annual precipitation may approximate 26 inches, the mean annual temperature 25° to 35° F, the freeze-free period from forty to eighty days. Here at 8,500 feet, comparable figures might approximate 20 inches of precipitation, a mean temperature of 42° F, and as many as one hundred days free of serious frost. Proceeding down the valley will take us into a progressively warmer and drier climate.

Biogeographers have their own terms for the alpine and subalpine. They call them the Hudsonian and Canadian zones, implying a continuity with regions much farther north. Indeed many of the plants and animals do range into Canada, Alaska, and in many cases into northern Eurasia. Descending from the Joe Wright junction, we gradually enter

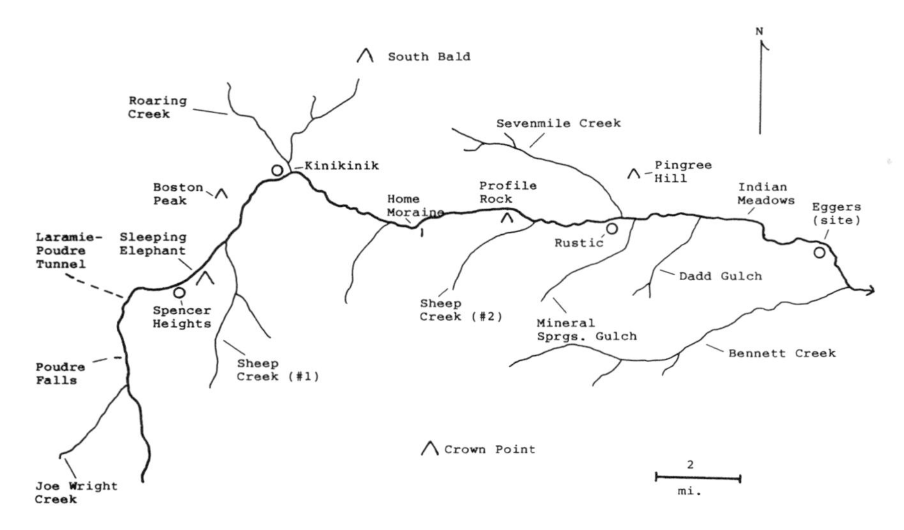

The upper canyon, from Joe Wright Creek junction to Bennett Creek junction.

the montane region — the Transition Zone of the biogeographers — transitional to the warmer and more arid zones below. Many of the plants and animals are more characteristically Rocky Mountain; they don't usually range into the Arctic or into the plains or deserts. We'll meet some of them as we descend.

There are no hard and fast lines between these zones; rather they grade into one another over several hundred feet of elevation. Further, the direction of the slopes bordering this basically west-east valley makes a great deal of difference. Slopes facing south receive more sun and may be sparsely, if at all, forested. The snow melts here quickly, spring flowers bloom and disappear early, and grasses, sage, junipers, and various bushes prevail. North-facing slopes tend to be heavily wooded, with loamy, moisture-holding soil. In many places in this winding valley, slopes face at angles that are by no means due south or north, and the vegetation may be still different, often unpredictable.

In the high country, streams have a more or less continuous strong flow, since there are active springs and melting snow even in late summer. In the Transition Zone, streams flowing into the Poudre in some cases have very little flow except in spring. This is less true of those flowing in from north-facing slopes, where the forest soil holds more moisture and releases it slowly. Smaller tributaries from south-facing slopes are sometimes dry for much of the year, but occasional summer thunderstorms can turn them into roaring monsters, flushing boulders and silt into the valley and destroying living things in their paths. On a sunny summer day, it is difficult to understand how the Rockies became so grossly dissected. But watch a flash flood on a normally tranquil or dry stream and consider how many times this must have occurred since the birth of the Rockies.

Joe Wright Junction to South Fork Junction

About a mile below the Joe Wright-Poudre confluence, the river makes the only descent abrupt enough to justify the word "falls." Poudre Falls is only a drop of thirty or forty feet, and the highway is so close beside it as to spoil any aura of wildness it may once have had. The falls were the bane of early loggers trying to float ties down to Laporte, where they could be collected by the workmen laying tracks. The logs tended to jam at the falls, and at least one logger was killed there while trying to untangle the mess. Poudre Falls had another but more or less forgotten function: it once held a small dam that provided power to the men who built the tunnel from the Laramie River. Remains of that dam are now barely visible near the top of the falls. The falls and its dam remnant are listed by the Colorado State Historical Preservation Office.

A bit downstream from the falls, the Laramie-Poudre Tunnel discharges its waters high on the north slope, an impressive artificial cascade. This tunnel, built during 1909–1911, diverts more of the Laramie River water. This is the second diversion from this river, and the fourth high-altitude diversion we have mentioned; there are others to be discussed later. At the time the tunnel was built, it was felt (at least in Colorado) that as Laramie River water was used only in a few hay meadows, it was needed more down on the Colorado plains where sugar beets were being grown. Wyoming ranchers disagreed but they lost the argument. The tunnel is about two miles long and adds an appreciable amount of water to the Poudre through the summer season.

At the time the tunnel was constructed, there was no road for the full length of the canyon, and equipment and supplies had to be hauled

Poudre Falls was once harnessed to provide power for the construction of the Laramie-Poudre tunnel, a short distance downstream. *Photo by W. A. Parsons, U.S. Forest Service.*

in by a circuitous route requiring at least two days' travel from Fort Collins. In spite of this, a camp was built that included bunkhouses, a commissary, and a small hospital. Water was piped from the dam above the falls to operate three water wheels that provided the power to drive the drills and supply lighting. Since the rock was a hard granite, a great

Lush meadows in upper Poudre Canyon provide winter grazing for bighorn sheep. *Photo by W. A. Parsons, U.S. Forest Service.*

many charges of dynamite were required to complete the task. Boring was done from both ends, but so accurate was the work of the surveyors that the bore from the Laramie met the bore from the Poudre with an error of less than an inch. When the tunnel was finished, there was a grand celebration during which 300 freshly caught trout were said to have been consumed.

Below the tunnel the valley becomes broader and flatter for several miles, with steep walls, the typical U-shaped profile indicating past glaciation. The small village of Spencer Heights provides various amenities for travelers, including tow service. Just beyond, Sleeping Elephant Mountain rises to 9,145 feet, thirteen hundred feet above the valley floor. While we tend to think people who give names to hunks of rock are presumptuous, we must admit that we, too, can pick out the ears and trunk of a reclining giant on the side of the formation — the side bordering Sheep Creek (the first of three of that name) as it slices its way to the Poudre.

This is a bright, open valley, with grassy meadows, groves of aspen,

Adult male bighorn sheep.

and thickets of willows and alders. Evidences of past forest fires are visible on distant hillsides. Along the stream a handsome deciduous tree now becomes common — the narrow-leaved cottonwood. Lewis and Clark discovered this tree along the upper Missouri River, remarking that the trees had a leaf "like that of the wild cherry." More like willow, some would say. These trees have little value as lumber, but they add a bright touch and welcome shade to many mountain streams. In the fall they rival the aspens with their golden foliage. Narrow-leaved cottonwoods follow the river all the way to the foothills.

The verdant meadows in this part of the valley provide the winter feeding ground of bighorn sheep. In the summer the sheep can sometimes be seen high on the valley slopes. In the late 1800s, the population of these magnificent animals was decimated throughout much of the Rockies by unbridled hunting. The herd in the upper Poudre was started in 1946 by the introduction of sixteen from the Tarryall Mountains southwest of Denver. It now numbers more than one hundred. The sheep breed in midwinter, when the rams compete aggressively for ewes that are in heat. Their battles, now familiar to everyone through television documentaries, involve violent clashes with the great, coiled horns. These are true horns and are not shed annually like the antlers of deer and elk. In fact, the age of the animal can be estimated from the growth rings on them. The females have smaller horns that are curved only slightly. The ability of these animals to climb about on rocky cliffs is legendary. Unfortunately this herd, like many others, is subject to periodic declines resulting from lungworm infections.

Streams entering this part of the valley plunge down the steep slopes in cataracts; above the slopes they often follow a much more gentle gradient. These are "hanging valleys" typical of once-glaciated areas. Roaring Creek, which enters the Poudre from the north, is such a valley. A trailhead along the highway gives access to Roaring Creek and the high country in which it begins. The trail goes on to join the Green Ridge Trail, which goes all the way from Chambers Lake to the slopes of Deadman Hill, near the source of the Poudre's North Fork.

Near the trailhead is a cluster of homes called Kinikinik, named for a low, creeping, evergreen plant that was highly esteemed by the Indians. Since the word is Indian, it has been transposed into English in a variety of spellings. Botanists seem to prefer double *n*s: kinnikinnik. This is a member of the heath family, related to blueberries, laurels, and wintergreen. It produces small, pink-lipped flowers resembling inverted cups and in the fall red berries that resemble cranberries. The berries have a mealy, puckery taste, but it is said that when boiled they are more palatable. We have never tried them. Indians used to harvest them and combine them with other berries and with dried venison to make pemmican, which served them through the winter. The berries are choice food for grouse, rodents, and black bears; in fact bearberry is an alternate name, and the scientific name, *uva-ursi,* means bears' grape. The Indians also smoked the dried leaves, usually mixed with other ingredients. Apparently they have a mildly intoxicating effect. They also contain glycosides said to be useful in the treatment of urinary infections and kidney and bladder stones. Whatever its chemistry, kinnikinnik is a treasured plant, growing in poor soil or over rocks, stabilizing and enriching the soil so that the other plants can take root. The deep green foliage, delicate blossoms, and red berries are a joy to behold, and without the berries a good many wild creatures would have a tougher time making it through the winter.

Kinnikinnik grows in many parts of the Poudre drainage, but the settlers in this part of the canyon must have had a particular affection for it. The Kinikinik store and cabins, now closed, represent one of the oldest resorts on the river. The adjacent ranch was settled in 1867 by an Englishman named Blackmer and is still occupied. The log blacksmith shop still stands and is said to be the oldest remaining building in the canyon. About two miles downstream, the broad valley is

The delicate, bell-shaped flowers of kinnikinnik are later replaced by tart red berries.

occupied by a trout-rearing facility operated by the Colorado Division of Wildlife. The meadows in this part of the valley are dominated by big sagebrush and by Colorado wild rye grass, as well as by several wildflowers of unusual interest to botanists. This is one of several areas along the Poudre that are being studied as part of the Colorado Natural Areas Inventory.

A short distance below the fish hatchery, a dilapidated log structure is all that is left of a cabin built for the TV miniseries based on James Michener's novel *Centennial*. Poudre Canyon is normally a sleepy place in March and April, when there is still plenty of snow about. But in the early spring of 1978, during the filming of *Centennial*, the highway was jammed with vehicles carrying filming crews, actors, and equipment. Among the props they carried, according to the Fort Collins *Triangle Review*, were "canoes, jugs of artificial blood, stuffed deer, animal traps, and enough frontier muskets, knives, and bows and arrows to fight the American Indian wars all over again." Even, it was added, barrels of genuine buffalo chips. The cabin was that of fictional mountain man Alexander McKeag, played by Richard Chamberlain. Now, helped by vandals, it is falling apart, and cattle graze in the surrounding flower-filled meadows.

In 1896 a resort hotel was built not far downstream from this point, but it was torn down in 1946 and few evidences remain. This was the Keystone Hotel, built and operated by John and Mike Zimmerman and their families and for half a century a major tourist attraction on the upper Poudre. The Home Post Office was formerly located in a cabin near the present site of the fish hatchery. When it was founded in 1880, application was made for the name "Mountain Home," but the U.S. Postal Service felt that there were already too many Mountain Homes, so the name became simply Home. Later the post office was moved to the hotel, and the name has been applied to the Home Moraine Geologic Site, a short distance downstream. This is a classic terminal moraine, consisting of soil and rocks gouged from the valley floor and sides and left as a barrier across the valley when the glaciers melted back. Now it is covered with grass and pine trees, and the river cuts through its north side, closely paralleled by the highway. A bulletin board in the parking area describes the formation of the moraine. The site is on the National Register of Historic Places.

In the summer the canyon is alive with hummingbirds taking nectar from the abundant wildflowers and from the feeders that residents maintain for them. The only locally breeding species is the broad-tailed hummingbird. Males of these fragile birds sometimes return from the south as early as April, when they may have to endure spring snowstorms. Males produce a high-pitched whistle while in flight. Often they fly high in the air, then descend quickly, like a stone being dropped, doubtless demonstrating their vigor to the quieter, more modestly colored females. We have occasionally found their nests, tiny baskets of moss and lichens attached to the limbs of trees.

The whistle of the male is produced by air rushing through slots between the two outer wing feathers. It has been assumed that the whistle is an important signal to other males in defense of courting territories. Working at the Rocky Mountain Biological Laboratory near Crested Butte, Colorado, two researchers from the University of Maryland, Sarah Miller and David Inouye, set out to test this experimentally. They silenced several males by applying a thin film of glue to the slot in the outer wing feathers; others had an equal amount of glue placed on other feathers to rule out any possible effects of the glue. The glue did not deter flight and could easily be removed with acetone. Silenced birds were less aggressive, perhaps as a result of lack of feedback from the whistle, and tended to lose their territories to other males. Silenced

A fisherman tries the waters of the Cache la Poudre, near Kinikinik. *Photo by W. A. Parsons, U.S. Forest Service.*

males often went unnoticed within the territories of other males, though they were eventually chased away. When the glue was removed, they resumed their normal aggressive defense of territories.

In July and August, rufous hummingbirds make their appearance, having bred farther north, even as far as Alaska. These are smaller but even feistier than the broad-tails. The wing sounds made by the males are quite different, more like a supercharged electric wire. We Americans tend to take hummingbirds for granted, forgetting that these remarkable fliers occur only in North and South America. They are mainly tropical birds, and of the many species only twenty enter the United States to some extent and only four occur in the Colorado Rockies.

If hummingbirds are the most minuscule of birds, living on nectar and tiny insects, peregrine falcons are the most formidable of predators, and now and then they can be spotted along Poudre Canyon. Once they were extinct here, but as a result of recent releases of birds bred in captivity, at least one pair has nested in the valley. These magnificent

Profile Rock guards the valley a short distance above the village of Rustic. *Photo by E. H. Mason, U.S. Forest Service.*

birds often prey on songbirds, which they overtake in flight, but they are part of the original predator fauna of the area, and it is good to have them back. Their decline in the fifties and sixties was at least in part a result of the fact that, as top predators, they often consumed prey that had ingested DDT. This produced physiological changes such that the eggs they laid had thin shells that were often crushed by the brooding parents. In the fall peregrines migrate to Mexico and points south, where DDT is still in use, so they are not entirely safe from that threat. Falcon eggshells in the wild are currently about 15 percent thinner than before the advent of DDT, but those laid by captive birds have normal thickness. The facility for rearing peregrines was formerly located near Fort Collins, and several years ago we had a chance to tour the station and observe these and other falcons at close range. The facility has now moved to Idaho, making way for approaches to a new brewery.

Below the Home Moraine, the valley is narrower and continues on down for about three miles until it reaches Sheep Creek (number two), which enters from the south just beyond where Poudre Canyon Chapel now stands. Various dwellings, mostly cottages and cabins, dot the riverside through this section. A prominent landmark, Profile Rock, looms up on the south side of the river. It is hard to miss and no doubt has served as the basis for many a story about earlier times. At the chapel is an old log schoolhouse that has been moved there from Eggers, a former settlement some seven miles downstream; it now serves as a library. Nearby a short trail leads to an old chimney that is all that remains of the Poudre City Stamp Mill, once used for processing ore from the surrounding mines. Poudre City once had a store, hotel, and saloons, serving some fifty residents. The village was destroyed when the Chambers Lake dam broke in 1891. The place is now a state historical site, and the name "Poudre City" has now been usurped by a modern resort a mile or so down the river.

In this section the valley is once again broader and relatively flat bottomed, not as a result of past glaciation, but because the river has entered a section of relatively easily eroded metamorphic rocks. The village of Rustic, a short distance below Poudre City, was started as a camp for loggers cutting ties, but it became important when a road was built down Pingree Hill from the north and on up the canyon to logging and mining camps, this before there was a road through the rugged lower part of the canyon. Rustic itself was a center of mining activity for a time. The Rustic Hotel, built in 1881, was still standing when we first became acquainted with the area in the 1970s, but it is now gone. Rustic is now a small community of homes, restaurants, and gift shops. The narrow gravel road over Pingree Hill from the north descends over 1,000 feet in three miles. It is a challenge to modern cars and must have been even more so to the teams of horses that once hauled people and supplies to the upper Poudre or down to the plains. "Many were the blocks and rocks placed behind the back wheels of the wagons, the Stanley Steamers, and the Model Ts to ease them down Pingree Hill," wrote Norman Walter Fry. Fry himself first entered the valley via Pingree Hill in 1889, and late in life he commented, "I guess I thought the Poudre Canyon was Heaven on Earth. And I still do."

At Indian Meadows, just below Rustic, the valley floor is especially broad and open. Dadd Gulch enters here from the south, said to have been named for an elderly African American who once had a cabin in the gulch. Whether his surname was Dadd or whether he was simply called "Dad" with a "d" added later is unknown (some of the early maps call it "Dad's Gulch"). We have hiked the gulch several times; like other streams that enter the valley from either side, it has something different to offer. The names of some of these side canyons are sufficiently intriguing to now and then lure curious people from the highway: Black Hollow, Mineral Springs Gulch, Poverty Gulch, Oskaloosa Gulch, Skin Gulch. Roosevelt National Forest headquarters in Fort Collins provides excellent maps showing established trails as well as many side canyons that invite exploration.

Not far below Indian Meadows, at about 6,900 feet, a road branches off to the south, winding its way through the hills to Pingree Park, where Colorado State University has its mountain campus. (George Pingree, for whom the hill and the park were named, we'll meet in chapter 7.) The road leaves the site of Eggers, now only a few foundations overgrown with bushes. After several miles the road enters the drainage of the South Fork of the Poudre. The South Fork itself enters the Poudre four miles below this point.

Two of the more popular camping and picnic areas are not far downstream from the intersection of the Pingree Park road with State Highway 14. These are Kelly Flats and Mountain Park. Norman Walter Fry tells that in the 1890s Jimmy Kelly had a three-room cabin on the flats that bear his name. "He was quite a picturesque figure," says Fry, "always dressed in buckskin shirt and pants which he made for himself from his skins. He was a small man, and unscrupulous." Kelly agreed to supply the crew working on the Skyline Ditch with elk meat, which he packed to their camp on his burros. But John Zimmerman found that some of his cattle were missing, and there was a strong suspicion that Kelly had "mistaken" some of them for elk. Kelly was eventually persuaded to leave the canyon.

Two short and easy trails leave from Mountain Park Campground. The Mount McConnel Trail provides an excellent overview of the canyon, while the William B. Kreutzer Nature Trail provides an introduction to the wildlife and the common trees and shrubs of the area. The latter is a candidate for National Recreational Trail status. Kreutzer has often been called "America's first forest ranger." In 1898, at the age of twenty-one, he was assigned as ranger to the Plum Creek Timber Reserve (this was well before the formation of the U. S. Forest Service). For a salary of $50 a month, he watched for fires and illegal harvesting of timber. In those years the equipment of a forest ranger consisted of a good horse, a pick, a shovel, a handsaw, and a tough constitution. Kreutzer wore his polished silver ranger's badge beneath his coat so that it would not serve as a target for ranchers and settlers who resented the federal presence in their forests. He was later transferred to the Gunnison Forest Reserve and finally to Colorado (now Roosevelt) National Forest, where he was supervisor from 1921 until his retirement in 1939. He was awarded an honorary doctor of science degree by Colorado Agricultural College (now State University), and Mount Kreutzer, a 13,120-foot peak in Gunnison National Forest, was named for him. Many of the campgrounds along the Poudre were built or improved during his tenure as supervisor.

The campgrounds at Kelly Flats and Mountain Park are shaded by ponderosa pines and Douglas-firs. These are the dominant evergreens not only here but in many parts of Poudre Canyon below the subalpine zone as well as in much of the surrounding country. Of the two, Douglas-firs prefer slightly cooler and moister sites, so are plentiful on north-facing slopes, while ponderosas are more abundant in drier and sunnier sites. But often the two are intermingled. Neither tree forms as dense a stand as lodgepole pine, and ponderosas, in particular, are often well spaced, with broad crowns, producing a park-like landscape. Along the moist, shaded valleys of the Poudre and its major tributaries, both trees occasionally reach a height of eighty feet or more, with massive trunks, but away from the streams the trees rarely exceed fifty feet.

Douglas-firs are not true firs, nor are they spruces, though they look superficially like both. The cones are very different; they are pendant, with bracts extending from between the scales. Each bract has a double, rounded end, with a slender filament between, rather like the tail ends of tiny animals plunging into the cones to escape a hawk circling overhead. The name of these trees was proposed in recognition of David Douglas, who was employed by the Royal Horticultural Society in the 1820s to explore western North America to obtain seeds to enrich English gardens. He joined the Hudson's Bay Company's outposts on the Columbia River, where he discovered several of the West's most distinctive trees. He met with a variety of misadventures and finally, at the age of thirty-four, was trampled to death by a bull — a dismal end for a person said to have had more plants named in his honor than anyone else in the history of botany. It is good to remember some of the discoverers of the plants and animals we see about us; often they endured extreme hardships, some losing their lives in the search for knowledge of the environment.

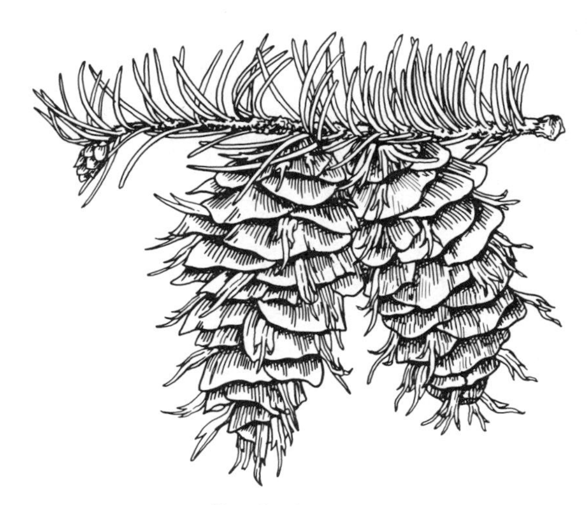

Douglas-fir cones.

Douglas-firs are known to be attacked by over 200 kinds of insect pests. In the early 1980s, spruce budworms defoliated many trees for two or more successive years, and extensive stands of dead trees can be seen in many places along the Poudre and its tributaries. The budworms have many natural enemies, including several kinds of parasitic flies and wasps as well as chickadees and other birds. But when budworm populations are low, many of the natural enemies are scarce, and it takes them several years to catch up and contain an outbreak. However, dead trees are soon replaced by others. These are resilient trees, and those that escape serious insect attack may live several hundred years. While old trees are often gnarled, misshapen, and bear numerous dead limbs, they still challenge the elements. Even after falling they provide living space and nutrients for mosses and fungi and living spaces for beetles, rodents, and other creatures before adding their substance to the forest soil.

Like Douglas-firs, ponderosa pines have a wide distribution, occurring from Canada to Mexico in mountainous areas. These are handsome trees, with relatively long needles and large cones. The bark of mature trees is yellowish-brown or somewhat russet, suggesting the alternate names western yellow pine and western red pine. David Douglas is reputed to have first suggested the name *ponderosa*, for in the Pacific Northwest they do indeed attain ponderous stature. Lewis

Mistletoe thrives on ponderosa pines in many parts of the Poudre basin.

and Clark called them "longleaf pines," and John Muir said of them, "Of all pines this one gives forth the finest music to the winds."

Ponderosa pines, too, have their insect pests. In the 1970s many were destroyed by mountain pine beetles, which feed beneath the bark and carry a fungus that stains the wood blue and chokes the tissues that carry the tree's nutrients. These beetles are always present in low numbers, and periodic outbreaks can be expected from time to time. The beetles and their larvae provide food for woodpeckers and nuthatches, and the dead trees supply homes for a variety of birds and mammals. While they may be unsightly to our eyes, dead trees are not a disaster to many creatures, and in time they will be replaced by wildflowers, by aspens, and by young ponderosas.

Dwarf mistletoe is another major pest of ponderosa pines. This is a yellow to orange epiphyte with small, scale-like leaves that lack chlorophyll. The plants send small rootlets into pine branches and take up nutrients from the tree. Often they form ugly growths on trees, including swellings and "witches' brooms." Gradually the trees weaken and in time may die. In the spring the mistletoes produce tiny blossoms, and in July or August small seeds that mountain bluebirds feed on with gusto. In the Poudre drainage, many of the pines suffer badly from these parasites, and weakened trees are more likely to be attacked by insects such as mountain pine beetles. There seems to be no easy way of control apart from cutting off infected branches or culling dying trees. Three species of caterpillars feed on mistletoe and on nothing else. One of these is the larva of a handsome butterfly called the thicket hairstreak. All three caterpillars occur widely in the West, but unfortunately are rarely abundant enough to have much of an impact on the mistletoes. With effort it might be possible to rear these insects in great numbers in laboratories and release them in nature. However, ponderosa pines along the Front Range are not considered to have enough monetary value to justify such a program. So far, human society has been unable to devise ways of recognizing ecological and esthetic values such that they can be used to justify the expenditure of very much money or effort.

Speaking of parasites, two rather remarkable ground-dwelling plants, like mistletoe devoid of chlorophyll, can sometimes be found in these forests. They bear no close relationship to the pines except that they prefer shaded places where there is loamy soil and rotting logs. Their roots probe the soil and come in contact with decaying organic matter and soil fungi, which they exploit for food. Pinedrops grow as a reddish-brown stalk, sometimes two feet tall, from which many small, whitish, bell-shaped flowers are suspended. There are no leaves except for a few scales at the bottom of the stem. Oddly enough, pinedrops belong to the same family as kinnikinnik, the heath family.

The second parasite is a member of the orchid family, called spotted coral-root. Superficially it is rather similar to pinedrops, rising on a tall stalk that bears a series of blossoms. But these are of typical orchid form — a broad, white lip speckled with red, overhung by slender, brownish petals and sepals.

It may not be quite correct to call these two plants parasites; they live primarily on decaying organic matter, so are usually classified as saprophytes. Michael Moore, in his book *Medicinal Plants of the Mountain West,* provides directions for collecting and preparing coral-root, which is said when boiled to be useful for "nervous fevers" and particularly recommended "for angry or frustrated states." The roots consist of closely interwoven fibers, remotely resembling coral. Out of respect for Colorado's few precious orchids, we have never dug one up.

Orchid admirers — and who is not? — will find another kind in damp places in these woods, and this is a real charmer. Calypso orchids,

Fairy slippers are the most elegant of the few species of orchids that grow in forests along the Poudre.

or fairy slippers, are normal plants that produce their own food via a single, succulent, basal green leaf. Each plant has a short stem surmounted by a slipper-shaped pink flower. Finding a group of these flowers in a secluded nook is a very special treat reserved for true lovers of the forest. These and many other plants tend to become trampled around picnic and camping areas and along the paths of anglers. So it takes a bit of hiking to find some of the more delicate plants and to catch a glimpse of some of the more elusive birds and mammals.

South Fork Junction to North Fork Junction

We have lingered long here at midcanyon, but even so we have barely begun to explore it. But it is time to move on; the most winding and steep-walled part of the canyon still lies ahead. At the point where the South Fork enters, the river and highway make a loop to the north and partially enclose an area of rolling meadows sprinkled with pines and junipers known as Dutch George Flats. George Weari, locally known as Dutch George, lived here in the 1870s, trapping and hunting in the surrounding hills and canyons. Elkhorn Creek, which enters the

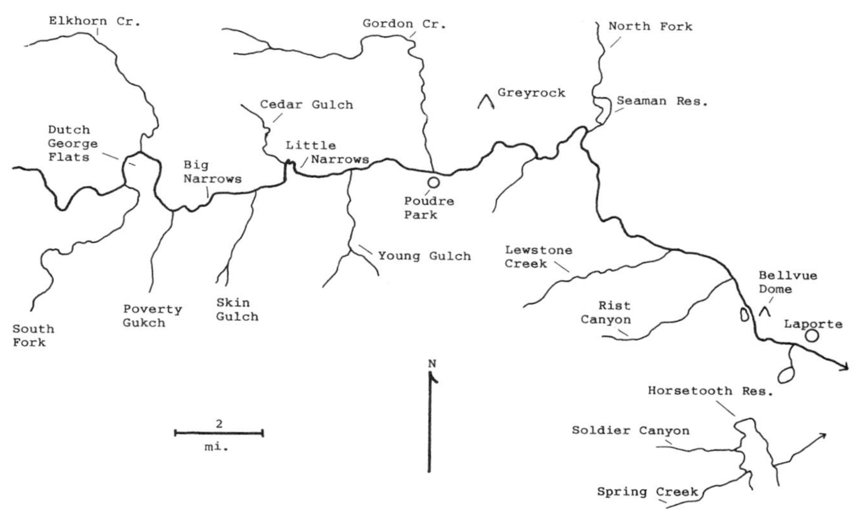

The lower canyon, from South Fork junction to Laporte.

Poudre from the north just opposite the flats, was his special hunting area, an area he is said to have protected vigorously from intruders. He got his comeuppance when he was killed by a bear, or, according to a different story, accidentally shot himself when his rifle fell down while he was skinning a bear.

Elkhorn Creek winds through a particularly wild canyon, walled in by spectacular rock formations and harboring unusually large ponderosa pines and Douglas-firs as well as a tangle of smaller trees and bushes. In its upper reaches, there are meadows strung with beaver ponds. Here and there the remains of old buildings leave one wondering what families called them home and struggled with the landscape for a living. George Weaver's Pinecroft Ranch once occupied over three thousand acres of the Elkhorn drainage. In 1959 it was purchased and presented to the Boy Scouts by Ben Delatour, a Nebraska rancher and banker who had retired to Fort Collins. Some ten miles west of the Ben Delatour Boy Scout Ranch, the Elkhorn has its beginnings on South Bald Mountain, only about four miles in a straight line north of Kinikinik.

We have spent many hours on the Elkhorn, since it is not far from our home. It is here that we first learned to know spotted saxifrage, a moss-like plant that clings to moist rocks and sends up delicate white blossoms speckled with purple and orange. And here we learned to recognize *Besseya*, sometimes called kittentails (as if kittens had lavender tails!). These individualistic plants were named for Charles Edwin Bessey, who wrote an early and much-used botany textbook. Bessey was a professor at the University of Nebraska and spent many summers in the 1890s studying plants in the Colorado Rockies. The Elkhorn is a special place to us, though we use it differently than did Dutch George. We even overlook the fact that it is improperly named, elk having antlers and not horns.

Below the confluence of the Elkhorn with the Poudre, the river loops south of Sheep Mountain, so called because early settlers found it a good place to hunt for bighorns. In time they eliminated them, but in 1975 the Colorado Division of Wildlife took twenty-five from the herd on the upper Poudre and moved them to Sheep Mountain. They were captured by baiting a drop net, then blindfolded and trucked to the new site. When released, the sheep left the truck in frantic haste and scattered widely. Some disappeared, but others assembled to form a herd that now numbers fifty or more, roaming Sheep Mountain and surrounding hills.

Where it passes Sheep Mountain, the river has cut a deep, tortuous ravine between cliffs of resistant metamorphic rocks in which the ancient strata are distorted in strange patterns. Here the river drops an average of 152 feet per mile as compared to 25 to 65 feet per mile in other parts of the canyon. Boulders in the stream result in cataracts that during spring runoff produce a roar that reverberates through the canyon. These are the Big Narrows, impassable prior to 1919, when convict labor succeeded in blasting a trail along the river.

Crevices in the canyon walls are filled with plants struggling to gain a foothold, and in July larger gullies are bright with thimbleberry, a species of raspberry that offers generous white blossoms but flavorless fruits. Everywhere lichens encrust the rocks, adding their own subtle colors to the formidable rock walls. These little-appreciated plants are highly sensitive to pollutants and so can tell us when we have overloaded the air with toxins. Most plants store undesirable chemicals in vacuoles in the leaves, then shed the leaves in the fall. But lichens have no deciduous parts. Furthermore they absorb water from rains, so toxins can build up and cause degeneration and death of the lichens. Although acid rain is currently perhaps less serious in the West than it is in the Northeast or in Europe, the lichens may be the first to tell us when the threat is severe. Sulphur dioxide from coal-burning power plants and ozone from automobile exhausts have both been shown to have serious effects on lichens. Many of the lichens in the mountains around Los Angeles, for example, have disappeared or become discolored. Lichens in the Poudre basin remain healthy, but as human populations increase, drive more cars, and demand more energy, lichens may some day provide a warning we cannot ignore.

Below the Big Narrows, the river flows a few miles through a less awesome section and is met on the south side by a small creek and a road descending from Stove Prairie, a verdant, park-like valley between mountain ridges. The origin of the name is uncertain; presumably an early camper left an old stove that was discovered by a settler who wanted a name for the area. Before there was a direct route up the lower part of Poudre Canyon, there was access to the river from Stove Prairie; the point at which the road reaches the river was called Stove Prairie Landing. Thus travelers could come through Fort Collins and Bellvue and up Rist Canyon, a small, sometimes dry canyon that parallels the Poudre to the south, and then through Stove Prairie and down to the Poudre, avoiding the longer route through Livermore and Log Cabin and down precipitous Pingree Hill to Rustic.

Not far below Stove Prairie Landing, the river enters another narrow, steep-walled section called the Little Narrows. It is here that in 1916 a tunnel was blasted through a rock barrier that nearly spans the canyon. Near the tunnel tall pillars of resistant metamorphic rock guard the outlet of Cedar Gulch on the north side of the river. Before the tunnel was completed, the road up the canyon ended at Mishawaka, a small resort a mile below the tunnel.

Another mile or so downstream, Young Gulch enters from the south. Parts of this north-facing valley are shaded by thick forest; there is a permanent stream containing dark pools alternating with musical falls and riffles. The trail up the gulch crosses the stream innumerable times. One of our most vivid memories on the trail is of a pygmy owl that was clutching a mouse and was being mobbed by noisy chickadees. These day-flying owls have a body length of only seven inches, considerably less than that of a robin.

Invariably we encounter mule deer staring at us, eyes bright and ears cocked, trying to decide at what point they need to disappear into the hills. Mule deer are plentiful in many parts of the Poudre basin.

The Little Narrows challenge experienced rafters during the high waters of June. *Photo by W. A. Parsons, U.S. Forest Service.*

Not until 1916 did a tunnel make it possible to go through the Little Narrows with a vehicle. *Photo by E. H. Mason, U.S. Forest Service.*

They were staples of the Utes and Arapahoes, and they are the most popular game animals of modern-day hunters, who flock to the hills in the autumn hunting season. It is hard to beat Ivan Doig's description of these splendid animals in his book *Winter Brothers*.

> As I watch . . . the motion of the doe's each step seems to recoil slightly into her as if some portion of poise is being pulled back each time in reserve. This tentative grace of deer which stops them just short of being creatures of some other element. Hoofed birds, perhaps, or slim dolphins of the underbrush. Who would have thought, on a continent of such machines of the wild as bison and elk and the grizzly, that it would be deer to best survive? For once, the meek have inherited.

On the Poudre near the bottom of Young Gulch is a campground named for Ansel Watrous, who for many years was editor of the Fort Collins *Courier* and who in 1911 published a *History of Larimer County*. In 1911 Larimer County was young and sparsely settled; Fort Collins had a population of only 8,500. There was little interest in history and

Steller's jays have the largest crests of any North American bird, adding a rakish appearance that well suits their disposition. *Photo by David Leatherman.*

few copies were sold, so much of the stock was destroyed. Fortunately, it was reprinted many years later and is frequently cited as a source of information on the early days of the area.

The Ansel Watrous campground is perhaps the most popular in the canyon, close enough to the plains to be readily accessible to city dwellers, yet deep enough in the mountains to enjoy their serenity and to become acquainted with some of the native plants and animals. Even the most casual picnicker is likely to be visited by chipmunks, golden-mantled ground squirrels, and jays, all prepared to clean up any crumbs that may be left. There are three common jays in the Poudre basin — grays in the high country, blues on the plains, and Steller's in the pine forests in between. (Scrub jays can also be seen occasionally near the mouth of the canyon.) It is rather fun to compare their habits and vocabularies. Steller's jays have a variety of harsh calls, including some quite like the calls of red-tailed hawks, but at times they also produce a soft, melodious warbling.

It is easy to condemn these rather noisy birds, which in winter often fatten themselves at feeders designed for smaller birds and in summer are inclined to steal and consume eggs from the nests of other birds. But Steller's jays are among our most beautiful birds, breast and tail blue as the late evening sky, back and head like the night sky, white streaks about their eyes giving them a roguish appearance that suits them well. Ornithologist Elliott Coues described them well: "a tough, wiry, independent creature, with sense enough to take precious good care of himself." We once saw a sharp-shinned hawk trying to catch a Steller's jay in a Douglas-fir. The jay hopped about where the branches were thickest rather than taking wing, where he would surely have been caught. The hawk left without a meal.

The jays are named for Georg Wilhelm Steller, who first discovered them in 1741. Steller, a German naturalist, was attached to a Russian expedition that left Kamchatka in two ships to explore the "Great Land" to the east, now called Alaska. It was headed by Vitus Bering, a Dane, for whom the Bering Sea and Bering Strait are named. Steller found the jays during a landfall not far from present-day Valdez. He recognized them at once as relatives of the blue jays of eastern North America, which had been described a few years earlier. "This bird," he said, "proved to me that we were really in America." The return from Alaska was disastrous. Violent storms drove the ships off course and eventually they were shipwrecked on what is now called Bering Island, where Bering and many of his crew died of scurvy in the course of a bitter winter. Steller ultimately reached Kamchatka but died a few years later while wandering about Siberia, still finding plants and animals new to science. It is good to be reminded of him by so visible a bird.

North America's most elegant squirrel can often be seen in pine forests along the Poudre. This is the tassel-eared (or Abert's) squirrel. These squirrels have a limited range, from the Wyoming border to northern New Mexico and Arizona. In the northern Front Range, they are usually deep brown to black, but gray, white-bellied individuals sometimes occur. Farther south the gray form is much more common, and on the North Rim of the Grand Canyon still another color form occurs with an all-white tail. It is difficult to understand what advantage (if any) there may be in being black here along the Poudre. Unlike ground squirrels and chipmunks, these squirrels are active all winter long, and a solid black squirrel sitting on a snow-covered rocky outcrop is not exactly camouflaged.

In winter the tassels are especially long and can often be seen being blown by the wind as the squirrels cavort on the rocks or in the pines. The "ear muffs" are shed in the summer and replaced in the fall, rather a neat arrangement for this climate. The squirrels live mainly on pine buds and seeds, though snacking now and then on fungi, berries, or seeds from bird feeders. They live in hollow trees or nests of twigs fifteen to twenty feet up in pine trees. Three or four young are born in May or early June and will be fully grown by winter.

The squirrels must have been a surprise and delight to their discoverer, Samuel Woodhouse, a Philadelphia physician who preferred natural history to medicine and joined several expeditions to the West in the 1850s. He discovered the squirrels on the San Francisco Peaks of Arizona. (He also discovered Woodhouse's toad and Woodhouse's aster.) Unfortunately he was bitten in the hand by a rattlesnake, which for a time cramped his style as a collector. But, being an M. D., he used the opportunity to study the effects of the bite and his treatment of it. Woodhouse named the squirrels after another early explorer-naturalist, J. W. Abert, who accompanied Frémont on one of his expeditions and may have been the first to see the squirrels. Watching these wonderful animals today, it is possible to feel some of the thrill experienced by men who trudged the "Wild West" in the effort to chronicle the plants and animals for science.

All is not pure joy in these forests and streamsides even on a halcyon day at the height of spring. On almost any day from April to June, ticks are likely to be waiting on the tops of bushes with their legs extended, ready to attach to any warm-blooded animal that passes. On people, they are likely to crawl up the legs and attach to the skin beneath the belt or among the hairs of the pubic area, the armpits, or back of the head. Here they bury their proboscis and begin to suck blood, forming an itchy welt. We well remember one spring hike on which we took our dog (not the best idea anyway, if one wishes to see wildlife). On returning we stripped and deticked ourselves, then spent the rest of the day removing nearly one hundred ticks from the dog. Since we are inveterate hikers, no spring passes without a few encounters with ticks.

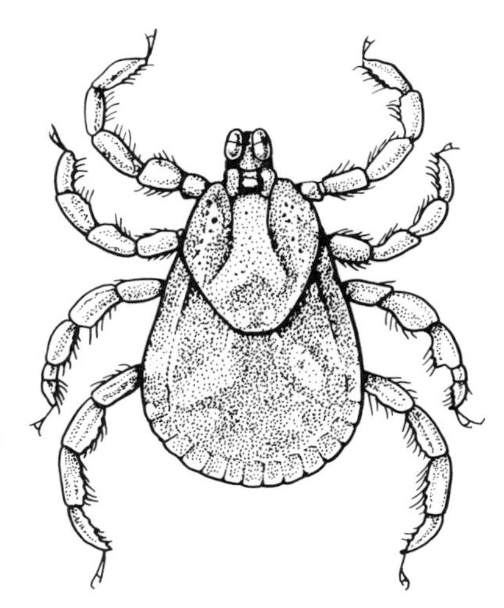

Rocky Mountain wood tick.

Rocky Mountain wood ticks have an interesting scientific name: *Dermacentor andersoni*, from the Greek *derma*, skin, and *centor*, pricker. The species name honors John F. Anderson of the U.S. Public Health Service, who did much of the original research on the ticks. The ticks first attained infamy when they were incriminated as vectors of Rocky Mountain spotted fever during an outbreak in Montana around the turn of the century. We now know that they are also capable of transmitting tularaemia and Colorado tick fever. Fortunately these are uncommon diseases nowadays, though several hundred cases of tick fever are reported each year. So far as is known, Rocky Mountain wood ticks do not transmit Lyme disease.

The ticks that attach to large mammals and to people are adult males and females. Over a period of ten days or so (unless removed), they engorge themselves slowly with blood, then drop off. After a few days, the female lays several thousand eggs on the ground. Tiny six-legged "seed ticks" emerge a few weeks later and attach themselves to rodents such as ground squirrels and wood rats. Here they feed for a while before dropping off and molting to an eight-legged stage that hibernates through the winter. In the spring they feed for a while on small mammals, then molt to adults, ready to attach themselves to larger animals. At any stage, if no suitable host comes along, they can live for many months waiting for a meal, even a full year. Closely observed, these ticks are really rather attractive creatures, having a pattern of lines on their backs rather more interesting than some modern art we have seen. And a dispassionate person must admire their persistence. But perhaps there are no dispassionate persons where ticks are concerned.

There are, of course, many redeeming features about spring along the Poudre. It is the beginning of an ongoing drama of blooming. As early as March, a small, pink, five-petaled flower springs unexpectedly from sheltered places where the snow is gone. These are spring beauties, *Claytonia,* named by Swedish naturalist Carl Linnaeus for John Clayton, one of the first American amateur botanists. Spring beauties occur in many parts of the world, always heralding the spring with wide-eyed expectancy. They have tubers that were used as food by the Indians; according to the Craigheads and Davis, when raw they taste a bit like radishes, when boiled, more like baked potatoes. The plants are so tiny it would take a great many to satisfy one's appetite, and in any case a person would have to be very hungry to destroy the first flowers of spring.

Spring beauties are soon joined by others: the white, star-like blossoms of sand lilies hugging the ground; the smaller but taller stars of chickweed; garish stands of golden banner, otherwise known as false lupine, since the flowers resemble lupines that have been dipped in the wrong paintpot. Soon wild geraniums join the cast, *Geranium fremonti*, the ghost of John Charles Frémont haunting many a western scene. Wild geraniums are also called cranesbills, since the erect, pointed seedpods resemble the bill of a crane (or perhaps a minirocket about to take off into space). In secluded places the sunflower-like blossoms of heart-leaved arnica shimmer like fleeting spots of sunlight on the forest floor. Arnica is reputed to have many medicinal uses, particularly when combined with alcohol to make a liniment useful for sprains and sore muscles. Left alone it serves a better function: to lift the spirits of a tired hiker.

Nighttime along the river, too, is filled with life, though the stirrings of rodents and the chippering of bats usually pass unnoticed.

As the sky darkens, nighthawks appear overhead, dashing about on slender, white-barred wings and emitting their distinctive "peenk." Now and then the males dive and produce a booming sound that can be a bit frightening if a person doesn't know its source. It is actually produced by the vibrations of the primary wing feathers just as the male comes out of his dive. We have several times found the "nests" of nighthawks, nests in quotes since the two speckled eggs are merely laid on a slightly cleared place on the ground. Nighthawks are among the last birds to arrive from the south, about the first of June, and by Labor Day they have already left.

Unless one is camped on the brink of the noisy river, he or she may be lucky enough to hear the two-syllable call of the poorwill, a shy relative of the nighthawk. Meriwether Lewis discovered the poorwill while he and Clark were crossing the Dakotas. The ones he found were torpid in October. This was a novel discovery; in fact poorwills, in contrast to nighthawks, often remain well into autumn; on cold nights their body temperature is depressed and they remain dormant. Eventually, one warm day, they take off for Mexico. Nighthawks and poorwills are related to the whippoorwills of the East, a group of birds with the curious name "goatsuckers." It is said that goat herdsmen in early times flushed nightjars (the European equivalent of nighthawks) from their pastures, assuming that their goats' failure to give milk was the result of the nighttime activities of these mysterious birds.

A fortunate camper may be wakened by the hoots of a great horned owl or by the yapping and howling of coyotes. Though not often seen, coyotes are common enough along the Poudre, taking advantage of ground squirrels and other small rodents as well as insects and whatever offal presents itself. Coyotes should be cherished as the sole surviving larger predators after the others that once roamed these valleys have either been eliminated (wolves, grizzly bears) or reduced to so few individuals that they are not part of the experience of most of us (black bears, mountain lions, martens).

Ranchers, to be sure, have a low opinion of coyotes. Mark Twain observed coyotes when he traveled through the West as a young man and reflected a common opinion of their character. "The coyote," he wrote in *Roughing It*, "is a long, slim, sick and sorry-looking skeleton, with a gray-wolf skin stretched over it, a tolerably bushy tail that forever sags down with a despairing expression of foresakenness and misery, a furtive and evil eye, and a long, sharp face, with a slightly lifted lip and exposed teeth. . . . The meanest creatures despise him, and even the fleas would desert him for a velocipede."

For an alternate opinion, listen to Ernest Thompson Seton: "O Wonder Dog of the West! . . . If only I could voice the fierce, sad joy that you engender in me! . . . If ever the day should come when one may camp in the West, and hear not a note of the Coyote's joyous stirring evening song, I hope that I shall long before have passed away, gone over the Great Divide, where there are neither barbwire fences, nor tin cans, nor hooch-houses, nor improvement companies . . . but where there is peace, and the Coyote sings and is unafraid."

That one animal can elicit such diverse opinions — and such extravagant prose — is a tribute to the coyote's impact on the psyche of the West.

The only community in the lower part of Poudre Canyon is Poudre Park, only about five miles from the mouth of the canyon. There is a store, fire station, community building, and the homes of about thirty families, many of whom make their living in Fort Collins. Fortunately the village is tucked in a valley that will not permit much expansion, so the residents are safe from the machinations of developers. At Poudre Park, Gordon Creek flows in from the north through a canyon called Hewlett Gulch. This broad, south-facing valley is in strong contrast to that of Young Gulch, only a few miles upstream. It is much more open and sparsely wooded, and there are evidences of abandoned homesteads and old mines. We'll have more to say about Gordon Creek in chapter 8.

The massive cliffs bordering Hewlett Gulch to the east are part of a highland that is crowned by Greyrock Mountain, a granite monolith reaching 7,613 feet and visible for many miles around. Greyrock Trail begins on the Poudre at 5,560 feet, so the six-mile round-trip hike is a challenging one. This is the most used trail in the Poudre system, being only a few miles up the canyon from the cities of the plains and open for most of the year. It was built by the Civilian Conservation Corps in the thirties and is now maintained by the U. S. Forest Service with the help of local environmentalists. It is a candidate for listing on the National Register of Recreational Trails.

We have hiked the Greyrock Trail many times. After crossing the river on a footbridge, the trail passes through groves of wild plums that are a mass of bloom in April and, in some years, hung with fruit in September. After numerous switchbacks the trail reaches the base of

Hikers to the top of Greyrock discover a pond nestled among the rocks. *Photo by E. H. Mason, U.S. Forest Service.*

Greyrock itself, looming so far above that to climb it seems out of the question. Yet the trail does make it to the summit, using the less formidable east side. There is a surprise almost at the top — a small pond — and at the extreme top a view on all sides that makes the climb more than worthwhile.

The return can be made by way of Greyrock Meadows, which occupy a broad, bowl-shaped clearing not far from the overlook into Hewlett Gulch. These meadows are alive with butterflies all through the warmer months of the year. Some of them have overwintered under the bark of trees and are out on warm spring days: mourning cloaks, their dark wings narrowly fringed with yellow, and red admirals, easily recognized by the slashes of red across the wings. Soon painted ladies will be migrating through, fueling themselves at whatever flowers provide them with a rich source of nectar. Since red admiral larvae feed on nettles, and painted ladies on thistles, these butterflies are to be cherished for more than their beauty.

In midsummer the meadows are filled with fritillaries, their orange wings flecked with black spots on top, underneath suffused with pastel

A swallowtail butterfly takes minerals from damp soil along the Cache la Poudre.

yellow, pink, and brown, spattered with blobs of silver. The pattern is so complex that one wonders what it means, for surely so much detail is wasted on the indiscriminate eyes of birds and other butterflies. It is known that male fritillaries respond to the orange of the female's wings — but they respond even more strongly to experimentally produced wings of solid orange. It is believed that the dark spots along the margin of the wings are "deflection marks," serving to divert the attention of birds from the butterfly's body. But that still leaves a great deal unexplained.

The largest and most common of these butterflies is Edward's fritillary, named for William Henry Edwards, who has had at least six other butterflies name for him and who himself named over eighty kinds of Rocky Mountain butterflies, over one third of all those occurring there. Edwards, a great-great-grandson of New England preacher and philosopher Jonathan Edwards, was a businessman who collected butterflies in the Rockies and commissioned others to collect for him. In 1868 he published the first part of a monumental, beautifully illustrated treatise, *The Butterflies of North America.* Edwards was more than a mere collector; he often caged females and collected the eggs, then reared the caterpillars on their appropriate food plant.

In late August the monarch butterflies migrate through on their way to wintering sites in Mexico. The bright orange patterns on their wings advertize their distastefulness. They retain in their bodies cardiac glycosides obtained by their larvae from their favorite food, milkweeds. Not that you or we would eat a butterfly, but birds often do eat them, and they soon learn to avoid monarchs, which make them ill. Monarchs are declining in numbers because their winter roosting sites are gradually being diminished as a result of what is commonly called "progress."

Not far below the Greyrock Trail, the river makes a tight loop to the north, where it is joined by the North Fork. The city of Fort Collins has had a water treatment plant at this point for many years but now pipes water from above the junction to a new plant closer to the city. This is a particularly attractive spot, with tall cottonwoods shading a flat, grassy area cupped among steep hills. The city has now leased the site to the Colorado Division of Parks and Outdoor Recreation, which is converting it to a park suitable for picnicking and fishing as well as for launching rafts and kayaks during the high water of early summer. There is hope that the buildings of the former water treatment plant may be converted to a conference center.

The part of the canyon that has been designated Wild and Scenic terminates near Poudre Park, leaving the lower several miles of the canyon open for development. This section of the canyon is especially popular with rafters, who are rewarded not only with a wet and exciting ride, but with a different perspective of the canyon's rock walls and its wildlife. Not far from the bottom of the canyon, at Picnic Rock, the Colorado Division of Parks and Recreation has provided facilities where rafters may disembark. From time to time, the Northern Colorado Water Conservancy has threatened to dam the Poudre opposite Greyrock Mountain, inundating the canyon nearly to Poudre Park as well as a distance of the North Fork. This would cause the highway to be rerouted through the hills and would produce another bland reservoir of vacillating shoreline to replace a particularly delectable section of the canyon.

5

A CLOSER LOOK AT THE RIVER

On our trip down the river, we have let ourselves become diverted by the trees, the flowers, the birds, the mammals, the people who have lived here or who have left their mark on the names of living things — almost as if the river were not there! Of course it is the river that has sculpted these landforms in their infinite variety and provided the soil and water that make all else possible. The river itself is filled with life, an ecosystem many miles long and only a few yards wide, slicing its way through diverse terrestrial ecosystems. In its own way, it is as complex as any on land, though much less obvious to creatures like ourselves, air-breathing as we are, and attuned to the larger forms of life.

The River in the Mountains

In the canyon the waters are still cold and free of major pollutants. Unlike many Rocky Mountain streams, the Poudre drains no significant mining areas that potentially add mercury, cyanide, and other toxins to the stream. Until fairly recently the water was safe to drink without treatment, but with increased human activity in the canyon, there is danger of picking up fecal contaminants, including *Giardia*. But still the waters are pure enough to provide home for a set of plants and animals very much the same as those that must have lived here before humans discovered the stream. At most seasons the waters are clear, and the stream is a peaceful place to cast a fly and watch the dippers cavort on the rocks. But during spring runoff, mid-May through early July, the waters are coffee-colored, replete with soils and detritus torn from the high country. The river is no longer soft-spoken but a raging extrovert, tearing at its banks and rearranging the rocks in its path.

High in the mountains, the river provides a rich habitat for the larvae of mayflies and stoneflies, with their predators, trout and dippers. *Photo by W. A. Parsons, U.S. Forest Service.*

The abundant life in the stream is all the more remarkable in the light of the great seasonal variation in stream flow. The average flow at Rustic is 248 cubic feet per second (cfs), but there are records of minimum flows of as little as 8 cfs and of maximum flows not uncommonly as high as 8,000 cfs, a thousandfold difference. When the

Chambers Lake dam broke in 1891, it produced a flow of 21,000 cfs. This was surpassed in 1904, during a flood produced by a freak thunderstorm. There were lesser floods in 1930 and in 1983. On the other hand, when the winter snowpack in the mountains is low and there are no unusual rainstorms in the summer, the Poudre may run low indeed.

During winter's low flow, ice forms over many parts of the river, glazing over pools and piling up on rocks in cataracts. During periods of thawing, ice rubble acts like a sand blast, clearing out crevices where insects or fish may be hiding, adding further to the hazards of life in the stream. Doubtless there is mortality during winter, as there is during spring and summer flooding. But one can only admire the adaptations that permit so many organisms to thrive in such a challenging habitat.

Plants form the bottom of the food chain in the river as they do on land. Plant life in the stream consists mostly of algae, often microscopic in size. The most abundant are diatoms, single-celled organisms encased in silica sheaths. Over sixty kinds have been found in the St. Vrain, a tributary of the South Platte a few miles to the south. In one transect of the Poudre, diatoms were found to vary from 60 to 60,000 per liter, depending upon the season. Other kinds of algae are composed of chains of cells without silica walls. Algae form the slippery film on rocks that anglers find treacherous. Like other plants they are photosynthetic, using sunlight to manufacture nutrients upon which all forms of animal life depend.

There are, however, other nutrients that come from sources outside the stream. Lichens, mosses, grasses, and flowering plants growing along the bank are often washed into the water, and leaves, pine needles, cones, and berries fall from above. All of this is grist for the mills of the many kinds of insects that form the next tier in the food chain. Fishermen are well aware that these larval insects, as well as the adult, flying insects they produce, are a major source of food for the fish that make up a still higher tier in the food chain. In fact they try to copy them in their flies and lures. Isaak Walton, as early as the seventeenth century, supplied directions for making dunflies from partridge feathers, blackflies from wool and "the herle of a peacock's tail," and many others. "Thus have you a jury of flies likely to betray and condemn all the Trouts in the river," he concluded.

Nowadays there are several lavish books devoted to stream insects and how fishermen may attempt to copy them. One of these, Doug Swisher and Carl Richard's *Selective Trout*, promises a "dramatically

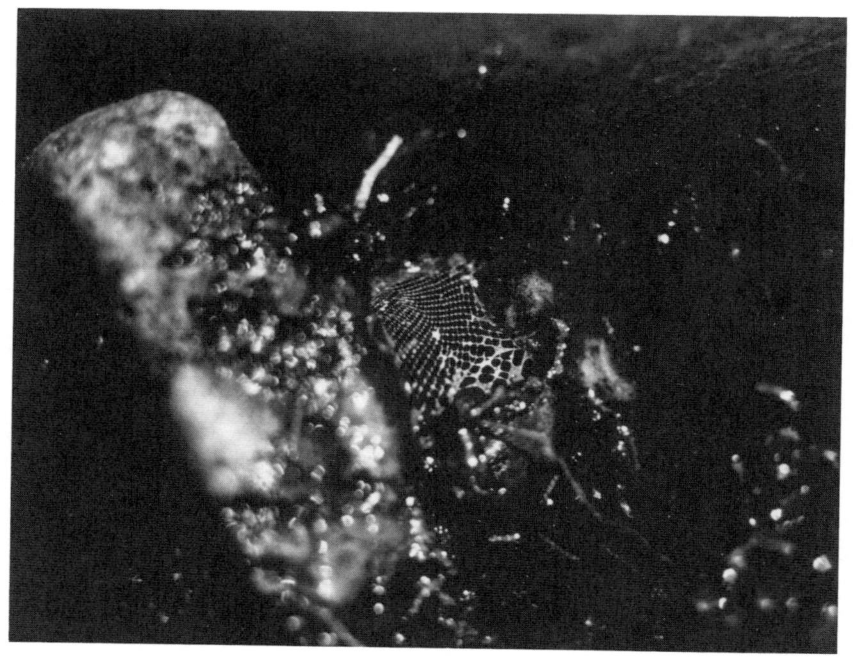

Larvae of caddisflies, *Hydropsyche*, spin silken webs in the current to capture small organisms on which they feed.

new and scientific approach to trout fishing." As the authors explain, the crowding of trout streams and the "activities of the great dam builders" make it imperative that fly fishermen, to compete successfully, learn what insects occur where and when they plan to fish and how to emulate them in their flies. They recommend using a butterfly net to capture flying adults and a seine to capture larvae in the stream, so that they can be properly identified. Each of the more commonly encountered stream insects is described and a recipe provided for approximating it, using various kinds of fur and feathers. Some are even illustrated in color. Isaak Walton would be amazed to learn how seriously he is taken three centuries later.

There are several different and quite unrelated kinds of insects occurring in the Poudre and in similar mountain streams. Even if one does not fish, they are well worth knowing. Finding them is as easy as turning over a rock. The undersides of most rocks in the current will reveal mayfly and stonefly larvae (often called "nymphs") scuttling away. Here and there are the cylindrical cases of caddisfly larvae, built of pebbles and bits of debris tied together with silk. Other caddisfly larvae build silken seines rather like miniature fishnets from which they harvest small organisms from the current. Blackfly larvae cling to rocks in the swiftest current; they also seine food from the stream, but do so by means of basket-like mouth brushes.

Insects that seine food particles from the current in this manner are spoken of as filter-feeders, in contrast to gatherers, which feed on deposits on the bottom; to shredders, which chew up large particles and to scrapers, which skim algae from the rocks. In addition, there are predators such as beetles and some kinds of caddisflies and stoneflies. Each is adapted to harvest and digest its own limited share of the stream's nutrients.

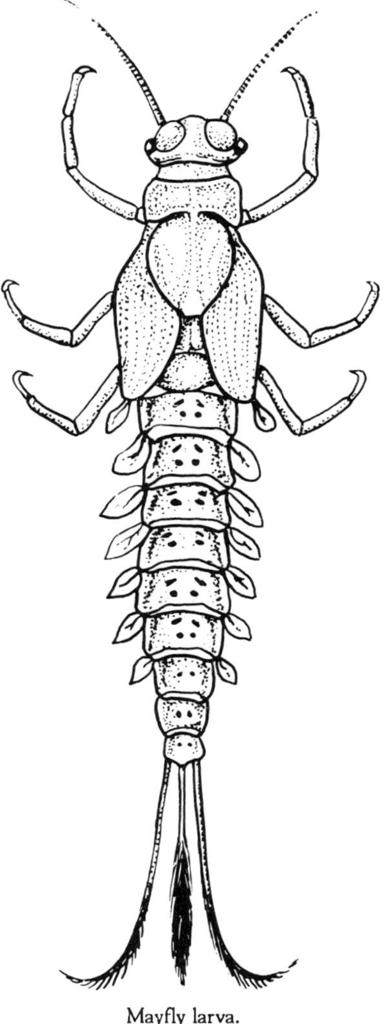

Mayfly larva.

Simply avoiding being swept away by the force of the current is a task in itself, and insects have evolved a variety of adaptations that permit them to hold their own in the stream. Some mayfly and stonefly larvae have exceedingly flat bodies, enabling them to fit so tightly to rocks that the current passes over them. The larvae of blackflies and others have suckers that fit tightly to rocks, and still others spin silken guy lines which they anchor to the bottom. Caddisfly larvae have stout hooks at the ends of their bodies, and riffle beetles enlarged claws that they attach to objects in the stream. In places where the current is less extreme, there are free-swimming forms, streamlined somewhat in the manner of fish. All of these insects extract oxygen from the water, and to do so they have evolved

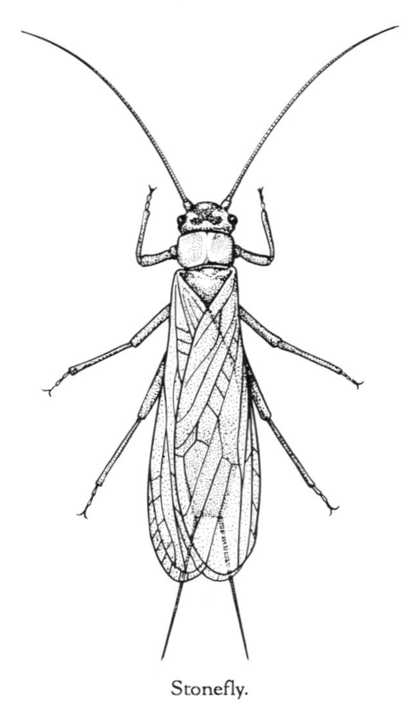

Stonefly.

a variety of external gills. To those first experiencing stream insects, they form a wholly new world of creatures far stranger than those sometimes imagined as inhabiting another planet.

Mayflies, stoneflies, and caddisflies all represent very ancient groups of insects with fossil records going back to the Paleozoic era, more than 250 million years ago. All three groups are confined to fresh water, where they thrive by having adapted in diverse ways to waters that are often cold, turbulent, abrasive, or sometimes subject to drying out. In the summer the winged adults emerge from the water, dancing over the stream or clinging to rocks and vegetation. For the most part, they are weak fliers, and they are often preyed upon by birds and bats or are devastated by a sudden storm. But soon after they emerge, they are ready to mate and lay their eggs, so they make good use of their brief time in the sun. Several kinds of stoneflies, against all reason, emerge not in summer but in the middle of winter, and it is fun to scout the streamsides on sunny days in February when these insects court, mate, and lay their eggs. These fragile insects presumably avoid being eaten by emerging when there are few birds or bats about.

To a casual observer, the behavior of these insects appears as simplicity itself. As is so often true, close study shows that there is much more to the story. Stoneflies, for example, drum with their bodies on leaves, twigs, and other objects. The sounds made by the larger species — and some that emerge along the Poudre are nearly two inches long — can be heard several feet away. Males drum to attract females, who answer by also drumming; in time the male approaches the female and mating follows. Only virgin females respond; females that have already mated are silent and reject males that approach. The "songs" of many species of stoneflies have now been recorded. Using computer-simulated calls modified in various ways, researchers have been able to determine which components in the songs are important in producing a response in the female of their species — such things as speed and number of pulses per call. It is a remarkable discovery that these ancient insects have developed a language, simple yet complex enough to assure that they find a mate during their brief time as adult, winged insects.

Mayfly.

Stoneflies are especially characteristic of cold streams flowing over rocks and gravel; they do not usually occur in lakes or in warm, silt-laden streams. Mayflies have evolved to occupy a greater diversity of habitats, even though they are seemingly even more delicate than stoneflies. Pioneer Cornell entomologist J. H. Comstock and his naturalist wife, A. B. Comstock, said of them: "So fragile are these pale beings that they seem like phantoms rather than real insects. No wonder that poets have sung of them as creatures that live only a day. It is true that their winged existence lasts often only a day or even a few hours; but they have another life, of which the poet knows nothing. Down in the bottom of the stream, feeding on mud, water plants, or other small insects."

Biologists call them Ephemeroptera, meaning "briefly winged," and of course the Comstocks are right that they have another life, living and growing within the stream anywhere from a few months to a year or two. In contrast to most insects, the adults cannot lower their wings over their bodies; fly fishermen call them "upwings." They are also unique in having two winged stages. When they first emerge, they have opaque wings and are called "duns" or subimagos. They simply fly to a sheltered place where they molt once more, wings and all. Only then are they sexually mature and ready to undertake their mating flights; they are now "spinners," in fishermen's jargon.

Most mayflies are incapable of much sustained, forward flight; they simply fly upward, drift down, fly up again, and so forth, generally in a

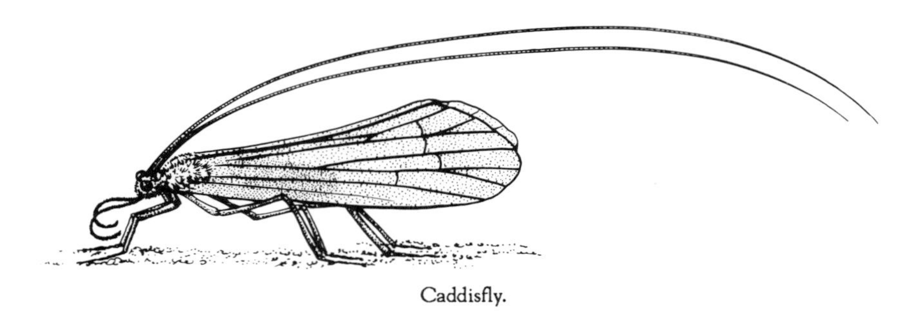

Caddisfly.

swarm. It is the males that form the swarm, their front legs thrust forward and their genital claspers extended, ready to seize a female that flies into the swarm. Two or three thread-like "tails" trail behind. The male's eyes, in many species, have enlarged facets on the upper side. These evidently assist them in coupling with the female as they approach her from below, often in dim light, because many mayflies swarm at dusk. An inborn response to certain landmarks serves to bring individuals together to form a mating swarm. The landmark may be the stream itself or a nearby patch of bushes or opening among trees. Two researchers from the University of Maryland, J. D. Allan and A. S. Flecker, working on Cement Creek, near Gunnison, Colorado, put out artificial swarm markers in the form of sheets of shining, black plastic of several sizes. They found that small sheets attracted only a few males, while larger ones, several yards square, often attracted a swarm that contained hundreds. They found that males lived several days and returned to the swarm several times, while females, after mating, laid their eggs and died soon after. The species they studied, *Epeorus longimanus*, also occurs along the Poudre.

Like mayflies, caddisflies are adapted to living in a diversity of freshwater habitats, but these are very different insects, with fleshy larvae quite unlike the moth-like adults. Unlike mayflies and stoneflies, they undergo a complete metamorphosis, with a pupal stage intervening between larva and adult. The larvae of many species live in cases which they drag around with them as they feed on algae and detritus. These are built of silk, with pebbles or bits of leaves or sticks incorporated into the walls. Most are circular in cross section, but some are semicircular or even square. One kind, appropriately called *Helicopsyche* (spiral sprite), even makes a coiled case resembling a snail. Other caddis larvae are predaceous. Species of *Hydropsyche* (water sprite) spin

Alternating stretches of riffles and quiet pools provide a diversity of habitats for stream insects. *Photo by W. A. Parsons, U.S. Forest Service.*

silken webs superficially like those of spiders, seining small organisms from the currents. These are abundant insects, and it is not uncommon to find numerous webs more or less uniformly spaced in a stream, so that each larva seines a different piece of the current. These larvae are known to produce sounds by rubbing body parts together, and it is possible that they warn each other of their location and so space themselves neatly in the stream.

Other caddis larvae are free living, moving about to capture prey in the stream. Many of these belong to the genus *Rhyacophila* (based on the Greek words *rhyacos*, stream, and *philia*, love; we admit that we, too, are afflicted with rhyacophilia, though with less dedication than these caddisflies). Robert Short and J. V. Ward of Colorado State University collected six species of *Rhyacophila* from a single riffle in Joe Wright Creek. In a small section of the stream, at about 10,000 feet elevation, these researchers collected eight species of mayflies, eight species of stoneflies, fifteen of caddisflies, about twenty of true flies, one kind of riffle beetle, and a few water mites, flatworms, and roundworms. Some of these were abundant, with as many as 200 individuals in a square meter. Altogether, in 1975 there was an average of 1,467 individuals per square meter. In 1976, apparently as a result of heavy summer rains, the density was reduced to 774 per square meter.

How can so many creatures live together in one small section of a small stream? Part of the answer lies in differences in feeding behavior. Short and Ward found that about half the insects were scrapers, about a quarter collectors, about a tenth shredders, and the remainder predators. But that still leaves a lot of scrapers competing for the algae on the rocks! Another dimension is added in that some feed on the exposed surfaces of rocks, others underneath, still others in crevices. When several kinds of net-making caddis live together, they tend to make nets of different mesh size, so that they filter different-sized particles from the stream. Other factors lessening direct competition are differences in microhabitat relating to streamflow at particular points, as well as lack of synchrony in the development of the various species. Still, that is a lot of species living together in a limited habitat, a tribute to the quality of the stream.

Working at about 8,000 feet elevation in Little Beaver Creek, a tributary of the South Fork, J. V. Ward and his colleagues found the primary shredders to be several species of winter stoneflies, while mayflies, caddis, beetles, and true flies were the primary collectors of particles shredded from or collected among the leaves. They put out packets of leaves from different kinds of trees, anchored them to bricks in the current, and then over time brought them in and counted the insects. They found that alder and willow leaves were processed more rapidly than aspen and much more rapidly than pine needles. In all, about twenty-five species were collected from the leaf packs, with pretty much the same species occurring irrespective of the kind of leaf in the pack. The major leaf fall is in the autumn, a time when young insects are growing rapidly from eggs laid in the summer, and leaves clearly provide a major source of nutrients at a critical stage.

In the broad view, one also finds altitudinal differences in stream life, although these are less marked than for terrestrial plant and animal life, since stream temperature is subject to much less variation than air temperature. J. V. Ward censused the life in the St. Vrain River all the way from the tundra to the plains and found nearly two hundred species of insects. (The St. Vrain is a sister stream of the Poudre some miles to the south, and his results should apply reasonably well to the Poudre.) In the tundra, streams are extremely cold and contain only a few fragments of grasses, sedges, and mosses, so relatively few kinds of insects occur there. Descending through the forest, leaves, pine and spruce needles, cones, and seeds are added, and there are more algae and other comestibles. Most tundra species also range into the montane region, where they are joined by a host of others, each with its own altitudinal range. For example, the mayfly *Epeorus longimanus,* which we met earlier, occurs from about 8,500 to about 6,000 feet, while a related species of the same genus goes all the way from the tundra to about 7,000 feet. In the case of stoneflies, Dr. Ward recognized one headwater species, several midaltitude species, several characteristic of the foothills, and two that range onto the plains; in addition there were several with broad ranges in the mountains. Species with broad altitudinal ranges tend to be most plentiful in one part of that range, often near the middle, where conditions are optimal for that species. At any one altitudinal transect, one finds a set of species best adapted to that particular combination of temperature, nutrients, and stream bottom conditions.

Small animals other than insects include segmented worms (related to earthworms), nematodes, and water mites, most of which have a broad altitudinal range. An unsegmented flatworm (or planarian) common all the way from tundra to foothills bears the attractive and meaningful name *Polycelis coronata* ("many spots, with a crown"). The name is an allusion to the many tiny eye spots that fringe the front of the head. When fully grown, these worms are no more than a third of an inch long, gliding over the stones and feeding on still smaller organisms, living or dead.

Those preeminent inhabitants of the watery world, the mollusks, are represented in the upper Poudre by only one kind. These are fingernail clams of the genus *Pisidium* (Greek for "little pea"). These clams, indeed smaller than a pea or a fingernail, are hermaphrodites — that is, they contain both male and female organs and are self-fertile. In the summer the body of the mother (who is also the father) is filled with young in various stages of growth; these are released into the water fully formed. These clams are rarely seen, as they live amongst the gravel on the stream floor, feeding on microscopic particles.

Perhaps the most remarkable organisms living in the Poudre belong to two related groups of insects called the mountain midges and the net-winged midges. Their larvae do not look like insects at all, the bodies consisting of nearly separate sections, each supplied with suckers that enable them to cling to rocks in waterfalls and other places where the current is especially swift. They require highly oxygenated water and move about slowly while skimming algae from the rocks. They eventually form pupae from which the adult midges emerge. But emergence from swift water by a delicate, mosquito-like insect can be hazardous. These insects have a remarkable adaptation that permits them to do just that. Most insects dry and expand their wings after they emerge from their pupal cases, a matter requiring several minutes. But these midges have their wings fully formed inside the pupal cases. They are folded up into a tight packet, rather like a parachute, so when the midges emerge they can "pop out" their wings immediately and fly off from the surface of the current. The wings retain evidence of the lines of folding, hence the name of one of the groups, "net-winged" midges.

Net-winged midges are worldwide in distribution but always rare and local, while mountain midges occur only in a few places in western North America (including the Poudre) and in a few places in central Asia. A disjunct distribution such as this is characteristic of ancient groups of plants and animals. Presumably they were once widespread but now cling to life here and there by having occupied a habitat too rigorous for most other organisms. They are among the least known of the Poudre's many secrets.

New kinds of insects are still being discovered in the Poudre. In 1987 C. R. Nelson of Brigham Young University and B. C. Kondratieff of Colorado State University collected a previously unknown stonefly in small tributaries just off the river between 5,800 and 6,600 feet elevation. It was named *Capnia arapahoe*, in recognition of the Indians

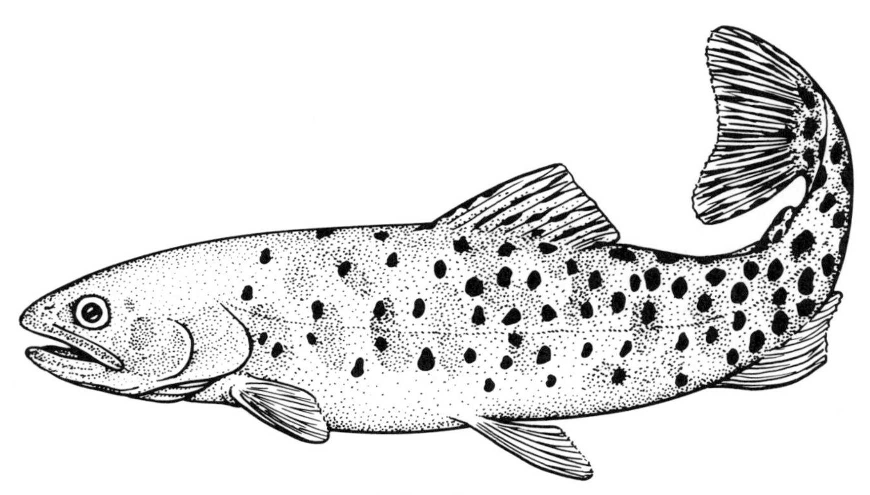

Greenback cutthroat trout.

that once hunted in the canyon (*Capnia* is based on the Greek word for smoke, with reference to the smoky-colored wings of these insects). Recently discovered species of mayflies and caddisflies have yet to be provided with names. It has been nearly two centuries since naturalists began reporting on the fauna and flora of the Rockies, but there remain species to be found — and a great deal to be learned about the life histories and ecological relationships of even some of the commonest plants and animals.

To those wishing to evaluate the amount of disturbance to a stream, it is important to determine the species present as well as the number of species and their relative abundance. Pollution results in lowered diversity, although a few tolerant species may thrive in moderately polluted water. The construction of a dam greatly alters water temperature, flow, and sedimentation, not only in the reservoir but downstream from it. Stoneflies, for example, tend to be greatly reduced in numbers below a dam, and midge larvae may increase. Logging, cattle grazing, road building, and other disturbances also influence the kinds and diversity of stream insects. There are many publications devoted to the identification of aquatic insects and other small organisms, since these are important indicators of water quality, both for human consumption and for fishing.

It is, of course, the fish that are of greatest interest to most people who visit the Poudre. Like the dippers we talked about in chapter 3, fish form a higher tier in the river's food chain, living primarily on the insects. Early settlers found the river filled with fish and depended upon them as food. Today the Cache la Poudre is a superior recreational fishing stream thanks to the efforts of the Colorado Division of Wildlife, for the native trout are long since gone. These natives were greenback cutthroats, recognized by the unusually large spots toward the tail as well as by the telltale red slashes on the throat. This race is now listed as endangered. It formerly had a restricted range, occurring only in cold-water tributaries of the South Platte and Arkansas rivers. It is believed to have evolved from the Colorado River cutthroat, individuals having been present in a tributary of the Colorado that was captured long ago by a tributary of the South Platte. Efforts are being made to bring back the greenback cutthroat, but so far they have met with mixed success.

These elegant fish disappeared as a result of stream degradation, overfishing, and competition with kinds of trout introduced from elsewhere: rainbows, browns, brook trout, and other races of cutthroats. Hybridization between rainbows and cutthroats is common. Actually all four species occur in the Poudre, thanks to periodic stocking. Unfortunately hatchery-bred fish lack some of the vigor of wild-bred fish, and the loss of native races means a loss of genetic diversity that might be used to increase survival and the fighting qualities of "domesticated" fish.

Brook trout, or "brookies," do especially well in smaller streams at high altitudes, while brown trout are tolerant of warmer water and a degree of turbidity and are thus useful for stocking low-altitude streams. Rainbows are especially versatile and do well in many streams and lakes. The Colorado Division of Wildlife stocks about five million rainbows a year, and private landowners still more. Rainbows were introduced from their native homes on the Pacific slope in the 1880s. Brook trout were introduced from the eastern states, brown trout from Europe. Cutthroats have half a dozen or so races that live in various parts of the Interior West. Rainbows and cutthroats breed in the spring, brookies and browns in the fall.

There are two trout-rearing facilities on the Poudre, one at Watson Lake near Bellvue, and another well up the canyon not far from Kinikinik. At the hatchery near Bellvue, eggs are stripped from females ready to spawn and fertilized with milt stripped from males. When the fingerlings reach two or three inches in length, they are transferred to one of the rearing facilities and kept until they reach catchable size (eight to twelve inches). With a diet of fish and soybean meal, yeast, vitamins, and other ingredients, they reach catchable size in only fifteen to eighteen months. After their release, they grow much more slowly, but may live several years if they are not caught or do not die from natural causes. Throughout the state, the Division of Wildlife annually produces 27 million cold-water fish and 30 million warm-water fish. The facilities on the Poudre produce rainbows, other species being brought from facilities elsewhere.

In the canyon the Poudre is believed to have a resident population of about 1,300 trout per mile (not counting those under 5.5 inches in length). To this are added each year over 2,000 hatchery-produced trout per mile, except in certain designated sections, which are not stocked and are posted as "wild trout waters," where only flies and lures are permitted. Most of the hatchery-bred fish are taken by anglers each year. One study found that 75 percent of stocked rainbows were harvested in no more than nineteen days, and by mid-September essentially all stocked trout had been caught, leaving only resident wild trout to overwinter.

Another game fish besides trout has been introduced into the upper Poudre: mountain whitefish. Some of the mountain lakes and reservoirs have been stocked with other nonnative game fish, including kokanee salmon, lake trout, and arctic grayling. Native fish occurring in Poudre Canyon include longnose suckers and longnose dace. The latter are slender, torpedo-shaped minnows no more than three or four inches long, with the wonderful scientific name *Rhinichthys cataractae* (nose-fish of the cataracts). Dace live primarily on small insects in the stream, while suckers scrape edibles from the bottom.

The highest tier in the Poudre's food chain is occupied by predators that feed on fish. Kingfishers patrol the stream in summer, and great blue herons and black-crowned night herons stalk the shallows here and there. When the ice is out in the spring, common mergansers ride the river in the lower canyon, snatching small fish in their serrated beaks. Of course it is we humans that are the most abundant and efficient predators, as everywhere.

In 1978 the Colorado Division of Wildlife introduced several river otters into the Poudre from stocks originally from Wisconsin. They have become established, though not often seen because of their elusive and mainly nocturnal habits. Otters feed primarily on fish, preferring

At low water, in the winter, the Poudre in Fort Collins flows sluggishly over a bed of cobbles. Life in these more alkaline and silt-laden waters is very different from that in the canyon.

easily caught bottom fish such as suckers and carp. They have been seen in many parts of the canyon, and undoubtedly take a few trout, but they tend to occur more frequently in the river after it leaves the canyon, as well as in ponds and reservoirs on the plains. River otters are classified as endangered in the state of Colorado.

THE RIVER THROUGH THE PLAINS

Since the river otter is at home either within or below the canyon, it provides a good point of transition. Of course the change from a cold, clear, swift stream to one that is warmer, gentler, and more silt-laden is gradual, and the changes in the stream fauna are also gradual. Fort Collins residents sometimes catch brown trout on the west side of the city, and longnose suckers and dace range well onto the plains. The North Fork, entering only a few miles from the canyon's mouth, adds a degree of turbidity and alkalinity to the river, and sediments and pollutants are added in abundance as the river flows through Laporte, Fort Collins, and beyond. Stream flow, except during spring runoff, is extremely niggardly, even absent in places, as water is diverted into irrigation ditches and through sewage treatment plants. The stream floor consists in many places of cobbles rolled from the mountains in times past, elsewhere of gravel, sand, or mud. Agriculture and industry reach to its very banks, and old tires, plastic containers, and other symbols of human ingenuity decorate the streambed.

A survey conducted in the 1970s by the Colorado Water Resources Research Institute compared water samples taken near Laporte to those taken below Fort Collins and just above and below Windsor. The changes resulting from urban and agricultural inputs were many and striking. Below Fort Collins, turbidity doubled, and below Windsor, roughly tripled. Alkalinity increased markedly below Fort Collins and continued to increase gradually, and phosphorus, nitrogen, potassium, and sodium showed increases along the course of the river. Most dramatically, bacteria associated with fecal material increased more than a hundredfold below Fort Collins. Clearly the Poudre has become a different stream than the one that tore, singing, through the mountains. Or, as the report put it more prosaically, "it is obvious that the intensive withdrawal of water and return downstream after use leads to a situation in which . . . the water . . . is only remotely related to the water flowing out of the mountain canyon."

This same survey also censused the fish at selected points by electroshocking, sorting the fish to species, and counting and weighing them before release. Longnose suckers were abundant above Fort Collins, white suckers much more plentiful below the city. Fathead minnows and sand shiners were reasonably plentiful at most sample sites. Both are small fish under three inches long, and both do well in warm and turbid water, even downstream of sewage treatment plants. Slightly larger fish, creek chubs and green sunfish, occurred in pools and undercut banks. And of course there were carp, technically members of the minnow family but sometimes reaching a weight of twenty pounds or more.

Carp were introduced from Europe in the 1870s, though actually native to Asia. When they were first introduced, there was much excitement about this prolific and versatile new game fish. According to John Madson in his chronicle of the upper Mississippi, *Up on the River,* "when a modest shipment of young carp arrived it might be greeted at the railway station by a brass band and paraded through town on its way to the river or pond." But disenchantment set in as carp began to replace native fish and to prove less desirable as game and food fish than had been hoped for. Nevertheless carp put up a good fight when hooked, and they are esteemed as food by people in many parts of the world. It is not unusual to see mating carp thrashing in side waters of the Poudre or in ditches and reservoirs. It takes experience to catch them. We have hooked one only once, and after nearly dragging us into the water it broke the light line we were using and escaped. One female carp was reported to have had over two million eggs, which accounts in part for the success of these fish.

In contrast to these common "trash" fish, there are some rarely seen and precious little fish that occur sporadically in the Poudre and some of its tributaries. The most noteworthy of these are two native species of darters, both more common east of Colorado but maintaining small populations here. They are the Johnny darter and the Iowa darter. Neither is more than three inches long. Aside from two other darters with limited distributions elsewhere in the state, these are the only members of the perch family native to Colorado (their larger relatives, yellow perch and walleyes, have been introduced). David Starr Jordan, the father of American ichthyology, spoke of the darters as "a royal series of little fishes," referring to their brilliant colors, and remarked on their "delicacy, wariness, and quaintness of motion." Darters lie half hidden among the stones and weeds in quiet pools, but when disturbed they dart abruptly forward with simultaneous beats of their large pectoral fins. At mating time the males establish territories and defend them vigorously. The females enter the territories and prepare a small depression in which eggs are laid and fertilized by the male; the eggs remain attached to the bottom by means of a sticky coating.

It is during the mating season that the males assume their most brilliant colors. The Iowa darter has alternating blotches of black and rust-red along the sides, a greenish-yellow underside, and a bright orange band along the dorsal fin. The Johnny darter is somewhat less vividly colored. Few people besides fish specialists have ever seen them — and we have not — but it is good to know that the river hides such secrets. The Johnny darter is listed by the Colorado Natural Resources Program as of "state special concern," and the Iowa darter is also regarded as a species worth monitoring.

Natural communities along the river are in a continual flux as the stream floods or changes its course. Banks are eroded away and sand

and gravel bars are shifted. Past floods have left vast deposits of sand and gravel that are now being mined in and near the cities. Some of the abandoned quarries are filled with water or grown over with reeds and cattails, providing wildlife sanctuaries where with luck one may hear the strange calls of rails or bitterns. Some of these ponds and some of the plains and foothills reservoirs contain bullheads, carp, and sunfish. The Colorado Division of Wildlife has also stocked some of them with yellow perch, largemouth bass, channel catfish, crappies, walleyes, or trout.

As the relatively rich fish fauna suggests, there are plenty of nutrients in the Poudre as it crosses the plains, as well as in ponds and reservoirs. Algae are abundant, including filamentous finds that often turn the water green in late summer. One of these, *Spirogyra,* is a favorite of biology classes, since the green photosynthetic elements form a spiral strand along each filament (hence the Greek name for "twisted in a spiral"). Higher plants include *Elodea* (waterweed), well known as an aquarium plant, water crowfoot, and duckweed, all of them common in still or slow-flowing water and all favorites of ducks and geese. Small tributaries with relatively clear water are sometimes choked with watercress, a plant of the mustard family introduced from Europe for its food value. According to H. D. Harrington, the Romans used it with vinegar "as a remedy for those whose minds were deranged." The leaves are considered a good source of vitamins and add piquancy to soups and salads. The plant is, however, rarely used locally, as many of the streams where it grows are polluted.

Insects are plentiful and more diverse than in the canyon. Stoneflies are mostly absent, but there are mayflies and caddisflies that are adapted to these waters. Larvae of various kinds of true flies are abundant, and there are dragonfly larvae, diverse beetles, and even aquatic caterpillars. There are snails, small crustaceans, and various segmented worms including leeches ("bloodsuckers").

The flatworms (planarians) of the lower Poudre and its tributaries are quite different from those occurring in the canyon. Their front ends (not really heads, as the mouth is at the end of a tube protruding from the middle of the animal) are triangular and have one oval eye spot on each side that is pigmented on the inner edge, giving them a cross-eyed look. Scientists place them in the genus *Dugesia,* named for Mexican biologist Alfredo Dugés. Dugés was an ardent collector of birds, insects, and plants, and his home in Guanajuato is said to have been crowded

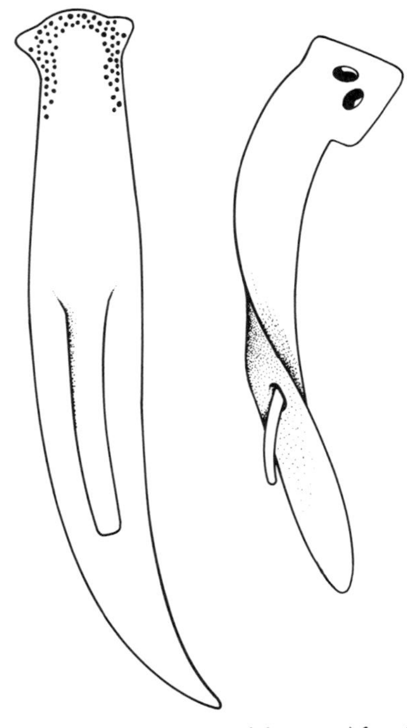

Two species of flatworms (planarians) found in the Poudre: *Dugesia* (on the right) at lower altitudes, *Polyscelis* (on the left) in the mountains.

with natural history specimens. We suspect he didn't mind having a worm named after him.

When we were still teaching, we used to go collecting in Spring Creek just below the dam on Horsetooth Reservoir for planarians to take to class for our students to watch. They are no more than half an inch or so in length, and can readily be found there on the undersurfaces of stones or decaying leaves and grasses. Planaria are not very complex animals, as such things go, but they have a couple of startling behavioral abilities. Their eyespots respond negatively to light, aiding them in seeking out dark places in which to hide from predators. Also, should any of these predators (such as fish or crayfish) manage to take a nip out of one, the flatworm can regenerate the lost part. This makes them a fun laboratory animal. They can be cut in half, and two animals will result when the lost halves are regenerated; or, an individual can be partially cut, and a two-headed or two-tailed "monster" can result. Perhaps the world would go on pretty much the same without planarians, but it would be a smidgen less interesting.

There are many more small creatures in the river and in side waters, swales, ditches, and reservoirs, some of them visible only with the aid of a good microscope. Many of them are as intriguing as planarians, perhaps more so. But the water world is one we humans can explore and enjoy only with difficulty. Perhaps it is time to change to dry shoes and look to the countryside, where we are more at home.

6

FOOTHILLS AND PLAINS

Below the junction of the North Fork with the main stem, the Cache la Poudre flows through semiarid foothills, first of igneous rock and then of hogbacks of sedimentary rock. After a few miles, it leaves the hills behind and wanders across the plains toward its junction with the South Platte. Between the North Fork junction and the city of Fort Collins (a distance of about twelve miles) there is a drop of about 400 feet; from Fort Collins to the South Platte (another twenty-five miles) there is a further drop of only 350 feet. (These are "as the crow flies" distances; no sane crow would follow the meanderings of the river.) The quiet-flowing river is no longer a sculptor of the landscape; it carves no canyons and gathers no major tributaries. With the bewildering array of diversionary canals and a fauna and flora of domestic animals and cultivated plants, and of importations such as Russian olives, leafy spurge, and house sparrows, it is not easy to reconstruct the original face of the land, and we shall not try. Nature is no longer natural, and the Poudre has become an inconspicuous sluice wandering across a vastly modified landscape.

Toward the bottom of the canyon, plants and animals characteristic of the Transition Zone gradually drop out and those of the biogeographers' Upper Sonoran Zone replace them. Narrow-leaved cottonwoods give way to broad-leaved plains cottonwoods; ponderosa pines become sparse and then disappear; Steller's jays are replaced by blue jays, mountain chickadees by black-capped chickadees; the big, black birds flying over are more apt to be crows than ravens. This is warmer and drier country, with a mean annual precipitation around 15 inches and as many as 150 frost-free days. Although the Poudre has lost its role as controller of the landscape, its waters, diverted and regulated by man, have been indispensable in converting much of the countryside to a relatively lush condition, home for many thousands of people in several growing communities and support for several industries and vast acreages of irrigated crops. The river has lost its poetry and often most of its water; like the cattle that have replaced the bison, it has become a docile servant of humanity.

During the Poudre's descent from the mountains, views are constricted by the canyon walls and by twists in the canyon. Now views are expansive, and from a promontory (such as Arthur's Rock in Lory State Park, just west of Horsetooth Reservoir) one can see much of the eastern third of Larimer County; a short way across one of the largest counties in the country, Weld County; and even a bit of Wyoming. One's sense of being cloistered in a limited realm whose inhabitants vary according to altitude is shattered. Now altitudinal differences are minor, but the land is divided horizontally. The foothills themselves are irregular in form and varied in the types of habitats they provide. Beyond are the extensive high plains, now urbanized, grazed by livestock, or converted to agriculture. Then there are the bands of trees that follow the Poudre and many of the diversion ditches and reservoirs of Poudre water. The native trees are largely lost among the nursery-bred trees in the cities, but elsewhere they follow the river across the plains to the South Platte.

THE FOOTHILLS

The distinction between foothills and mountains is an arbitrary one. We define foothills as any place with a clear view of the plains. In places that may be as high as 8,000 feet, though with an eastern exposure and a semiarid cast to the landscape. There are ponderosa pines in higher parts, junipers both high and low. Much of the country is clothed in grasses and low bushes. Here big sage, so common above 8,000 feet, is absent, but smaller species — prairie and fringed mountain sage — are plentiful and have the same classic aroma. In valleys of the intermittent streams that dissect the hills, there are taller bushes and small deciduous trees: wild plums, chokecherries, mountain maples, and others. Mule deer as well as whitetail deer do well here, often ranging close to the highways and not infrequently adding their bit to the "flattened fauna" that decorates our roads. In an average year, 7,000 deer, elk, and antelope are killed on Colorado highways, to say nothing of innumerable rabbits, skunks, and other small mammals. There seems no easy solution to this problem.

Much of the foothills landscape seems superficially rather dreary except for a brief period in spring when yellow wallflowers, blue penstemons, magenta locoweeds, and whiskbroom parsley brighten the slopes and small pincushion-like cacti erupt in pink blossoms. These are mountain ball cacti, *Pediocactus simpsonii*, named for early geologist and explorer James Hervey Simpson by George Engelmann, whom we met in chapter 3. Later these cacti will produce black seeds to which a small mass of protein is attached. Several kinds of ants harvest these seeds, carry them off, and feed on the protein, in the process planting the cacti in new places.

Prickly-pear cacti also abound in poor soils on sunny slopes, producing garish yellow blossoms in early summer and succulent reddish fruits later on. These are formidable but useful plants. Jelly made from prickly-pear fruits can be purchased in novelty shops, though our own success in making jelly has not been outstanding. Our attempt to make wine from the fruits was even less so; there is a stringy consistency to the fruit that resists liquefaction. The Indians made use of both the stems and fruits, rubbing off the spines first, of course. The larger spines are actually less of a problem than the tiny, barbed bristles that cluster close to the surface. H. D. Harrington reports that 90 percent of the ancient human feces found at Mesa Verde in southwestern Colorado contained these tiny spines.

Still another plant that we think of as characteristic of deserts grows commonly in poor soils of the lower foothills and adjacent plains. This is yucca, often called Spanish bayonet because of the stiff, sharply pointed leaves that can indeed pierce a person if he or she stumbles into them. During severe winters we have seen these formidable leaves chewed to the ground, especially on rocky hillsides where woodrats occur. For a brief period in June, the spires of waxy white blossoms add a flavor of the Southwest to hillsides and roadsides.

Yuccas are regarded as undesirable weeds in pastureland, but in times past they proved to be among the most useful of plants. The roots were used by the Indians and early settlers as soap, hence an alternate name for the yucca is soapweed. The roots contain saponin and when chopped up and boiled in water produce suds that have definite cleaning properties. Indians also soaked the leaves in water and after softening them pounded them to release the fibers, which could be woven into baskets or ropes. The fruits were also used as food, usually baked in the ashes of a fire. Euell Gibbons, in his book *Stalking the Good*

Pasque flowers are known by a variety of names: wild crocus, anemone, wildflower, and others.

Life, reported that the young fruits were good roasted and peeled, tasting "a bit like sweet potato." Many of the fruits in our area are infested with insects, so unless one is eager to increase protein intake in this way it is best to select them carefully — or to opt for sweet potatoes.

By no means are all the flowering plants of the foothills armed with spines or dagger-shaped leaves. Indeed, some of the most delicate of wildflowers occur here. Well before the last snows have fallen, pasque flowers spring up in sunny places. Their cup-shaped lavender blossoms, with a central cluster of yellow stamens, later give way to a clump of long, feathery seeds that will be carried off by the wind. In her account of her childhood on Lone Pine Creek in the 1880s, Carrie Williams Darnell told how she and her brothers looked for the earliest wildflowers: "Among these were the pasque anemone flowers, always known to the children as 'grouse blossoms' because that was what their father called them. Carrie searched for them in the early part of March and finding their little fuzzy gray buds in clumps would fall upon her knees kissing them in an ecstasy of joy at their appearance."

Pasque flowers also grow on the plains, and they follow the melting snows in the mountains up to about 9,000 feet. They are the state flower of South Dakota. They have been called by many names besides the ones used by Carrie Darnell: wild crocus, blue tulip, windflower, mayflower, Easter flower, and still others. "Pasque" is a French word for Easter; the paschal festival was originally a pagan rite dedicated to the goddess of spring, Eastre.

Pasque flowers belong to the buttercup family, like so many of our most attractive wildflowers, including clematis, columbine, and larkspur. Like other members of that family, the plants contain an irritating chemical, in this case sometimes poisonous to sheep that happen to graze on them. But to early spring bees, they are (along with pussy willows) a valued source of nectar and pollen. And to people weary of the drab colors of winter, they are a feast for the eyes and a foretaste of the heady days of summer soon to come.

As the pasque flowers begin to set their seed, yellow violets begin to appear in improbable places. Despite a lack of odor, violets have a quiet charm and a distinctive flower shape that is theirs alone. In fact, they need no odor, as they are self-fertile and have no need to attract bees. The violet's showy flowers rarely set seed; instead, inconspicuous flowers close to the ground that do not open are the ones that produce the seeds. Violets are edible plants, used by some Indian tribes as greens and by early settlers for thickening soups or making violet tea.

Viola nuttallii is the scientific name of the yellow violet, named for early botanical explorer Thomas Nuttall. Nuttall seems to have packed several lifetimes into one. Born in England in 1786 and devoted to natural history since childhood, he emigrated to Philadelphia when he was twenty-two and determined to spend his life exploring the plants of the New World. His first expedition was in the upper Missouri River, with John Jacob Astor's American Fur Company. Washington Irving said of him in *Astoria:* "Delighted with the treasures, he went groping along among the wilderness of sweets, forgetful of everything but his immediate pursuit." He was lost several times, but eventually made it back loaded with herbarium specimens.

Nuttall was later appointed as an instructor of natural history at Harvard, but he was lured to the West several more times. One of his former students, Richard Henry Dana, found Nuttall on a California beach stuffing shells into his bulging pockets, an event recorded in his classic *Two Years Before the Mast.* As a result of his energetic collecting, he not only had many plants named for him but several birds and mammals as well. The poorwill mentioned in the previous chapter was

Sego lily. "To look into this flower," wrote Francis Ramaley, "is to gaze into a cup of mystery."

named *Caprimulgus nuttallii* by Audubon; and as we write this, a cottontail rabbit, *Sylvilagus nuttallii*, is staring at us outside our window.

In June and July, the sego lilies begin to appear, each slender stem bearing a single tulip-like blossom. These are remarkable flowers, with three flaring, white petals and in the center a dark, purplish ring filled with yellow, clubbed hairs. They were favorites of Francis Ramaley, late professor of biology at the University of Colorado. "To look into this flower," he wrote, "is to gaze into a cup of mystery, to study it intently is to penetrate the very heart of nature."

Sego is said to be a Shoshone word. Many tribes of Indians esteemed these lilies for their edible bulbs, and the Mormons, in their lean early years in Utah, found them a good emergency food. (The sego lily is now the state flower of Utah.) H. D. Harrington says that the bulbs have a "crisp, nutlike texture." He mentions one person who placed raw pulps on a pizza and cooked the pizza for twenty minutes "with good success." But he adds that the bulbs should be used sparingly, if at all, because of the addition they make to the display of wildflowers on our hillsides. We surely agree.

In some places sego lilies are called mariposa lilies, mariposa being the Spanish word for butterfly; butterfly tulip is still another name. The scientific name, *Calochortus gunnisonii*, pays tribute to another early explorer of the West, John W. Gunnison, for whom the Gunnison River of western Colorado, and the city of Gunnison, are named. *Calochortus*, by the way, is Greek for "beautiful grass," referring to the grass-like leaves and of course to the flowers, for which the word beautiful seems an understatement.

In many places in the foothills, whole hillsides are covered with mountain-mahogany, a rather scraggly member of the rose family, quite unrelated to true mahoganies of the tropics. Evidently, the hard, dark wood suggested the name, although early settlers preferred to call it hardtack, or in the Southwest *palo duro* (hard wood). The wood is so heavy it sinks in water, but it makes a hot, slow-burning campfire. Its leaves are a favorite food of deer and popular with domestic livestock as well. According to Michael Moore, leafy branches can be placed under mattresses to repel bedbugs. We cannot vouch for the effectiveness of this procedure.

In late summer these unprepossessing bushes become things of rare beauty. The small whitish flowers give rise to fruiting bodies that are slender, two or three inches long, and covered with white, silky hairs. Each is loosely coiled like a corkscrew, with a seed at one end. For a few weeks, they remain on the bushes, and a hillside of mountain-mahogany with sunny backlighting becomes something out of a Japanese painting. Eventually the fruits are released and are blown in the wind, the coils spinning and driving the seeds into the soil. The scientific name, *Cercocarpus montanus* (tailed fruit of the mountains), is a good deal more romantic than hardtack and more accurate than mahogany.

Another member of the rose family, bitterbrush, is in many places even more abundant than mountain-mahogany. While its seeds are less unusual than those of mountain-mahogany, the small flowers produced in early summer are showier — creamy-white and produced in masses that often closely cover the entire bush. Serviceberry, still another member of the rose family, grows in protected places, sporting small clusters of large, white blossoms with narrow, twisted petals and, in the fall, purple berries that were a staple in the diet of Indians, who mixed them with bison meat to make pemmican. All three — mountain-mahogany, bitterbrush, and serviceberry — are major food for deer and are especially important in winter, when the tips of the branches extending above the snow provide essential browse during hard times. They withstand considerable browsing, but experimental clipping by

Even while gorging themselves at road kills, magpies appear dressed for a formal occasion, with black tie, immaculate white shirt, and tails. *Photo by David Leatherman.*

researchers of the Colorado Division of Wildlife has shown that if more than the current year's growth is removed, the plants may not survive. In severe winters deer and elk may be reduced to eating the woody stems, killing the plants.

The chokecherries and wild plums (also of the rose family) of moist gullies were also cherished by the Indians, and even today, when supermarkets offer us so much variety, it is great fun — and economical — to harvest these fruits for making jelly. And winter passes so much more congenially if one is stocked with chokecherry wine! When the cherries are ripe, black bears appear out of nowhere, sometimes breaking the trees in their eagerness to devour the berries and leaving their huge, seed-filled droppings here and there.

Valleys in the foothills are favorite haunts of an elegant bird that westerners tend to take too much for granted (it is absent over the eastern half of the country). Magpie nests are often spaced along the valleys near the tops of small trees; they also occur along the Poudre itself, from fairly high in the canyon all the way to the South Platte and beyond. These long-tailed, short-winged birds are a common sight and noisy enough to attract attention to themselves. There are no halfway measures about their plumage; no grays or pastels; deep black and pure white sharply defined, the black reflecting iridescent green in the sunlight. The huge bill is an efficient tool for handling a varied diet of carrion, insects, and vegetable matter. In summer, grasshoppers, caterpillars, and maggots plucked from carrion are the preferred diet. In winter almost anything even remotely edible will do, including road kills and suet filched from bird feeders.

It was in 1804 that Meriwether Lewis, then on the upper reaches of the Missouri River, noted "a remarkable bird (Magpy) . . . about the size of a large pigeon, a butifull thing." The magpies flew into their tents and snatched food; during the skinning of game, they lurked about and dashed in to steal pieces of meat. Although new to Lewis and Clark, the birds had long raided Indian camps for offal from their hunts. Indian boys sometimes kept them as pets.

No bird is more characteristic of the West, whether it is gliding down a canyon, pecking at a carcass, or chattering in concert with others from a grove of cottonwoods. The range of the magpie extends from New Mexico to Alaska and on into Eurasia, in fact all the way to England. In Europe, magpies are the stuff of folklore and superstition. One of the legends inspired an opera by Italian composer Gioacchino Rossini, *La Gazza Ladra* (The Thieving Magpie). The Spanish artist Goya included a magpie in his portrait of Don Manuel Osorio de Zuniga, a tribute to humanity's long fascination with this magnificent bird.

As for the name, some suppose that it is a contraction of "maggot pie," with reference to the bird's habit of picking maggots from flesh. Others claim it is compounded of the common French name Margot and the Latin word for woodpecker, *pica*. The latter word comprises the scientific name of the species, *Pica pica*, rather easier to remember than most scientific names.

Magpie nests consist of great piles of twigs, often two feet in diameter but sometimes much larger; one record nest measured seven feet from top to bottom. The base and sides are built of coarse sticks, often thorny ones such as Russian olive or thorn apple. Inside there is a cup of mud, lined with rootlets and horsehair; over the top is a canopy of twigs. There is an opening on each side, one for entry and another to accommodate the long tail. They start nest building in March, and in April the female lays seven to ten speckled eggs. When young magpies are taken from the nest and hand-reared, they can sometimes be taught a few words. Like their cousins the crows and ravens, magpies are counted among the more intelligent of birds.

In his monograph on the magpie, Jean Myron Linsdale comments that "the general manner of a magpie is that of a bird well able to take care of itself." Good for the magpie; we live in times when wild creatures must adapt to our curious ways or join the ranks of endangered species. Magpies have learned to live with people, but with caution. Surely Meriwether Lewis was right that a magpie is "a butifull thing." Hardy and adaptable, winging free over canyon and plain, it is one of the West's more accessible treasures.

Other birds of the foothills lack the dramatic plumage of the magpie but far excel it in song. Green-tailed towhees live among the rocks and bushes of the slopes, and rufous-sided towhees inhabit the stream valleys. Both are notable songsters. But of all the birds of the foothills, our favorites are the rock wrens. Four quite different series of notes are produced in unpredictable order, usually from the top of a rocky outcrop. All wrens seem to have songs louder than their small bodies seem capable of producing. House wrens also occur here, and if one is especially honored by the spirits of the wild he or she may hear, in a rocky foothills canyon, three kinds of wrens singing in the same area — rock, house, and canyon wrens. It has happened to us only once.

Rattlesnakes formerly abounded in the foothills of the Rockies, as well as on the plains, and Indians and homesteaders were well aware of the menace they presented. Arapahoe medicine men were often called upon to treat snakebite. One treatment consisted of chopping up the snake's head, drying and powdering it, and adding certain herbs such as snakeroot. The mixture was then put on a cloth that was tied around the patient's wrist after it had first been abraded until it bled. A piece of fat was added to the bandage and kept warm with a hot stone. Doubtless the patient usually recovered, since in fact most people do survive rattlesnake bite, though after many agonizing hours. During the twenty-year period from 1958 to 1978, only two individuals (both children) died from rattlesnake bites in Colorado.

Chronicles of early settlers are filled with anecdotes about rattlers. Hal Borland, who was brought up in eastern Colorado, tells of several adventures in his autobiographical *High, Wide and Lonesome*, including one in which his dog barely survived a bite by spending the night in a mudhole. Those on the eastern slopes of the Front Range are prairie rattlers, though they also occur in the mountains up to about 7,000 feet, sometimes higher on south-facing slopes. Although their numbers are now greatly diminished, it is not uncommon to find them sunning themselves or slithering through the grass in ravines and on hillsides. In our fifteen years of roaming the foothills, we have seen perhaps ten, and only once have we had a real scare — not nearly enough to cause us to worry about them very much. Unfortunately fear of snakes is very widespread even today, and some people will kill just about any snake they see. This is unfortunate, since snakes, including rattlers, do much to keep populations of rodents and other small animals in check.

Rattlesnakes occur only in the Americas, and "snakes that rattle" were a source of amazement and disbelief to Europeans who first heard reports from the New World. They are wonderfully well-adapted predators, members of a group called "pit vipers," a pit between the eye and nostril being an organ capable of detecting the warmth of potential prey at some distance so that the strike can be accurately directed. The large fangs inject a potent venom that quickly immobilizes the prey, which, as in all snakes, is then swallowed whole. And the rattle? That is a curious structure indeed. It is made up of a number of sections of a horn-like substance that vibrate together to produce the sound. Each time the snake sheds its skin, another rattle is added. However, the age of the snake cannot be told from the number of rattles, since older snakes tend to lose them; if all were retained there would be a long chain that would be more handicap than help to the snake.

There has been much speculation as to how the rattle may have evolved. Snakes of many kinds vibrate their tails when nervous or angry, and it may be that the rattle developed over time to enhance this reaction and to frighten enemies and deter large animals (such as bison) from stepping on them. Of course since rattlers don't have ears, they presumably can't hear the rattle. Recent research favors a different hypothesis. Many snakes lie motionless in the grass while they expose and twitch their tail, which serves as a worm-like lure for toads or shrews and a source of curiosity for birds and field mice. Frogs have been seen to be lured by the tip of a twitching tail, whereupon they were struck, killed, and devoured. Such a device might easily have become elaborated to the point that it also served as a warning to animals too large to serve as prey. Perhaps all of this does little to assuage anyone's fear, but it does highlight the wonder of these unique inhabitants of our plains and foothills.

North of Fort Collins and just east of the village of Livermore, along a hogback paralleled by U. S. Highway 287, there is an extensive stand of pinyon pines, small trees noted for their edible nuts. Presumably they were accidentally planted many years ago by Indians who obtained the seeds by trading with tribes further south, for there are no other stands for 150 miles to the south. Some of these trees have been found to be 300 to 400 years old. Portions of this hogback are being quarried, but 658 acres are preserved in the Brackenbury Natural Area, which is maintained by the Colorado Division of Wildlife. This natural area also includes several archaeological sites as well as an unusual fern. This is purple cliff brake, a fern that is widely distributed in the eastern states but rarely found in Colorado.

There are other rare plants secluded among the hogbacks and the plains just east of them. One of these is a modest member of the mustard family that has a limited distribution and is listed by the Colorado Natural Areas Program as being of special concern. This is Bell's twinpod, *Physaria bellii*. *Physaria* is a Greek word for "bellows," with reference to the inflated fruits. William Abraham Bell, according to Joseph Ewan in *Rocky Mountain Naturalists*, was "an Englishman gentleman of wealth and enterprise" who became an executive of the Denver and Rio Grande Western Railroad and served as a guide to Ulysses S. Grant on his tour of Colorado. Of course he collected plants on the side, or he would not have been honored by having a twinpod named after him.

At the foothills-plains intercept there are patchy stands of a bushy plant with narrow, gray-green leaves called rabbitbrush. Growing mostly in disturbed areas, these plants escape much attention until late August and September, when they explode into yellow bloom, among the last flowers of summer. They actually grow from far out on the plains well up Poudre Canyon, and they make very desirable (though seldom used) ornamentals in the cities, as they are adapted for semiarid conditions and require little water. ❧

Indians used to chew the inner bark of rabbitbrush as gum, and around 1900 it was discovered that the bark contains rubber of very similar composition to that of tropical rubber trees. One estimate has

nevertheless a grand ornament for prairies that sometimes go on for miles with little to break the monotony.

Russian thistle is another spiny plant of the plains, another thistle-like plant that isn't really a thistle. Unfortunately it has no showy blossoms to offset its prickly disposition; the flowers are small and cling closely to the stems. These are bushy plants that in late summer tend to draw in the tips of their branches to form a somewhat circular ball of bristly branches. When the plants are loosened by the wind, they roll across the plains, pile up against fences, and fill up irrigation ditches. These are the tumbleweeds that romanticized cowboys sing about and tourists from the East take back to show their neighbors. Oddly, this classic symbol of the West is not a native plant at all; it arrived in Colorado about a century ago. However, other weedy plants, pigweeds and others, also blow about in the fall, so presumably there have always been tumbleweeds of a sort.

These are pestiferous weeds of the worst kind. "It is possible that a good word could be said for the Russian thistle," wrote Francis Ramaley in *Colorado Plant Life*, "but the appropriate word does not easily come to mind." Yet in the past, these plants have sometimes saved people's lives. When the first shoots appear above the ground, in the spring or after a summer shower, they are tender and succulent. Many a pioneer, supplies exhausted, has survived on them until other food became available. According to H. D. Harrington, the young plants are "mild, pleasant, and crisp tasting, making one of the very best potherbs we have ever eaten." He recommends serving them with bacon or boiled eggs, or with a cream sauce and served on toast — though doubtless early settlers were happy to do without these embellishments. Young plants were also sometimes used as emergency hay for livestock.

Many other useful plants abound on the plains. Sunflower seeds were a staple for some tribes of Indians, who parched them, ground them into flour, and made a nutritious bread. They also used the oil for anointing their skin and hair. It goes without saying that sunflowers also add a great deal of color to the plains in late summer. Nowadays we use larger, cultivated varieties of sunflowers for a variety of purposes. A species of scurfpea called by early French trappers "pomme de prairie" has starchy tubers that are wholesome and nutritious eaten either raw or boiled with venison. Even wild licorice, a rather coarse member of the pea family with spiny cocklebur-like pods, was used by the Indians, who chewed the stems for their flavor and supposed tonic effects. There is something to be said for every living thing, no matter how ugly it may at first appear.

The plains are the home of Colorado's state bird, the lark bunting. These attractive black-and-white members of the sparrow family often sing their exuberant songs on the wing, flying up at a 45-degree angle to a height of twenty to thirty feet, then concluding their song as, with jerky wing movements, they descend slowly. It has been said that the buntings have the song of a lark, the bill of a grosbeak, the plumage of a bobolink, and the gregarious habits of blackbirds. "These characteristics," says H. E. Baumgarten in Bent's *Life Histories* of North American birds, "render the lark bunting unique and endear it to those with whom it spends the late spring and summer."

Their nests are built on the ground near the base of a plant, where three to six greenish-blue eggs are laid. The young are fed on insects, and the adults also live mainly on insects in the summer, with well over half of their diet consisting of grasshoppers. There is no question that these are highly beneficial birds, as grasshoppers are often overly abundant on the plains. Overgrazing and the conversion of the plains to farming cause the birds to move elsewhere; already they have abandoned parts of their former range, though fortunately they are still plentiful on the plains of the Poudre drainage.

True larks, called horned larks because they bear some partly erect feathers on the sides of their head, also abound here, though their songs are less ear-catching than those of lark buntings. Neither bird flies as high or has quite the ethereal song of the skylark of Europe that inspired Shelley's poem, but they will do. This is also meadowlark country, and the flute-like calls of these birds seem to ring from every fence post. One wonders what the birds perched on before there were fences and power lines. Now the fence posts are favored perches not only of meadowlarks but of kingbirds and shrikes; the electric wires are strung with swallows and mourning doves, and the poles provide an occasional perch for a red-tailed or Swainson's hawk.

We would be remiss not to say a word about that blithe spirit of the plains, the jackrabbit. Mark Twain was much intrigued by these animals as he crossed the plains by stagecoach as a young man. The jackrabbit, he wrote,

> has the most preposterous ears that ever were mounted on any creature but a jackass. When he is sitting quiet, thinking about his

Darkling beetles are among the insects most often noticed on the plains. They are sometimes called "circus beetles" from their tendency to "stand on their heads." They are, in fact, positioning themselves to discharge a noxious defensive chemical from their tails.

> sins, or is absent-minded or unapprehensive of danger, his majestic ears project above him conspicuously; but the breaking of a twig will scare him nearly to death, and then he tilts his ears back gently and starts for home. All you can see, then, for the next minute, is his long gray form stretched out straight and 'streaking it' through the low sage-brush . . . ears just canted a little to the rear, but showing you where the animal is, all the time, the same as if he carried a jib.

Once it was common to see the mounds of prairie dog towns on the plains, but these are becoming increasingly hard to find. The mounds that one sees on the grasslands are much more likely to be those of prairie mound-building ants. These ants make remarkably deep nests, sometimes reaching a depth of seven feet, piling up the soil in a conical mound with an entrance on one side (almost always the east or south side). The average mound of a mature colony may be two to three feet in diameter and five to eight inches high. Each mound is surrounded by a space cleared of vegetation. The mound is full of chambers where the ants live, and there are further chambers deep in the soil where the queen lives and to which all of the ants retreat in the winter.

Robert Lavigne, a professor of entomology at the University of Wyoming, excavated thirty-three nests, using a backhoe, with a trowel and forceps for following the tunnels in detail. He found 412 to 8,796 worker ants in various nests. These are fierce ants, which can both bite and sting, and digging up a nest is not something to be undertaken casually. The chambers are used for rearing the young and for storing seeds, for these are harvester ants, living primarily on weed and grass seeds which are kept in granaries deep in the soil. One striking thing about the nests is that they tend to be neatly spaced across a pasture, usually about twenty feet apart. Clearly this is an efficient use of the available seed-bearing plants: the resources are effectively shared because each colony has its own piece of the pasture. Boundaries between territories are reinforced by occasional combat between workers.

As in many ants, prairie mound-builders lead nest mates to good food sources by laying odor trails, in this case with the contents of the poison glands. In the nest, seeds are husked before storage, the husks being placed in special refuse chambers. Dead ants are removed from the nest and placed in a pile outside. Corpses are recognized by the odors of decomposition, particularly oleic acid (also produced by butter when it becomes rancid). When we were teaching, we used to take our classes to nearby ant mounds and place small sticks treated with oleic acid on the mounds. They were promptly picked up by the workers and carried to their refuse dump. Even healthy ants, if treated with this acid, are often carried off and dumped in the "cemetery." Like most ants, harvesters have small eyes and live mostly in a world of subtle odors.

Formidable though these ants are, they have a persistent enemy that preys exclusively on them. This is a small, attractively colored wasp called *Clypeadon*. The female wasps quickly seize and sting worker ants, even entering their nests to do this if none are available outside. The paralyzed ant is then carried to the wasp's nest, in the ground nearby, where it serves as food for the wasp's larva. Rather than holding their prey in their jaws or legs, as most wasps do, they carry the ant attached to their tail end by means of a unique "ant clamp." This frees their jaws and legs for quick entry into their nests.

As it flows through Fort Collins, the Poudre is a quiet stream flanked by shady cottonwoods and willows.

Byron Alexander, then a graduate student at Colorado State University, studied several of more than thirty *Clypeadon* nests not far from the banks of the Poudre within the city limits of Fort Collins. He found that larger wasps were able to provision their nests more rapidly than smaller wasps, either because they were better able to subdue the ants or better able to drive off smaller wasps that were competing at ant nests. He also found that some of the wasps stocked their nests primarily by stealing paralyzed ants from nests of their neighbors. The existence of "bullies" and "thieves" in the insect world may tell us nothing about these phenomena in our own society, but it does help us understand how some insects have evolved so as to live at the expense of other, related species.

The place where Byron Alexander did his research was severely flooded during the spring of 1983, and populations of both the ants and wasps were wiped out. But these insects are opportunists and may someday reoccupy the site. People living on the floodplain of the Cache la Poudre also had problems during this flood, as they have had during past floods — indeed Fort Collins owes its beginnings to the flood of 1864, in which Camp Collins (at the present site of Laporte) was destroyed. Floods not only cause much property damage but lead people to contemplate all the "lost water," inviting thoughts about more dams rather than more reasonable solutions, better care of the watershed and better uses of the floodplain than for homes, for example.

As the Poudre leaves the canyon and weaves its way to the South Platte, one tree more than any other dominates it banks, it tributaries, and many of the ditches and reservoirs — the plains cottonwood. These are sometimes regarded as "weed trees." It is true that the wood is inferior for building or for firewood; the female trees produce quantities of fluffy "cotton" that collects on window screens and clogs drains; the trees are often gaunt and irregular in shape, with dead branches that may descend without warning. Farmers resent the water their roots take from irrigation ditches along which they often grow.

But what would the West be without cottonwoods? To the pioneers they were salvation after crossing endless miles without shade or shelter — and they were a promise of water. As Donald Culross Peattie puts it, "these cottonwood groves were the wayside inn, the club, the church, the newspaper and fortress, when the wagon trains drew up in a circle beneath their boughs." The hollowed trunks of the larger trees provided primitive river transportation. In winter, when the ground was covered with snow, the inner bark made acceptable food for horses. William Ashley, ascending the South Platte and heading toward the Poudre in the winter of 1825, wrote in his journal: "I was . . . gratified at the sight of a grove of timber . . . it proved to be a grove of cottonwood of the sweet bark kind, suitable for horse food."

Cottonwoods captured the imagination of Worthington Whittredge, a member of the so-called Hudson River School of landscape painters. Although brought up in Ohio and trained in the East and in Europe, Whittredge traveled in Colorado in 1866 with General John Pope, who was inspecting Indian settlements after the Civil War. He was so taken by the plains abutting the Rockies that he returned twice and painted several idyllic scenes of its streams. One of his best, now in the Amon Carter Museum in Fort Worth, Texas, is *On the Cache la Poudre River, Colorado*. The quietly flowing river is framed by great, deep green cottonwoods, and four deer seem to be reflecting on nature's beneficence. The scene was painted near Greeley, and a reporter for the *Greeley Tribune* remarked that Whittredge had "lingered lovingly along the Cache la Poudre . . . for there can be no more picturesque stream in the world."

Even today, though the river is scarcely as pristine as Whittredge portrayed it, there is much to be said for cottonwoods. The reddish male catkins brighten the spring, and the rustle of the glossy green leaves enlivens the summer. To a person afoot on the plains on a hot summer day, there can be no greater pleasure than a siesta beneath a spreading cottonwood. Great, scraggly willows also hug the streamside, and on sandspits smaller, bushy sandbar willows. Other trees and shrubs that inhabit a narrow strip along the river include box elder, hackberry, hawthorn, wild rose, snowberry, and in places poison ivy. Snowberry, a low, bushy member of the honeysuckle family, has attractive, succulent white berries in late summer. Oddly, the berries seem not to have been used as human food, or to have found a use in folk medicine. Yet they are palatable and nonpoisonous.

People have an incurable tendency to use rivers and their banks as dumping grounds for wastes of all kinds. Fortunately the cities along the Poudre are beginning to appreciate the river's value for recreation and the need to preserve some of the original plant and animal life. Fort Collins has built seven miles of walking and bike trails along the river and another five miles of trails along Spring Creek, a small tributary that winds through the city. There are several riverside parks and open areas as well as a ten-acre plot along the river that has been developed as a nature preserve to honor Gustav A. Swanson, professor emeritus of fishery and wildlife biology at Colorado State University — a good friend and a well-known local naturalist. Gus has had much to do with the city's awakening to its natural beauties and the need to save bits and pieces for posterity.

As the Poudre leaves the city to the southeast, the Northern Colorado Environmental Learning Center provides 200 acres of reasonably natural river bottomland available to students, researchers, and bird watchers. The river, to be sure, has by now lost its youthful ebullience. It is a tired and turbid stream as it flows past the city, at times and places little more than a trickle over the cobblestones it has rolled from the mountains in times past. Walking the trails, one is often more impressed by past abuses than by the river's present charms. But the rattle of a kingfisher assures us that there is still life in the river, and the vaulting cottonwoods provide respite from the city's mad pace.

Recently the citizens of Fort Collins have formed the Poudre River Trust in the hope of controlling development along the river and perhaps restoring some of its original beauty and usefulness for recreation. There has also been much discussion about the feasibility of designating 18.5 miles of the river, through Fort Collins to the Weld County line, as a National Recreation Area. When the upper section of the Poudre was designated Wild and Scenic in 1986, Congress mandated such a feasibility study and allocated $75,000 for it. The study, conducted by Shakley Walker Associates, resulted in an impressive report which concluded that NRA designation was feasible. Whatever the final outcome of this process, the resulting focus on the problems and possibilities of the river as it flows through Fort Collins is certain to be beneficial. But despite our affection for the river, we question whether this part of the river can ever be transformed to the extent that it will be attractive on a *national* scale.

Past Fort Collins and the neighboring village of Timnath, the river winds a leisurely course southeastward, bordered by grassy bottomlands and by cottonwoods that cast their branches skyward in a thousand different patterns, as if each had a different story to tell (as doubtless each has). The surrounding fields, at one time mostly sugar beets, are now mainly corn and other silage crops to supply the numerous cattle feedlots. Windsor, once a small country town, is now thriving because of a large Kodak plant nearby. Greeley's Island Grove Park and Centennial Village occupy a spacious area along the Poudre as it wanders along the north side of the city. The huge trees in the park are those planted by the founders of Greeley in the 1870s. Centennial Village includes a sod house of the type built by the early settlers; when we visited, the walls of the hut were riddled with small holes, the nests of burrowing bees. The village also includes other buildings characteristic of Greeley's early years: log cabins, a one-room schoolhouse, Victorian homes, and the old Union Pacific Depot.

Greeley had been in existence for only a few years when a plague of Rocky Mountain locusts descended on the community. They flew in from the northeast by the millions, destroying grains, vegetables, and even small trees. "They had a peculiar fondness for onions," said David Boyd in his history of Greeley, "and resembled their human brethren in their partiality for tobacco . . . there was a time when it was doubtful whether the man or the locust was the fittest to survive on these plains."

David Boyd tells of a Greeley clothier who offered the best suit of clothes in his store to anyone who would bring him a million grasshoppers. A local Scotsman brought him what he estimated to be a million,

The Cache la Poudre flows from the right into the broad and shallow South Platte, east of Greeley.

but the clothier refused to accept them because they were dead. The Scotsman then returned in the evening with a sack of live ones. When the merchant insisted that he count them, the Scotsman threatened to dump them on the floor of the store since it was dark outside. At that, the clothier gave in, and, in David Boyd's words, "the canny Scot thereafter went around Sundays in a suit of the finest blue broadcloth."

Rocky Mountain locusts declined dramatically after the 1870s. In fact, by 1902 the species had disappeared altogether, an extinction never explained and never regretted. Other kinds of grasshoppers continue to have periodic outbreaks on the plains of eastern Colorado, but these are nonmigratory kinds that with vigilance can usually be contained. At present, a protozoan (one-celled animal) called *Nosema locustae* shows promise as a control that may avoid the widespread use of toxic chemicals with their many unpredictable effects on the environment.

Greeley today is the center of a rich agricultural area, much of it irrigated by Poudre water. Across the fields of potatoes, beans, onions, corn, and other crops, in the morning light, the mountains shine in the distance, a source of inspiration as well as the lifeblood of all this bounty.

On a warm day in early April, we visited the junction of the Poudre with the South Platte. Fortunately there is a public access, at the Mitani Tokuyasu State Wildlife Area a few miles east of Greeley. The wildlife area was littered with old tires and shotgun casings; a cornfield is closely adjacent, and across the road a cattle feedlot provides rich odors familiar to those who live in that part of Colorado. Still it was a peaceful place, a place to revere if one has experienced the Poudre in many of its other moods. Here the cold, clear waters that seeped from mosses in the high country, much diluted and clouded with algae, sediments, and contaminants, leave the river that embraced them for so many miles and begin a mingling of waters that will take them to the Gulf of Mexico. As we visited the junction, there were great flocks of noisy blackbirds in the trees, a solitary great horned owl perched in a tree across the river, and a muskrat stirred the water along the shore. Even here, the river did not deign to shed the last traces of its wildness.

7

NORTH FORK AND SOUTH FORK

The two major tributaries of the Cache la Poudre are streams of very different character, fathered many miles apart and in dissimilar terrain. The South Fork arises in the tundra of the Mummy Range, among ice fields, cirque lakes, and jagged cliffs, then follows a relatively short course to join the main stem of the Poudre near Dutch George Flats, many miles from the mouth of the canyon. In no more than about twenty miles, it descends from over 12,000 feet to about 6,700 feet, with an average fall of 264 feet per mile. From an origin in Rocky Mountain National Park, it passes for the most part through national forest, including parts of the Comanche Peak and Cache la Poudre wildernesses.

In contrast the North Fork begins in rolling, forested country near Deadman Hill, barely over 10,000 feet in elevation, and runs a course somewhat more than twice that of the South Fork before joining the Poudre not far from the bottom of the canyon at about 5,400 feet. The average fall is only about 100 feet per mile. Much of this is country of gentle slopes and broad, open areas. At one time the Union Pacific Railroad owned 38 percent of the land in the drainage, but most of this has been sold to individual owners. About 60 percent of the land in the drainage is now in private ownership. Well over half of the total area of the watershed is now grazed by cattle.

Altogether the North Fork watershed covers 566 square miles, of which 100 square miles are in Wyoming. There are 440 miles of more or less permanent streams. In spite of the size of the basin, at most times the North Fork is a leisurely stream, less well endowed with water than one might suppose. Although the watershed is over five times the area of that of the South Fork, the mean annual flow at the mouth is less (54 cubic feet per second as compared to 63 cfs for the South Fork). The two forks together provide slightly less than half the mean annual flow of the main stem of the Poudre at Rustic (248 cfs).

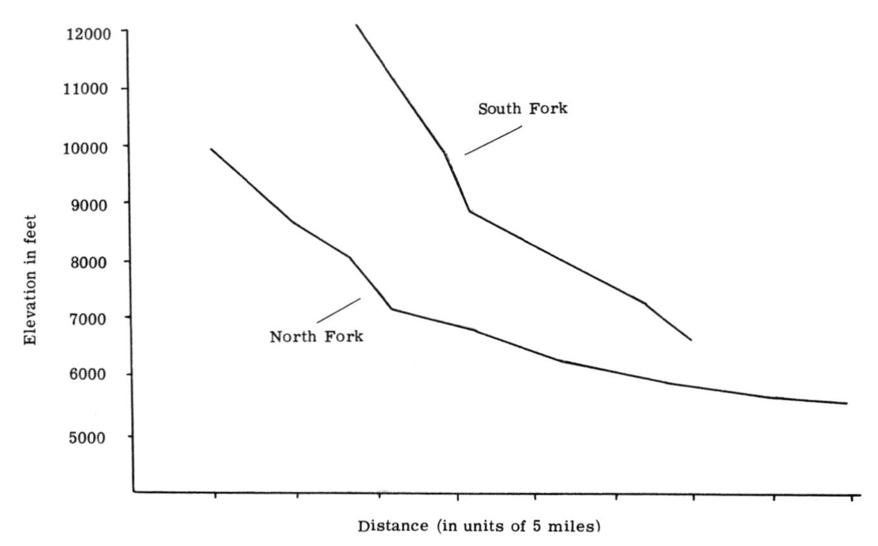

Profiles of the North and South Forks compared.

In many parts of the North Fork drainage, for example around the villages of Virginia Dale and Red Feather Lakes, there are great outcroppings of granite, sometimes rising a hundred feet or more above the general lay of the land. Some of these are rounded, others pyramidal or in shapes impossible to describe, and many have curious patterns of fissures. These striking rock formations, combined with the park-like appearance of much of this country with its scattered ponderosa pines, make this one of the most beautiful parts of Colorado.

The North Fork

We have not explored the sources of the North Fork, which drain the south slopes of Deadman Hill, cresting at 10,711 feet. No one now remembers when and by whom the hill was named. A "deadman" is a stationary log that may be used as an anchor for a wagon descending a steep slope or for rolling other logs, so it is reasonable to suppose that the name came to be applied to the hill at an early date. Ted Dunning, a longtime resident of Red Feather Lakes, had a more colorful story. According to him, "an old Swede" long ago trapped on the hill during

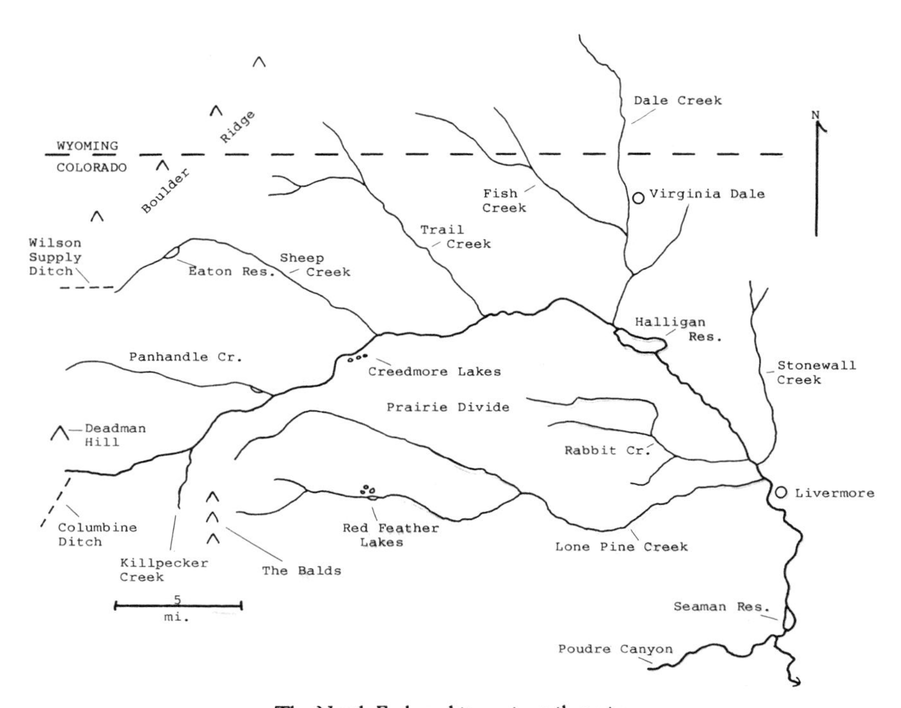

The North Fork and its major tributaries.

the winter, but one spring failed to return. When Lou Young, a local cowboy known for his abilities with a rope, was driving cattle over the hill a year or two later, he found the bones of the old Swede and his horse. Presumably the horse had been tied and starved to death. According to Young, a bear had been caught in a trap, but before the trapper could take out the bear, it "reached out and belted [the old trapper] and killed him." How Young could so precisely reconstruct the scene is not clear, but a good bear story is its own excuse for being. Young brought back the trap as evidence and gave it to Dunning, who nailed it to the front of his store along with other paraphernalia; later it was given to the Fort Collins Historical Museum.

In an effort to increase the flow of the nascent North Fork, a connecting ditch was dug many years ago from one of the branches of Nunn Creek, a west-flowing tributary of the Laramie River. This is the third capture of Laramie River water we have mentioned, and the sixth transmountain diversion. It is called Columbine Ditch, and like similar

Green gentian blossom.

ditches it is a tribute to the energy of those who wielded picks and shovels in remote forest areas — and to the value they placed on water resources.

Where the North Fork is joined by Killpecker Creek, at 9,150 feet elevation, the U.S. Forest Service has built a campground, deep in aromatic forests of Engelmann spruce and lodgepole pine. A musical background is provided by the stream, still no more than an exuberant infant, and by the haunting strains of hermit thrushes. Charles Hartshorne, a professor of philosophy at the University of Texas, once made an evaluation of birdsongs on the basis of such things as tone, complexity, loudness, and continuity. Of all North American birds, he rated the hermit thrush first (the western meadowlark was not far behind). Catskill naturalist John Burroughs had a special affection for hermit thrushes, describing their song as "pure and serene, as if a spirit from some remote height were slowly chanting a divine accompaniment" to other forest sounds. These thrushes live only in wild, heavily forested areas, and those of us who love such country find them kindred spirits but far more appropriately articulate than we can hope to be.

On the upper reaches of the North Fork, as in other parts of the Poudre drainage of comparable elevation, one of the Rockies' most eccentric plants can be seen: green gentians. It is hard to believe that these are true gentians, related to the azure fringed gentians that grace mountain meadows. When in bloom, green gentian plants are often three or four feet tall, with great numbers of flowers in a tapering spire (monument plant is a fitting alternate name). The flowers are green, as the name implies, and the four large petals are speckled with purplish dots; at the base of each petal is a jagged appendage that overlies some rather large nectar tubes; between each petal is a long, pointed, green sepal; finally, there are four long, pollen-bearing anthers and a central stigma. There is nothing even remotely like these flowers.

But that is only part of the story. A green gentian in flower can be remarkably old for an herbaceous plant. Some of them live as long as sixty years as a rosette of large, succulent green leaves before sending up a flowering stalk and dying afterward. Others live much shorter lives before flowering and dying. At one time, in one area, there are likely to be numerous green gentians in flower, while elsewhere few or none are in flower. This unusual variability in life-span and the tendency for synchronous flowering have puzzled researchers at the Rocky Mountain Biological Laboratory for many years, and some tentative explanations are now available. Obviously these unusual life history features are successful, since green gentians normally set many seeds before succumbing.

Generally speaking, a short-lived plant should be at an advantage over a long-lived plant that flowers only once, since it produces a series of seed-bearing generations during the life-span of a long-lived plant. So why should many green gentians live as rosettes for many years before flowering? Rosettes grow from year to year, and the larger the rosette the taller the flower stalk that can eventually be produced. These taller plants, all flowering at once, compete strongly for pollinators (mainly bumblebees) in a setting where many other kinds of plants are blooming and attracting bees. Assurance of pollination means that more seeds are set, and taller plants are able to disperse their seeds more widely.

Many alpine flowers lose many of the blooms or seeds to insects. For example, lupine, which commonly grows in the same meadows as green gentians, often has over half the blossoms or seeds consumed by caterpillars. But green gentians rarely lose more than 5 percent of their potential seed production to insects. Since lupines flower each year, certain insects have adapted to their regular availability as food. But green gentians, flowering infrequently and unpredictably, do not present a source of food to which insects can readily adapt. So it seems probable that the unique features of green gentians represent uncommon solutions to common problems of survival in a world full of competing plants and of insects that may either insure or diminish seed set. Elk often feed on rosettes, cattle eat and trample them, and shade and moisture conditions often change over time. So there are possible hazards in living so long before flowering. While admiring the beauty of green gentians, one must admire, too, the unusual ways in which these plants manage to make a go of it in a highly competitive world.

Much of the country in the upper North Fork basin can be reached via a gravel country road, which is closed in winter. Leaving the village of Red Feather Lakes, the road winds upward toward the west, providing views of the valley below and access to trailheads. It also crosses a vast area that has been devastated by fire — the Killpecker burn of 1978. A different road from Red Feather Lakes leads to the North Fork at Beaver Meadows, about three miles downstream from the North Fork campground. This is a resort area located on the sides of a broad, open valley along the winding, willow-fringed river. The meadows in June are bright with marsh marigolds, and the hillsides clothed with big sage and Oregon grape (also called mountain holly, though actually a barberry). The berries of Oregon grape are said to make good jelly, and the juices, diluted and sweetened, to taste much like grape juice. The Indians made a yellow dye from the berries and from the wood and used it for decorating their clothing and baskets.

Not far downstream from Beaver Meadows, the North Fork is joined by a major tributary, Panhandle Creek. The creek is dammed not far upstream from its confluence with the river, providing a recreational lake for a community called Crystal Lakes. Much of the land in this area is in private ownership, but several miles downstream there is national forest access to Creedmore Lakes, a series of three small, shallow lakes without obvious inlets or outlets, set close beside the river but on a plateau several hundred feet above it. One is located in a rocky setting and is stocked each year with rainbow trout. The other two are unstocked and so not often visited, though they have much to recommend them, including an assortment of colorful dragonflies hawking through the rushes for midges and mosquitoes. The lakes were named after a hunter who long ago had a camp there.

Flowing in a northeasterly direction, the North Fork is soon joined by Sheep Creek (the third creek of that name), a major tributary rising in the hills some forty miles to the west. Near its headwaters there is a ditch, the Wilson Supply Ditch, that takes water from Sand Creek in the Laramie River drainage (for the record, the fourth diversion from the Laramie and the seventh transmountain diversion). The ditch helps to supply water to Eaton Reservoir on Upper Sheep Creek. Benjamin Eaton, a governor of Colorado in the 1880s, was a great believer in dams and ditches for irrigation, and at one time he owned the land where the reservoir is located. Parts of Sheep Creek are closely paralleled by the Cherokee Park road, and there are good campsites and, at times, good fishing. Just southeast of the junction of Sheep

Creek with the North Fork is Chicken Park, which we have already mentioned as a one-time source of diamonds.

Five miles downstream, Trail Creek enters from the north. Both Sheep and Trail creeks arise on Boulder Ridge, which has an elevation of about 9,000 feet and separates the Laramie and Poudre River watersheds. The road crosses the North Fork near the point where Trail Creek enters. Trail's End Ranch, at the intersection, was operated as a dude ranch and small zoo in the 1920s by Frank and Peggy Miller.

Below Trail's End the river winds through forests past a prominent pinnacle of granite called Turkey Roost. It is easy to imagine early hunters finding the place a good one to hunt turkeys. In her story of her childhood on Lone Pine Creek around the turn of the century, Carrie Williams Darnell tells of Thanksgiving Day turkey shoots, followed by a "wonderfully good" dinner and a night of dancing. Wild turkeys were pretty well hunted to extinction in Colorado, and those now found in small numbers in the Poudre drainage are the result of reintroductions. Persons who wish to hunt turkeys nowadays must apply for a permit and follow regulations issued by the Colorado Division of Wildlife. Gone are the freedoms of the frontier — and with reason, for otherwise turkeys would once again disappear from our fauna.

We have often hiked to the North Fork below Turkey Roost. We especially remember a sunny day in late May when we made camp inside a U-shaped bow in the river, still high and turbid from spring runoff and noisy enough that from our tent we could barely hear the birds or the wind in the trees. There were dippers diving for insects in the stream and the usual jays studying our campsite for a handout. Four brown trout made an ample evening meal. No turkeys; but a mallard duck obligingly left a single egg on the riverbank, so we scrambled it for breakfast, splitting a fried egg being a more difficult operation.

A hillside near our camp was covered with pasque flowers, and there were also wallflowers, larkspur, heart-leaved arnica, and the generous blue blossoms of rock clematis. In places sand lilies matted the ground so thickly that we had to walk carefully to avoid stepping on them. These white, six-petalled blossoms have no stems, but have tubular bases that extend well into the ground. The seeds are formed underground, and how they are dispersed is anybody's guess. The scientific name is *Leucocrinum montanum*, "white lily of the moun-

Sand lilies are stemless true lilies that spring from the ground in May and early June.

tains." True enough, though we ourselves might have chosen a more hyperbolic name.

As we hiked back through Douglas-firs and across the meadows to our car, we disturbed a small herd of pronghorns, which ran away flashing their white rumps, then stopped and looked back at us, trespassers in their domain. Although often called antelopes, these handsome animals are not related to the true antelopes of Africa and in fact have no close relatives anywhere in the world. They are one of the West's most treasurable animals, and to see a herd racing across the plains — sometimes as much as forty miles an hour — provides a thrill even to hardened westerners. Once the herds grazed alongside those of bison, and nowadays they often share the grasslands with cattle. The two are not serious competitors, since pronghorns prefer to nip off succulent plants while cattle gorge themselves primarily on grasses. According to wildlife biologists, the diet of cattle and pronghorns overlaps by only 8 percent. Unfortunately pronghorns do not usually leap over fences the easy way that deer do. They prefer to go under them, and unless the rancher has left a large enough space below the lowest wire or used unbarbed wire for the lowest strand, they may be

Male pronghorn antelope.

unable to cross. In severe winters, pronghorns sometimes die by the hundreds if their way to better grazing is blocked by fences they cannot cross.

The bifurcate "pronghorns" of the males are true horns, and not antlers, but unlike the horns of bison and cattle they are deciduous, being shed annually from a permanent bony knob. The females have small, unbranched horns. During mating season, in late summer, the bucks fight to maintain harems of up to fifteen does. The young are born in May or June, young does usually having a single fawn, older females twins. Colorado has an estimated 56,000 pronghorns, Wyoming many more. Controlled hunting results in some thinning of the herds, but these are resilient animals and continue to be abundant. When we drive across the plains of Colorado or Wyoming, we often try to relieve the monotony by counting pronghorns. They are a good deal more entertaining than billboards.

Photographs cannot really do justice to Phantom Canyon, on the Poudre's North Fork.

Turkey Roost is in the last piece of national forest on the North Fork. Shortly the river enters Halligan Reservoir, named for an Irishman, Daniel Halligan, who had a ranch at the site around 1860. At the upper end of the reservoir, Dale Creek enters from the north. This stream has its origin deep within Wyoming and its drainage includes nearly 100 miles of streams. The creek and the village of Virginia Dale on its banks were named by the notorious Jack Slade for his wife. Virginia Dale has a post office and school serving surrounding ranches. The old stage station still stands, but there is little else to suggest its former importance as a stop on the Overland Stage Route.

Below the dam on Halligan Reservoir, the North Fork enters a deep gorge known as Phantom Canyon. Names are usually filled with history or legend, but that is not true of Phantom Canyon. A few years ago, when local ranchers tried to persuade the state to buy the area for a park, they needed a name quickly and came up with an overworked name that by no means reflects the uniqueness of the area (there is a Phantom Valley Ranch in the upper Colorado River valley, not all that many miles away, a Phantom Canyon thirty miles south of Cripple Creek, Colorado, and of course a Phantom Ranch deep in Grand Canyon National Park). The state legislature was not interested in

Aletes humilis, one of the Rockies' rarest plants, blooms on a cliff overlooking Phantom Canyon.

acquiring the canyon as a park, but fortunately, in 1987, The Nature Conservancy purchased 656 acres, with a conservation easement on another 500 acres. With volunteer help, The Nature Conservancy has fenced the canyon area and built an interpretive center and a trail to the bottom. The fence is a three-strand, solar powered electric fence, without barbs and designed so that deer can jump over it and pronghorns easily pass under it.

The gorge provides nesting sites for red-tailed hawks, golden eagles, white-throated swifts, cliff swallows, and rock doves. Bobcats, bighorns, black bears, and mountain lions have been seen there. On cliff tops there are populations of a small plant of the parsnip family with the scientific name *Aletes humilis*, an appropriate name meaning "wanderer low over the ground." The total range of this rare plant encompasses only a score of square miles in these foothills.

On a warm and windy April day, we hiked the east-facing rim of the canyon, finding many clumps of *Aletes* in bloom, each forming a bright patch of yellow among the rocks. On the way we saw many pasque flowers, spring beauties, and salt-and-peppers in bloom, the last another member of the parsnip family but having little in common with *Aletes*. There was also a *Besseya* (kittentail) we had never seen before.

Some 500 feet below the cliffs, the river wound through meadows just turned green.

On another occasion, in August, we hiked to the bottom of the canyon. Here there were giant ponderosa pines and Douglas-firs, and in open places junipers, hackberries, mountain-mahogany, and skunkbush, with alders and chokecherries close to the stream. Two weedy, alien plants were much in evidence: Canada thistle and great mullein. Of the two, mullein is the more admirable, and as we often do we scanned the plants to find the tallest one — it measured more than nine feet. Mullein has a long history in folk medicine, flowers, leaves, and roots all having diverse uses — including, according to Michael Moore, the prevention of bed-wetting. And speaking of the leaves, Moore comments, "Although not comparable in luxuriance to two-ply scented bathroom tissue, it is sort of floral designed and may be used similarly . . . and there is no chance of confusing it with poison oak."

Of course we learned a new plant on this trip, as we often do. It was wirelettuce, a plant with slender, sedge-like leaves and small pink flowers, an individualistic member of the sunflower family. The books describe it as a weedy plant, but it is a native, attractive in a modest way, and deserves a better press.

A few miles downstream from Phantom Canyon, the North Fork is joined by Stonewall Creek from the east and by Rabbit and Lone Pine creeks from the west. Stonewall Creek is named for the vertical cliffs that border it for a distance (close beside U.S. Highway 287); to the north of the "stonewall" section, it drains a broad valley just west of Steamboat Rock and Red Mountain, picturesque landmarks visible for miles around.

Lone Pine Creek drains a large area; with its two major branches and several tributaries, it has a total stream length of nearly eighty miles. The two branches both have their origin on the east slopes of North and Middle Bald mountains, not far from the origin of the Elkhorn on South Bald. On the long trip eastward to join the North Fork, the south branch of Lone Pine Creek passes the community of Red Feather Lakes. Early settlers in what was then called Westlake built a series of dams and ditches and diverted and captured water from the Lone Pine drainage, resulting in a series of small lakes. In the 1920s enterprising developers gave the lakes Indian (or pseudo-Indian) names such as Pocahontas, Nokomis, and Papoose, and renamed the settlement Red Feather Lakes. "Princess" Tsianina Redfeather was a young Indian lady, part Cherokee and part Creek, who was trained in voice and traveled and concertized with composer Charles Wakefield Cadman. Since Cadman and Redfeather had in fact visited the area, promoters seized the opportunity to rename the village with a striking and unusual name. In her book *Red Feather Lakes: The First Hundred Years*, Evadene Swanson tells the story in greater detail and provides several photographs of Redfeather. The lakes are now partly private and partly in national forest, and they are popular with anglers and with those who simply wish to escape the heat and turmoil of the cities on the plains.

Lone Pine Creek received its name from a prominent solitary pine that formerly stood near its point of entry into the North Fork. The pine served as a landmark to persons heading into the mountains. The broad valley surrounding the confluence of Lone Pine Creek with the North Fork is the site of the village of Livermore. There is a hogback of colorful, tilted rocks to the east, parts of it plastered with mud nests of cliff swallows. As we mentioned in our first chapter, some of the reddish sandstones in this area extend several miles to the west as horizontal layers, rather than being tilted like most of the sedimentary rocks. There are rolling, grassy meadows ideal for grazing, and not surprisingly Livermore was founded as a ranching community, which it remains.

Two early settlers, Adolphus Livernash and Stephen Moore, built a one-room cabin here in 1863 and prospected for minerals. Neither stayed long, but a combination of their names provided a name for the area. Over the next decade, hunters and tie-cutters traversed the Livermore valley, and the attractions of the area for ranching became apparent. One of the prominent early families was that of Robert O. Roberts, who in addition to ranching became the first postmaster and also built the Forks Hotel at the intersection of the Overland Stage Route with the road to the mountains. When the hotel was finished in March 1875, there was a grand ball attended by everyone from miles around. "What a time we had!" wrote Robert's son George. "The boys danced in their high heeled boots. Some had brand new overalls. The ladies wore calico and gingham. . . . We danced until the golden sun warned us that another day was born."

When the Forks Hotel was sold in 1887, an advertisement in the *Fort Collins Courier* described it as "large and commodious with 17 rooms and a large dance hall . . . situated at the junction of the three well traveled roads to Cheyenne, Laramie City and the mining camp of Manhattan." The hotel underwent several modifications and numerous ownerships until it was consumed by fire just before Christmas in 1985. It has since been rebuilt as a restaurant and store. Livermore remains as a quiet country town where the cattle far outnumber the people. Near the site of the Forks Hotel, a stone marker pays tribute to Robert O. and Mary E. Roberts, "pioneers of this valley, 1874."

Since the major route into the mountains in the early days was through Livermore, the hotel served as an important stopover on a long trip. For a time there were two hotels in Livermore, as well as one in Log Cabin and one at Elkhorn, some miles to the west. When it was planned to build a road through Poudre Canyon, residents of the area signed a petition of protest, since the road would (and did) divert much of the traffic to the canyon. Ultimately it was the automobile that spelled the doom of most of the local hotels, since it was now possible to drive deep into the mountains and return on the same day.

Many tales have passed down from early times in the Livermore valley, tales of Indians, animals, floods, blizzards, feuds, cattle rustling, and so forth. One of the best concerns a swarm of grasshoppers that descended on the ranches in 1873. Turkeys have a voracious appetite for grasshoppers, and it was hoped they would help clean up the infestation. But the grasshoppers were so thick they covered the turkeys and ate their combs. Like many yarns, this may be a bit exaggerated, but like bear stories, grasshopper stories are part of the heritage of the West.

Below Livermore the river winds through a canyon of varied rock formations and fine meadows and forests, once the home of several pioneer families but now well known only to the cattle that roam its reaches. Finally it emerges in Seaman Reservoir, owned by the city of Greeley, the third of the major reservoirs on the North Fork. From here it is only a few hundred yards to the junction with the main stem of the Poudre, near the site of Fort Collins's now abandoned water treatment plant. The waters of the North Fork are more alkaline and sediment laden than those that flow from Poudre Canyon, so some of the river's crystalline quality is lost at the junction. Fort Collins still pipes its water from above the junction, but to a new treatment plant closer to the city.

When the Cache la Poudre was declared Wild and Scenic in 1986, only major parts of the main stem and the South Fork were so designated. The North Fork was omitted, probably in part because there are major grazing allotments on the river and more than half of the river's course is in private ownership. Recently, at the urging of the Colorado Environmental Coalition and American Rivers, Inc., the U.S. Forest Service has been weighing the feasibility of requesting a Wild and Scenic designation for the upper part of the North Fork, from its source to Dale Creek junction just above Halligan Reservoir. Of these twenty-nine miles, some 46 percent is in private ownership, the remainder controlled by the U.S. Forest Service or the Colorado Division of Wildlife. The area is a popular one with hikers, hunters, and anglers, and some sections of the river are certainly scenic, but whether these values are to be granted formal federal designation remains to be seen.

The South Fork

It can be argued that the South Fork, or "Little South," begins anywhere in a number of places on the north slopes of the Mummy Range. Cartographers favor a source on Rowe Peak, close to 13,000 feet and not far from Hague's Peak, highest in the range. The peak was named for Israel Rowe, who came to the Estes Park area in 1875. He was a great bear hunter and discovered that hordes of Rocky Mountain locusts had died on the snow trying to cross the mountains, attracting bears to an unaccustomed feast. Rowe described his discovery to William Hallett, an inveterate mountain climber. Hallett explored on his own and fell into a crevasse thirty feet deep, from which "he extracted himself by the grace of God and extreme caution" (in the words of Louise Arps and Elinor Kingery in their book *High Country Names*). Hallett had his own peak named for him, not quite as high as Rowe Peak but one of the most picturesque peaks in the Front Range.

Rowe Glacier, on the side of the peak opposite the source of the South Fork, forms the headwaters of the North Fork of the Big Thompson River. The South Fork of the Poudre begins on the south side of the peak, then drains permanent snowfields at Icefield Pass before dropping down to join a stream beginning in ponds and soggy fields near Mummy Pass. All of this is well above timberline and has many of the features we discussed in chapter 2. Altogether about 10 percent of the South Fork drainage is in alpine tundra.

A mile or two below Mummy Pass and three miles from Rowe Peak, the stream descends through a steep-walled, heavily forested canyon.

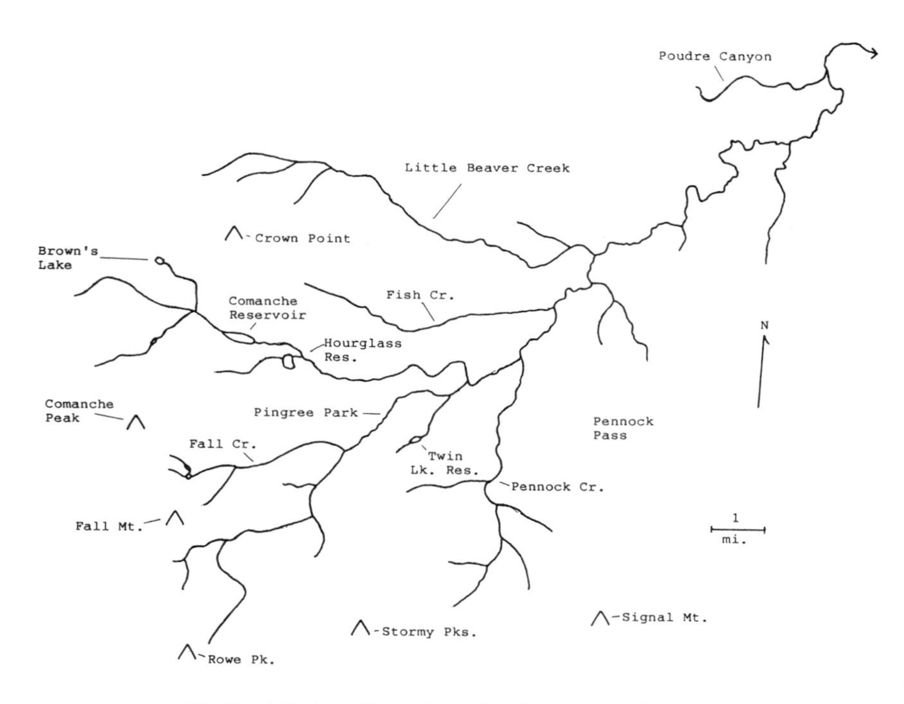

The South Fork, or "Little South," with its major tributaries.

In about four miles, this canyon drops from 11,000 to about 9,000 feet, so there must be many cascades and many stretches of difficult passage for hikers. There is no trail through the canyon, and we have never explored it. It is clearly visible from our house, which is thirty miles or so to the north. When surfeited with the news of human foibles that the radio delivers to our aerie, we often look to the Mummies and particularly to the deep canyon of the upper South Fork, a bit of inviolate wilderness protected by being partly in Rocky Mountain National Park and partly in the Comanche Peak Wilderness of Roosevelt National Forest. That we have never seen it close at hand does not bother us. There should always be something beyond experience. In Wallace Stegner's words, "The reminder and the reassurance that [the wilderness] is still there is good for our spiritual health even if we never once in ten years set foot on it."

We have explored Fall Creek, which plunges in from the west just as the South Fork passes from its canyon into Pingree Park, a meadowed valley nearly two miles long and a quarter of a mile wide. Fall Creek

The young South Fork pours through forests of spruce and fir. *Courtesy of the U.S. Forest Service.*

has its origins on the slopes of Fall Mountain, Comanche Peak, and the intervening ridges. A good trail leads to Cirque Lake and Emmaline Lake, two jewels cupped beneath cliffs splashed with patches of snow even in late summer. Cirque Lake is hardly a distinctive name; the high Rockies are full of small lakes formed in cirques or basins hollowed out by past glaciation. Emmaline Lake was named by Frank Koenig, an early resident of Pingree Park, in honor of his mother. He also named Hazeline Lake in the drainage of Hague's Creek for his wife, Hazel, adding a suffix so that it rhymes with Emmaline — he must have been a bit of a poet. Hazel was the daughter of Hugh Ramsey, another early settler in the area. Frank Koenig named Ramsey Peak for his friend and father-in-law. Ramsey Peak towers above the canyon of the upper South Fork. (Arps and Kingery's *High Country Names* is, as usual, a rich source of information on these matters.)

A good base camp for exploring this wonderful country is a campground named for Tom Bennett, who in the 1920s had a ranch and resort in the area. Already the stream is noisy and turbulent. Among the plants along its banks are twisted-stalks up to three feet tall, members of the lily family bearing individual small flowers and later red berries from stems arising in leaf axils. Other, more bushy plants bear yellow flowers, and later purplish berries, in close pairs cupped in leaf-like bracts. This is twinberry, also called bush honeysuckle. The berries of neither twisted-stalk nor twinberry are particularly tasty, but bears eat them, and Indians collected them to add the their pemmican.

Among the commonest and tamest birds at the campground are juncos. These belong to the grey-headed race, with pale heads and reddish patches on their backs. This is the usual color form seen in the summer, but winter feeders attract others: Oregon juncos, with black heads and a reddish streak on the sides; white-winged juncos, without reddish but with white bands on the wings; and sometimes eastern slate-colored juncos. Some are intermediate in color, suggesting that members of the four races sometimes interbreed, although for the most part they breed in different parts of the country. At one time they were considered four separate species, and they are so listed in our copy of Roger Tory Peterson's *A Field Guide to Western Birds* (second edition). Now they are lumped as a single species, called the dark-eyed junco to distinguish it from the yellow-eyed junco of Southern Arizona and Mexico. People who keep lifetime lists of birds they have seen suddenly found their lists reduced by three! The cheerful trills of juncos are among the most welcome sounds of summer in the high country, and watching the diverse plumage of juncos on feeders makes the winter seem shorter.

The Rockies have few broad-leaved evergreen shrubs, but one of these grows in abundance along the Fall Creek Trail. This is sticky laurel, also called snowbrush, mountain balsam, deerbrush, tobacco-bush, and soapbloom. The many names suggest the major features of the plant as well as the uses to which it has been put. The dark green, somewhat sticky leaves are aromatic and balsam scented and have occasionally been used as a substitute for tobacco. The flowers form balls of white blossoms suggesting snowballs, and they contain saponin, which is a pretty fair substitute for soap. Deer and elk often consume the leaves in winter, when there is little green foliage available other than the harsh needles of conifers.

The trail follows Fall Creek through stands of spruce and fir, with mushrooms adding spots of color to the forest floor. Where springs ooze from the hillsides, there are bog orchids, their small, waxy white flowers clinging to a stalk one to two feet tall. What could possibly pollinate these flowers in dark forests, largely devoid of bees and butterflies? Of course there are plenty of mosquitoes, as campers soon discover, and it is mosquitoes oddly enough, that pollinate these orchids as they add nectar to their usual blood diet. Brian Hocking, late professor of entomology at the University of Alberta, spent much of his life studying mosquitoes, and other unpopular insects. In his book *Six-legged Science*, he has this to say about the matter:

> In some orchids the pollen is carried as a pair of special structures known as pollinia, which have long stalks with sticky pads at the base. From a mosquito's viewpoint these are one of the unkindest inventions of the botanical world. When a mosquito visits the flower seeking nothing more than a sip of nectar, one or perhaps both of the sticky pads becomes permanently stuck on its face close to the eyes, like an extra pair of monstrous antennae. No matter how one dislikes mosquitoes, one cannot but feel sorry for the unfortunate victim as one watches its frantic attempts to remove the unwelcome addition to its head on withdrawing from an orchid.

When the mosquito visits another flower, some of the pollen is brushed off onto the stigma, and this may be repeated until the mosquito dies. One mosquito was found with seven pollinia stuck to its head. Brian Hocking comments that a man who takes flowers to a wife or girl friend is assuming that she has tastes similar to the insects that visit them, since flowers, after all, evolved to attract pollinators. He adds that "a man who takes along a bunch of our little woodland orchids is paying his lady love the doubtful compliment of likening her tastes to those of a mosquito."

The Fall Creek Trail in time opens out into Cirque Meadows, where the creek wanders through low willows and bog birches, permitting a glorious view of the peaks beyond. The trail then returns to the forest, but this gives way to krummholz and tundra before reaching Cirque and Emmaline lakes at about 11,000 feet elevation.

Still another trail starting near the Tom Bennett campground more or less follows Beaver Creek past Sky Ranch (now a Lutheran summer camp), Hourglass Reservoir, and Comanche Reservoir. There are further trails to Comanche and Brown's lakes, both about 10,000 feet and so below timberline. These are the only natural lakes in the drainage other than small ones above timberline and beaver ponds along the streams. There is one additional reservoir, Twin Lakes, just east of Pingree Park. Hourglass and Twin Lakes reservoirs were built around the turn of the century, Comanche, by far the largest, in the 1920s.

Cirque Meadows provide a scenic rest stop for hikers to the sources of Fall Creek, high in the Mummy Range.

Pingree Park was named for the same George Pingree we met in chapter 4 in connection with the road he built down the steep slopes north of Rustic. Pingree first came into the area when still a soldier and stationed at Camp Collins. According to Ansel Watrous, he was under the command of Colonel John Chivington during the infamous Sand Creek Massacre of 1864. During the massacre he received an arrow in his cheek, dislodging several of his teeth. Later in life he covered the scar with a heavy beard. According to one account, he took several Indian scalps during the battle and later exchanged these with a Denver barber for free haircuts. After a year cutting ties on the upper Poudre, he moved to what is now called Pingree Park and did some hunting, trapping, and prospecting while supervising the tie camp there. Later in life he roamed widely in Colorado and Wyoming, ranching, hunting, and serving as a guide. In old age he lived in Platteville, chopping his own wood and telling stories to anyone who would listen until he died in 1921, over ninety years of age.

In the late 1860s, homesteaders began to take up 160-acre allotments in the Pingree Park area. These included Hugh Ramsey and Frank Koenig, whom we have already mentioned. When Rocky Mountain National Park was formed, Frank Koenig became one of its first rangers, at a salary of $900 a year. He liked the backcountry better than homesteading and left the ranch to the care of his wife, Hazel. To augment their meager income, Hazel collected and sold butterflies and herbs to interested parties. She cherished her "butterfly checks" but regretted being unable to collect any of the rarer and more valuable species. Among the herbs, she tried in vain to find ginseng, then in much demand, but was able to supply Oregon grape root, widely used in those days for fevers and constipation.

Frank Koenig interested his cousin Charles Lory, president of Colorado Agricultural College, in the area, and in 1914 Lory acquired over one thousand acres at the northeast end of the park as a summer campus, primarily for the Forestry Department. The campus still serves as a place for summer classes and occasional conferences. Some of the old buildings of the Koenig ranch still stand adjacent to the campus.

Other parts of Pingree Park contain summer cottages, and at the southwest end there are many beaver ponds. Since both Beaver Creek and Little Beaver Creek are in the South Fork drainage, it seems a safe assumption that early trappers made a good harvest in this area. For a mere rodent, the beaver's influence on both the history and the natural history of the West has been remarkable. From the seventeenth through the middle of the nineteenth century, upper-class Europeans were addicted to the wearing of beaver hats. As early as 1600, hardy Frenchmen penetrated deep into the continent, often in log canoes, collecting pelts and often taking Indian wives. Later the Hudson's Bay Company, the American Fur Company, and the Rocky Mountain Fur Company were all dedicated to harvesting beaver, and most of the legendary mountain men of the West were associated with this endeavor. Experienced French voyageurs often accompanied trapping and fur-trading expeditions — hence names such as Platte, Laporte, and Cache la Poudre. Early trappers in the Poudre basin left no written records; perhaps Joe Wright, for whom the creek was named, was one of them.

Beaver underfur is nearly an inch thick, soft and velvety, with a reddish tint. The longer guard hairs are coarser and are removed in the manufacture of hats and fur coats. Aside from the pelts, trappers also often kept the large musk glands and used the contents in various animal lures. The contents of these glands (called castoreum, after the scientific and original Greek name of the beaver, *Castor*) were also much in demand in perfumery, and a number of medicines were compounded from it. In nature, during the breeding season, beavers of both sexes use the musk glands for marking objects and so informing other beavers of their presence.

The powerful incisor teeth of beavers are quite capable of gnawing down a fair-sized tree in a few hours. Since these incisors grow continually, beavers must in fact use them regularly, or they become too long to be useful. Because of their tree-cutting and dam-building activities, beavers have profound effects on the terrain in which they occur. Enos Mills felt a special attachment to beavers, calling them "little conservationists." "His dams and ponds," Mills wrote, "have saved vast areas of soil, have checked many a flood, and helped to equalize stream-flow."

Each beaver colony is usually an extended family: parents with offspring of the past two years. Their food consists primarily of the bark and young shoots of aspen, willow, and other deciduous trees and shrubs. In winter they feed on branches they have stored under the ice, taking them into their mud-and-stick homes. The major function of the dams is to raise the water level so they can retrieve their food from the water through the winter. In their living chambers, which are above the water level, several young are born in early summer. Beavers are quiet animals, but when alarmed can produce a loud report by slapping their broad tails on the surface of the water. It is a good sound, reminding us that these remarkable animals, after centuries of persecution, are still making a go of it.

Beaver Creek flows into the South Fork from the west about two miles below Pingree Park, and about a mile further Pennock Creek comes in from the south. Pennock Creek drains a broad area between Stormy Peaks and Signal Mountain, both reached by U.S. Forest Service trails. Horse-thief Cabin, near Signal Mountain, was once the hangout of rustlers who stole unbranded calves from some of the local ranchers and sold them to others. John Derbey, whose Lazy-D Ranch was at the junction of Pennock Creek with the South Fork, had an unusually prolific herd of cattle. He claimed his cows usually had twins, but it was suspected that he was one of the rustler's best clients.

After it leaves Pingree Park, the road winds along the 8,800-foot contour for a while, then dips into the Pennock Creek valley. Here it is soon joined by another gravel road from Pennock Pass to the east. This road, from the Buckhorn valley, was the first route of entry to the upper South Fork, the present Pingree Park road not having been completed until 1923. Both the pass and the creek were named for

Charles Pennock, whom we met in the previous chapter as an early resident of Pleasant Valley.

Below the junction of Pennock Creek with the South Fork, the road follows the twists and turns of the river for about three miles, through national forest, old ranches, and summer cabins. The valley is filled with Colorado blue spruce, handsome, symmetrical trees often having a bluish cast to the needles. It is not always easy to tell blue spruce from Engelmanns, which also sometimes have bluish tints in the foliage. Blue spruce needles are stiffer and more prickly than those of Engelmanns, and the cones are larger. Generally, blue spruce grow along streams at moderate elevations, while Engelmanns grow in subalpine forests. But the two sometimes hybridize, so perhaps it is excusable to simply call both species "spruce." Horticultural varieties of blue spruce are commonly planted as ornamentals in the cities.

Not far below the Pennock Creek junction, two tributaries come in from the west — Fish Creek and Little Beaver Creek. Evidences of the old Flowers Road can be seen in this area. Built by Jacob Flowers of Bellvue in the 1870s, this road was designed to reach Lulu City across the Continental Divide. The road is listed by the Colorado State Historical Preservation Office. When the Poudre was declared Wild and Scenic in 1986, all of the South Fork was included except for a section near the Little Beaver junction, as both Fort Collins and Greeley have for many years had designs on this section for a dam, to be called Rockwell Dam and Reservoir, since the old Rockwell Ranch at the site will be flooded.

Shortly the Pingree Park road climbs out of the South Fork valley and winds its way through the hills to State Highway 14 on the Poudre. On the way it gives rise to a dead-end road passing west beyond Crown Point, an outlier of the Mummy Range reaching 11,463 feet. The road leads to trails to Brown's Lake and the Comanche Peak Wilderness, as well as to the upper reaches of Sheep Creek, Black Hollow, Dadd Gulch, and other streams draining north to the main stem of the Poudre. The Crown Point road follows Bennett Creek for much of its length. This is not truly part of the South Fork drainage, since Bennett Creek enters the Poudre separately at Kelly Flats, about two miles upstream of the South Fork.

After the Pingree Park road leaves the South Fork, the river plunges in a northeasterly direction through a wild and winding canyon for several miles before reaching the main stem of the Poudre. This

The South Fork races through two wilderness areas before joining the main stem of the Cache la Poudre. *Photo by J. Higgins, U.S. Forest Service.*

section of the South Fork is in the Cache la Poudre Wilderness. There are no well-defined trails, and we have explored it only by following the river up for a mile or two from its junction with the Poudre. This is a difficult hike when the water is high because of the steep, enclosing banks, but in the fall, when the water is low, it is easy to wade the Poudre and follow the South Fork for a ways. The fall and early winter are particularly fine times to venture up the stream, though best not in hunting season. It is then that the Townsend's solitaires seem to sing from every copse — the only birds in good voice at this season.

Solitaire is a word for hermit, a being that is self-sufficient and in little need of companionship. Solitaires, indeed, are rarely seen in flocks, and they disdain feeders, surviving the winter perfectly well on juniper berries. In the fall they establish territories where there are plenty of berries, defend them from other birds, and advertise them with song. T. Luke George, while a graduate student at the University of New Mexico, showed that fall and winter territories average about 3.5 acres in extent, but are smaller where juniper berries are plentiful, larger where they are sparse. Males and females are individually territorial and equally proficient songsters. It is not only a delight to hear them singing in the fall or winter, but a surprise to learn that females sing as well as males.

Male and female solitaires are identically colored: gray, with a white eye ring, a dash of buff in the wings and of white on the tail. In the spring they disperse from their winter quarters, and the males establish breeding territories that they announce with a particularly prolonged melody. The young, after they leave the nest, are striking birds, completely covered with white polka dots, as if ready for a masquerade ball. When we first saw one, we rushed to our bird guide, thinking we had spotted a stray from another continent.

John Kirk Townsend discovered the solitaire in 1836 while trekking through Wyoming. In his *Narrative of a Journey Across the Rocky Mountains to the Columbia River,* he remarked that he had found "a beautiful new species of mocking bird." Indeed, solitaires do resemble mockingbirds in many ways, though they are thrushes. Townsend was a Philadelphia Quaker, trained in medicine but from youth fascinated by birds. When he was in his twenties, he joined an expedition to the Pacific, where his companion was botanist Thomas Nuttall. Nuttall named the common easter daisy of the Rockies *Townsendia grandiflora* as a tribute to a man with whom he had shared a great many adventures.

Townsend's solitaire occurs widely in the Poudre basin but seems especially suited to wild canyons such as this. Overall, the South Fork drainage has been less modified from its original form than that of the North Fork or the main stem of the Poudre. Less than 10 percent of the area is in private ownership as compared to 15 percent in Rocky Mountain National Park and 75 percent in Roosevelt National Forest. Cattle do graze in some areas in the summer, and there are a few ranches and summer homes as well as the Pingree Park campus. Even so, the watershed has been touched lightly by the hand of humanity: 100 square miles without a paved road, post office, store, or gas station, where solitaires sing appropriately to the pine-scented forests and the snow-spangled peaks.

8

SOME FAVORITE TRIBUTARIES

Dozens of small streams contribute their flows to the Poudre and its two major forks. All of these are worth exploring, though some are on private land or have their accesses blocked by private land. Even in fall and winter, there is life in the streams and there are birds in the trees, tracks and scats of mammals, patterns of lichen-colored rocks and of ice and snow. In spring and summer, even the smallest rivulet has much to offer.

Here we will record our impressions of four streams that are particular favorites of ours, selecting ones at various altitudes and diverse parts of the Poudre system. There are others that might have done just as well. Small streams have a particular intimacy; they bare their hearts in ways larger streams cannot. To follow such a stream as it twists its way through forests and meadows is to grow wiser in the ways of nature.

TRAP CREEK

Trap Creek has its beginnings well above timberline on the eastern slopes of the northern part of the Never Summer Range between Cameron and La Poudre passes. Descending rapidly to about 10,500 feet, it enters a meadowed valley nearly two miles long but only about a quarter of a mile wide: Trap Park. Many years ago several bear traps were dug along the valley, supplying a name for a stream that perhaps deserves better. There is no longer any evidence of the traps, but the remains of sawmills suggest that railroad ties were once harvested here, as they were in many parts of the upper Poudre watershed.

The stream is clear and icy as it winds tortuously through the meadows, in most places tightly enclosed in a tangle of willows. In late June the damp meadows are so thick with white marsh marigolds and

Marsh marigolds carpet the ground in wet places soon after the snows have melted.

yellow buttercups and cinquefoils that it is impossible to pass without treading on a few. Over the next few weeks, death camas, elephant head, and bistort will take the stage, while in drier places stonecrop, penstemon, and pussytoes will fill the spaces between the short grasses and rocks.

Perhaps the most fascinating plants in the meadows and adjacent forest borders are several kinds of lousewort, plants often with feathery leaves and spikes of complex blossoms that suggest a variety of nonfloral objects. One of the more showy kinds has white blossoms in which the upper petal is pointed and curved downward, suggesting the common name, parrot's-beak (elephant head, too, is a lousewort). The blossoms of the several species differ in color and in depth of the blossoms as well as in floral structure. None of them have flowers that suggest a louse, however. Evidently there is an ancient belief that livestock acquire lice by feeding on the plants. Aware of this, Linnaeus, in the 1750s, dubbed the genus *Pedicularis*, based on the Latin word for louse. There is no evidence that lousewort either favors lice or can be used to control them, but tea made from the leaves has been used as a relaxant and analgesic. Too much of it, says Michael Moore in his book on medicinal plants, may produce "befuddled lethargy." Perhaps the ancients who saw their livestock acquiring lice had themselves overindulged.

Lazarus Macior of the University of Akron, who spent many summers studying the ecology of Rocky Mountain plants, found that louseworts are pollinated almost exclusively by bumblebees. When he enclosed the plants in bee-free cages, they set no seed at all. The differing structure of the blossoms in each species of lousewort suggests that each might be specialized for pollination by a different species of bumblebee, but this is not the case. Rather, young bees of several species have to learn to harvest the pollen in these complex blossoms, but once they have learned, they tend to return to the same type of blossom, thus insuring cross-pollination. Blossoms of some kinds of lousewort release pollen only in response to wing vibration, while others have to be entered upside down. The various strategies employed by the bees were recorded on film by Dr. Macior, not a bad way for someone from Ohio to spend his summers enjoyably and productively.

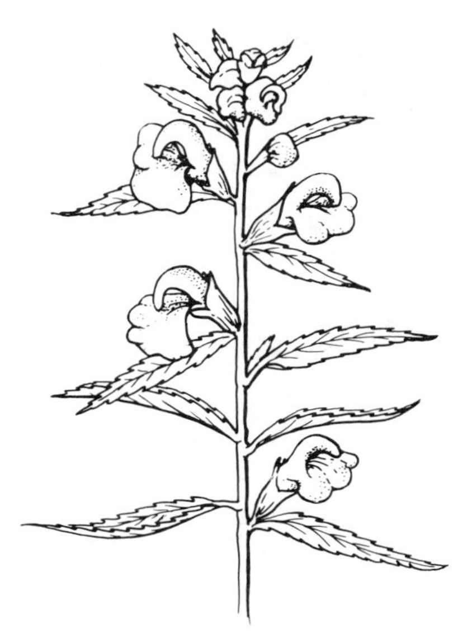

Parrot's-beak lousewort.

Below Trap Park the stream enters the forest, and off to one side, not directly connected to the stream, is a shallow pond, Trap Lake. This is a well-known habitat of Colorado's smallest frog, the striped chorus frog, *Pseudacris triseriata* (*Pseudacris* is Greek for "false grasshopper," with reference to the trilling song; *triseriata*, Latin for "three-rowed," descriptive of the three rows of spots on the back). The call produced by the males in the spring is a sweet but somewhat scratchy series of notes that ascends the scale. These frogs have a wide distribution from Colorado eastward, but here in the Rockies they show some puzzling variation, a matter that Dr. David Pettus and his students at Colorado State University have been studying for several years.

The frogs occur in a number of ponds and pools at this altitude where there is no strong current of water. They are diverse in color;

A chorus frog, one of the most often-heard songsters of wet places in the Rockies. *Photo by Steve Corn, U.S. Fish and Wildlife Service.*

they may be brown, green, or reddish, and on each background may be superimposed spots of either brown or green. Each pond differs in the relative abundance of particular color forms. During 1966, for example, Trap Lake contained 43 percent "browns," 11 percent "reds," and 2 percent "reds with green spots." In contrast Lily Pond, only about two miles away, had only 21 percent "browns," 40 percent "reds," and 19 percent "reds with green spots." Other ponds had still other proportions of these and other color forms, and these proportions remained relatively constant from year to year. How might this be explained? The frogs suffer great mortality from predators both as tadpoles and as adult frogs, so that only about 1 percent of the eggs ever produce a mature frog. It seems possible that the ponds vary in the background they provide for the frogs, whether it is green algae, brown or red soil, detritus, or whatever. Frogs that blend best with their backgrounds are probably less frequently taken by predators and are therefore likely to contribute a higher percentage of the eggs.

To test this hypothesis, Pettus's colleague Walter Tordoff placed frogs in chambers containing a background of either brown or green terrycloth and exposed them to gray jays, which are important predators in nature. The jays were allowed to feed for a certain time, then the remaining frogs counted. He found that when the background was brown, many more green frogs were eaten, and when the background was green, the jays spotted and devoured many more of the brown frogs. So it does seem possible that color variation bears at least some relationship to characteristics of the ponds.

It is also curious that high-altitude chorus frogs are appreciably larger than those occurring below the mountains. Here at Trap Lake, at 9,900 feet elevation, they average about 1.25 inches in length, while at Fort Collins (4,950 feet) they average slightly less than an inch. (At altitudes in between, they are intermediate in size.) The larger frogs at high altitudes lay larger eggs; the frogs are sexually mature in two or three years and may live for five. In contrast Fort Collins frogs lay smaller eggs that give rise to smaller tadpoles that produce sexually mature frogs the following year and may live no more than a year. Probably the larger size of alpine frogs is an adaptation allowing them to lay larger eggs that produce tadpoles that mature rapidly in the short summer. The longer life of the high-altitude frogs may simply reflect the fact that summers are short and they spend proportionally much more time sleeping away the winter than do those at lower altitudes. There may also be more predators down below; garter snakes, bass, and several kinds of birds are known to feed on them.

Larger frogs, because of the greater size of their vocal apparatus, produce calls of lower pitch than those of smaller frogs. Also the number of pulses per call increases slightly with body size. So if a Fort Collins frog met one from Trap Lake, they would find themselves speaking a different language. Biologists find variation of this kind of great interest in understanding how different species evolve, for clearly if ponds throughout the Front Range were more completely isolated, with little migration of frogs between them, barriers to interbreeding would soon become complete and several species might be produced.

Observing Trap Lake on a summer day, there is little to suggest that it played a role in significant research. Caddisflies dance over the surface and mosquitoes hum in the surrounding bushes. It is a tranquil place, scarcely conducive to profound reflections on frogs or any other subject. Below the lake, Long Draw Road parallels Trap Creek for a while before the creek plunges off to the northeast toward its terminus in Chambers Lake. There is no trail here, and the forests are filled with fallen trees and rocky outcrops.

We once followed this part of the creek for a space, stumbling over rocks and logs and brushing away mosquitoes, to be rewarded, in a shaft of sunlight, by the sight of one of the Rockies' most spectacular flowers: Parry's primrose. The Craigheads and Davis speak of these as "blood-red," but Ruth Nelson, in her book *Plants of Rocky Mountain National Park,* describes them as rose-purple; both agree that the plants have a disagreeable odor. Our reaction to the plants was too breathless to respond to their odor or to try to categorize their color.

What might we have found if we had followed the stream for the rest of its course?

KILLPECKER CREEK

The three Balds — North, Middle, and South — rise in the forests between Kinikinik on the Poudre and the National Forest campground on the North Fork. They barely break the treeline, at about 11,000 feet, but they are visible for many miles around and give rise to several streams: the east fork of Roaring Creek to the south, Elkhorn and Lone Pine creeks to the east, and Killpecker to the north. Killpecker is the least of these, running a course of only a little over two miles from the slopes of North Bald to the North Fork of the Poudre. A good trail provides access to fine forests and the secrets they hold.

It is a rare treat, hiking in country that is not overly endowed with rain or snow, to come upon a series of springs. Those near the source of the Killpecker are especially generous, their waters issuing from the hillside in unexpected places and forming translucent pools among moss-covered rocks. Mayflies dance over the springs, as if to celebrate so delightful a break in a forest that is otherwise almost a monoculture of lodgepole pine. Arrow-leaved yellow ragworts and blue delphiniums tower over the springs two to three feet tall, capturing and seeming to magnify the sunlight that filters through the pines. Both seem more appropriate to a tropical rainforest than to these subalpine woodlands.

Ragwort seems an inadequate name for so radiant a plant. Fortunately there are some alternate names: butterweed, groundsel, squawweed. The genus is *Senecio,* based on the Latin word *senex,* meaning an old person and alluding to the somewhat ragged appearance of the blossoms. There are several species of *Senecio* in the Poudre drainage, but none as tall and showy as these.

Delphiniums are well known from the horticultural varieties we grow in gardens. With our usual fascination with names, we discovered that the word is based on the Latin word for a dolphin, *delphinis*, a curious association presumably suggested by an imagined resemblance of the nectaries to a dolphin. Its alternate name, larkspur, is believed to be descriptive of the blossoms, the splayed petals suggesting the forward toes of a lark, the spur the long back toe. None of this is very helpful to ranchers, who heartily dislike larkspurs of any kind, since cattle like to eat the young foliage and often become ill, sometimes dying if they eat too much. Oddly, sheep are immune to the poisons and have sometimes been used to clear larkspur from a pasture before admitting the cattle. Livestock grazing on national forest land are always at risk of overconsuming toxins in the diverse vegetation they encounter in their wanderings.

Following the Killpecker Trail below the springs, one passes through shadowed forests of lodgepole pine with a uniform ground cover of broom huckleberry (also called whortleberry, bilberry, or grouseberry). It is unusual to find berries on these bushes; evidently they often do not set fruit, and when they do the berries are quickly consumed by birds and rodents. The berries are tiny and it would take a great many to make a pie. Indians used to dry the berries and use them in soups or in pemmican. Early settlers used the leaves to make tea, as they did the leaves of a variety of plants.

Through the forest one sees many piles of pinecone fragments, a result of the work of pine squirrels, and it is unusual to walk very far without being challenged by one of these feisty animals. The pine squirrel of the Rockies is actually a subspecies of the red squirrel of the eastern states, although it is predominantly grayish. *Tamiasciurus hudsonicus fremonti* is an imposing scientific name for so small a squirrel, but it is appropriate: *Tamia-sciurus* is Greek for "hoarder-squirrel" (hoarder of evergreen cones, in this case); *hudsonicus* refers to Hudson's Bay, well within the range of this cold-adapted animal; and *fremonti* is of course for John Charles Frémont, for whom so many western animals and plants are named. These were favorites of Enos Mills, who called them Frémont squirrels and succeeded in taming several, even though normally they have little use for anyone who invades their territories. As Mills says, if you approach "he may come down on a low limb nearby and give you as torrential and as abusive a 'cussing' as trespasser ever received from irate owner."

Pine squirrels do not hibernate, though they may sleep in their nests through winter storms. Much of the summer and autumn is spent harvesting and caching food supplies, mostly pine or fir cones but sometimes fungi and berries. They have the curious habit of picking mushrooms and drying them on limbs of trees; when they are dry, they are added to the winter stocks of food. Like many rodents, they also gnaw on bones and antlers, apparently obtaining calcium and phosphorus from this source. Most of their feeding is done at one site, resulting in a pile of cone fragments and other scraps, a "kitchen midden." Cones, mushrooms, bones, and berries are sometimes stored in the middens, sometimes in other hiding places in the ground or in logs.

Having stored a winter's supply, pine squirrels defend their territories vigorously. Usually these are one to two acres in size, enough to assure a good crop of cones. The squirrels are remarkably agile as they leap from tree to tree; leaps of twenty feet are not uncommon, though they prefer to live in dense trees where such leaps are unnecessary. After clipping off several cones, they descend to the ground and collect them, always appearing in a great hurry. In spring territorial borders are relaxed, and males enter territories owned by females. From two to six young are born in June in a nest of grasses and leaves in a hollow tree or amidst dense branches. Although pine squirrels are favorite food of martens and goshawks, their numbers are controlled more by the abundance of cones than by predators. Lodgepole pine forests in the Poudre basin present a relatively dependable source of cones, and almost any hike in the high country is likely to be enlivened by these hardy and energetic animals.

The birds that chipper in the trees along the Killpecker Trail are more often than not mountain chickadees. These are easily distinguished from the black-capped chickadees of the plains by the pale line over the eye. They are among the tamest of birds, and in the winter will often take sunflower seeds from one's hand. In the summer they are ardent insectivores, and when spruce budworms are abundant they take them in great numbers. They will nest in almost any cavity they can find, and if disturbed will sit very tightly on the nest, often hissing and fluttering their wings. The female lays an unusually large clutch of eggs, usually seven to twelve.

Mountain chickadees bear the scientific name *Parus gambeli*, named for a Philadelphia naturalist, William Gambel, who, at twenty-three, joined a party of trappers so that he could explore the West for birds and plants. Eventually he reached California, on the way discovering not only the chickadees but also Gambel's quail, Gambel's oak, and several other plants and birds. On a second trip to California in 1849 when he was 28, Gambel tried to cross the Sierras in midwinter, but stumbled into Rose's Bar on the Feather River, suffering from exhaustion. He died of typhoid fever a few days later. One of his fellow travelers described him as an amiable, excellent fellow. It is good that he left a bit of himself in the name of one of our commonest birds, also in its way amiable and excellent.

The Killpecker Trail is not only a good place to become familiar with small birds such as chickadees but also with one of the mountains' largest birds. Ravens are birds of tall forests and rocky cliffs. They are experts at finding food in the coldest and most barren places, either carrion, small mammals, the eggs and young of other birds, or occasionally berries or other plant food. They are the largest of the passerine or "song" birds, with a wingspan comparable to that of many hawks. Often they ride on updrafts, like hawks, and at times seem to ride motionless in the air. Courting pairs sometimes soar with their wingtips touching and perform various acrobatics. In the words of Arthur Cleveland Bent:

> With the springtime urge of love-making, the otherwise sedate and dignified ravens let themselves go and indulge in most interesting and thrilling flight maneuvers and vocal performances. Chasing each other about in rapid flight, they dive, tumble, twist, turn somersaults, roll over sidewise, or mount high in the air and soar in great circles on their broad, black wings. Their powers of flight shown in these playful antics are no less surprising than the variety of their melodious love notes, soft modulations of their well-known croaks, varied with many clucking and gurgling sounds. Their exuberant spirits seem to be overflowing at this season.

Ravens mate for life and may live for thirty years. Pairs have a home territory which they patrol for food, sharing carcasses or whatever other food they can find. Although ravens sometimes harass large animals and will kill rabbits and other small mammals, they are remarkably cautious when approaching a newly found carcass. They land some distance away, approach slowly and when close to it jump up and down while flapping their wings. After a while they may peck at the carcass, then resume their jumping behavior. In a provocative essay, "Why Do Ravens Fear Their Food?", Bernd Heinrich, of the University of Vermont, has speculated that this behavior may have evolved to insure that ravens do not approach a sleeping or sick animal that might attack them. In his words, "The jumping-jack maneuvers may function in eliciting a reaction from live animals, letting the approaching bird know whether or not it is safe to try to feed." Dr. Heinrich found that hand-reared, inexperienced ravens behaved in the same way, so evidently this is not a learned response.

Ravens do not attain sexual maturity for several years, and juveniles and unmated individuals are nonterritorial and often roost together at night. Territorial pairs feed quietly on a carcass, but when the food is discovered by one of these vagrants he may recruit others by "yelling," a type of call very different from the usual hoarse "croak" of these birds. Only by recruiting a crowd can the vagrants overcome the defenses of the resident pair and share in the feast. Even so, the residents take the best pieces of carrion, asserting their dominance by standing tall and fluffing out their feathers, while the vagrants draw their heads into their necks submissively and make the best of it. Only by force of numbers can the vagrants be assured of a meal — an unusual example of competitors calling upon rivals to help them gain access to a resource.

These, too, are recent discoveries of Bernd Heinrich, who observed the birds from a blind or a nearby treetop, using a great many carcasses and chunks of slaughterhouse offal to attract the birds. In order to follow individual birds, he captured forty-three of them and marked them with tags, and two were fitted with radio transmitters. After many days in the cold winter woods, he developed a genuine affection for these often maligned birds. Because of their black plumage and hankering for corpses, ravens have acquired a reputation as birds of death, as in Poe's haunting poem. To those of us who looked forward to seeing ravens riding the air currents or to hearing them call across a valley, these are very much birds of life, a life that seems to revel in the wild forests and crystalline air of the mountains.

Too soon the Killpecker Trail ends at its junction with the Deadman Hill road, where the stream joins the North Fork. But there will be other days and other trails.

Gordon Creek

Gordon Creek has its beginning in several sloughs and soggy meadows in the broad ridge between the ravines cut by Elkhorn Creek to the south and Lone Pine Creek to the north. Its north branch begins just west of Haystack Butte, an imposing pyramid of rock near the Livermore-Red Feather road, then winds through meadows blue in June with wild iris before joining its south branch about two miles to the east. The south branch, too, begins near a great mass of granite, a globular monolith called Manhead Mountain. Both are tiny streams, easy to step across and during dry seasons running only intermittently. They come together in a swale thick with willows and bordered by a grove of aspens and junipers.

Since the south branch of Gordon Creek courses the valley below our house, we know it especially well. It begins as drainage for a broad, sloping, forest-rimmed pasture, where Winfred Holley, a retired professor of horticulture at Colorado State University, maintains a home and runs a few fortunate cows. Below the ranch the valley is ungrazed and allowed to grow to tall grasses and great splashes of wildflowers. Willows fringe the stream, with now and then a clump of river birch. Back from the stream, there are groves of aspen and dense stands of chokecherries that are visited in late summer by black bears and by local residents eager to begin their yearly round of jelly making and wine making. The north-facing slopes are forested with ponderosa pines and Douglas-firs, while the south-facing slopes are grassy, with an abundance of cacti and yuccas. The meadows along the valley floor are interrupted by patches of snowberry, skunkbush, and squaw currant.

We have roamed these meadows so often that they have become a series of places very special to us. A grove of dying aspens is each year home to a pair of Lewis's woodpeckers, birds of bizarre color and behavior — they often catch insects in the air as if they were flycatchers. A thicket of hawthorns each June is the source of the curious hoots and chuckles of a yellow-breasted chat, another eccentric of the bird world (it is a warbler that doesn't warble). In one soggy place along the stream, we can often flush a snipe, which we suppose one could call a sandpiper gone berserk. Just beyond, in a shady glen, shooting stars spring from the grass each spring. These, too, are eccentrics, primroses that flex their petals upward so that the blossoms seem to be "shooting downward."

In full summer, wetter parts of the meadows are rank with members of the parsnip family, their umbels of white flowers often head high. Cow parsnip is the most robust of these, and the best known, as it occurs throughout the Northern Hemisphere and in the Rockies from the foothills to the subalpine. It is a somewhat malodorous plant but is said to be relished by sheep and elk and to have been used as both food and medicine by the Indians. Often growing close beside cow parsnip is angelica, easily told by its more circular clusters of blossoms. Angelica is named for its supposed healing properties; various kinds grow in diverse parts of the world, and the roots and seeds have been used for a variety of ailments.

Still a third tall member of the parsnip family growing here is water hemlock, recognized by its deeply divided leaves, slender stems, and small flat umbels of white flowers. The roots of this plant contain cicutoxin, a poison so potent that a small lump is enough to kill a cow; yet the leaves and fruits, which sometimes contaminate hay, are relatively nontoxic. It is odd that this plant's roots are so poisonous when its neighbors and relatives have been used as food and medicine — and of course cultivated parsnips and carrots are part of our regular diet.

There is still more to this story. We tend to think of toxins in terms of their effect on people and higher animals, but of course insects are major herbivores against which plants must protect themselves. (Some of the substances that plants have evolved to defend themselves against insect attack we use as insecticides, such as pyrethrum, derived from daisies.)

May Berenbaum of the University of Illinois has studied the problem of why certain members of the parsnip family are toxic to certain insects while other insects actually feed exclusively on them. The foliage of water hemlock, she found, contains xanthotoxins that deter feeding by many insects, for example armyworms; but the caterpillars of black swallowtail butterflies thrive on it. Cow parsnip and angelica contain both xanthotoxin and another substance differing only in molecular configuration, angelicin. This is toxic even to black swallowtails, but parsnip webworms feed only on plants containing angelicin, even using it as a feeding cue. By having evolved means of detoxifying these substances, the webworms have been able to exploit plants that are otherwise free of insects.

There are other examples like this in the plant world, plants that have evolved substances that shield them from insect attack, only to have certain insects evolve ways of breaching the defenses. In some cases the plants may evolve further defenses, so that certain insects must evolve a still more sophisticated ability to overcome them, an evolutionary "arms race." Interestingly, May Berenbaum found that since xanthotoxins are primarily effective in sunlight, species of the parsnip family that grow in forests lack these poisons. They are fed upon by diverse insects, but no specialists have evolved to exploit them.

Other tall plants growing in these meadows have developed quite a different method of defense — prickly spines. Canada and musk thistles are immigrants from abroad, now occupying spaces once filled by native plants. They are admirably protected from being eaten by deer and by livestock, and ranchers justifiably detest them. But they do have their good points. The blossoms are attractive and provide nectar for butterflies, bumblebees, and hummingbirds; in late summer, goldfinches and pine siskins gorge themselves on the seeds. Spines do not protect thistles from insect herbivores; the larvae of painted lady and pale crescent butterflies feed exclusively on thistles, and small black weevils ar often abundant on them. However, none of these insects are usually abundant enough to have much effect on thistle populations.

These meadows are alive in summer with bumblebees taking nectar and pollen from wildflowers and incidentally pollinating them and so insuring a crop of seeds that will guarantee more flowers next season. We have found eight kinds here, four of them black and yellow, four black, yellow, and orange. The bees have their nests in the ground, usually in abandoned rodent nests. These are founded each spring by females that had mated the previous fall and overwintered in the ground or in an old log. These large females, or queens, are often seen in the spring, but later in the season one sees mostly the smaller, sterile workers produced in the nests. Toward midsummer a crop of large females is produced, the potential queens of the following season. Males are produced at this same time. We have been using this meadow for research on the mating behavior of bumblebees over the past few years. It has been a great deal of fun and has added a good deal to knowledge about the lives of these exciting (if not exactly cuddly) little animals. To be sure, we have been stung a few times (by the females, since the males have no sting). But what are a few stings suffered in a good cause?

The males are wonderfully alert and energetic creatures. Beginning in mid-July, one finds males of certain of the species perched on the top of small bushes, sagebrush, or other plants, each with is body tilted

A male bumblebee perches on a sagebrush, defending his territory from other males and on the alert for passing females.

upward slightly and his antennae extended rigidly forward. These males (unlike most other bumblebees) have enlarged eyes, and as they rotate on the perch they scan the air for anything that passes. When males occupy adjacent territories, they continually respond to one another and spend much time in aerial combat. When a large insect passes (or even sometimes a bird), the males fly up and pursue it. When a male first arrives in the morning (and he uses the same territory day after day), he flies to stems in and around his perch and rubs his body along them. He is in fact applying a volatile chemical to the stems from specialized glands in his head. We assume that virgin queens are attracted to this chemical, as we have several times seen females flying over territories, whereupon the males took off as if shot from a cannon, seizing the females and dropping to the ground to mate. There is still much we do not understand, so we have an excuse to spend more summers in this flower-filled and bee-filled meadow, fully appreciating Thoreau's classic remark, "I had no idea that there was so much going on in Haywood's meadow" (Weixelman's meadow in our case, but no matter).

These meadows are filled with history as well. Just before the two branches of Gordon Creek come together, beside the highway stands

The Batterson barn, built around 1900, is one of the prominent landmarks of the upper Gordon Creek drainage.

the Batterson barn, a well-preserved relic of the days when people squeezed a living from these reluctant hills. Solomon Batterson arrived in the area in 1870, and he and his son Will kept dairy cattle and sold milk as well as venison and trout to villagers. Will's sister Azubah, who died of scarlet fever when she was ten, is buried in a well-marked grave on a hillside just above the barn. Will himself died a mysterious death in 1908. It was rumored that he was poisoned by his hired man, William St. Clair. This may or may not have been true, but St. Clair had a dubious reputation, having been accused as a train robber — and he did soon marry Will Batterson's widow. The story is told in Wesley Swan's *Memoirs of an Old Timer*. The Swan family lived and ranched for many years a short distance down Gordon Creek, beginning in 1907.

The creek has been dammed at several points, and the resulting small lakes are named for several of the early inhabitants of the valley: Batterson, Crellin, Riddle, and Currie (in the West, any pond too wide to spit across is called a lake). Gordon Creek itself is named for Cyrus and John Gordon. John was a mail carrier for several years before building a house on the creek in 1863. Many of the "old-timers" are buried in Adams Cemetery, dating from 1880 and located on a hillside overlooking the valley about a mile below the junction of the two branches. The cemetery and a couple of old stone walls are all that is left of Adams, a settlement that once boasted a post office, store, and stage stop in the 1880s and 1890s.

Much of the country in the upper Gordon Creek basin was for many years ranched by Clarence Currie and his family, and his barn still stands, as does the elegant brick house he built overlooking Currie Lake. Currie was an avid big game hunter, and his trophy room was filled with heads and skins of leopards, water buffalo, and African antelopes, with a stuffed grizzly mounted in attack posture and reaching nearly to the ceiling of the room. The house, now in other ownership, is locally known as the Lox house, since Currie had his cattle brand, LOX, built into the side of his chimney. The brand dates from 1884 and had passed among several ranchers before being acquired by the Curries. It is a curious brand, perhaps designed so that it could not easily be changed by cattle rustlers. Most of the old Currie ranch is now called Glacier View Meadows, a housing development and a place where a person may rent horses and imagine himself pioneering this radiant landscape. The "glaciers" are the snowfields in the distant Mummy Range.

Below Currie Lake the valley is especially broad, and the stream meanders east for a mile or two through open meadows, punctuated only here and there by clumps of small willows. Then hills encroach from the south, and the stream is shunted north in a broad loop before turning south toward the Poudre. There are several homes on the loop, reached only by a gravel road that is not always in the best condition. There are tall willows and plains cottonwoods along the stream, and the hills are clothed with mountain-mahogany, rabbitbrush, and diverse wildflowers in season. This beautiful section of the valley, enclosed by hills on all sides, is only about thirty miles from Fort Collins, yet it could be a thousand miles from the turmoil of the city.

The lower section of Gordon Creek tumbles south through a twisting canyon called Hewlett Gulch. Presumably Hewlett was another early settler, but he seems to have left few traces. Once, a primitive road passed through the canyon, but now there is only a trail that is popular with hikers and trail bikers. On the east side of the canyon, the walls rise steeply for over 1,200 feet, culminating in Greyrock Mountain at 7,613 feet elevation. On the west side, the hills are rolling and sparsely wooded. Enriched by springs and side canyons, the stream is now big enough to nourish a few brown trout that have

Clematis (virgin's bower) was in bloom when Frémont traversed the lower Poudre basin in 1842.

made their way up from the Poudre. The upper part of the canyon is shaded with towering ponderosa pines and Douglas-firs, along with smaller trees such as junipers and mountain maples. Enclosed within walls of metamorphic rock in variegated colors and odd formations, the canyon is a cloistered place with a choir of birdsong and eloquent discourse from the stream.

Hiking the canyon one June day, we could hear cicadas clicking from almost every tree. These small cicadas of early summer have no elaborate sound-producing organs like those of most cicadas, but converse in clicks apparently produced by wind movements. We were impressed by the abundance of clematis (virgin's bower) climbing over rocks and bushes, and thought of Frémont, who commented on the clematis as he trekked through the lower part of the Poudre basin in 1842. Snowberry, too, carpeted the valley in many places, here in bloom, though still in bud when we left the headwaters of Gordon Creek earlier in the day.

Along the stream, western flycatchers advertised their presence with a simple, two-syllable call, while solitary and warbling vireos filled the trees with more musical offerings. Now and then we caught sight of more brilliantly colored birds, western tanagers, black-headed grosbeaks, and lazuli buntings, each with its own characteristic song. There was one song we could not identify. Of course no hike would be complete without one unidentified birdsong or half a dozen plants that couldn't be named with certainty.

In winter the migrants will be gone, and the canyon will be left to its permanent residents, Steller's jays, mountain chickadees, hairy woodpeckers, and now and then a golden eagle scanning the ground for a meal. The flowers will be gone and many of the bushes and trees leafless, but the pines, Douglas-firs, and junipers will still stand green above the snow. It is a good place to hike at any time of year, and even the heaviest snows usually melt back within a few days at this altitude.

Hewlett Gulch is now part of Roosevelt National Forest, but it was not always so. There are two abandoned mines reaching deeply into the canyon walls, as well as the remains of several homesteads. Some were landscaped with trees and flowers that still flourish long after the people who planted them have gone on to other realms. In places there are groves of ornamental, lavender-flowered locust trees, and one glade is filled with the brilliant blooms of oriental poppies and a bush of yellow roses that we have been known to trim back a bit to decorate our home. Scattered apple trees provide a crop of small, wormy apples that we much prefer to the immaculate, polished apples that supermarkets sell for ridiculous prices.

The lower part of the canyon is unfortunately filled with weedy plants, especially Canada thistles and leafy spurge, and the stream, in many seasons, flows beneath the sand before reaching the river at Poudre Park. So there is little to suggest that this is the terminus of a stream that traverses some wonderfully diverse country and provides sustenance for a vast array of plants and animals. Not that this stream is notably different from many others in the Poudre system, but like all streams it has its individuality. We hope to continue to hike its banks as long as our legs will carry us.

Soldier Canyon

Soldier Canyon is, by most reckoning, a rather no-account canyon. It begins in the foothills west of Fort Collins and runs a mere three miles before entering Horsetooth Reservoir. Years ago the stream breached the hogback along the east side of the reservoir and found its

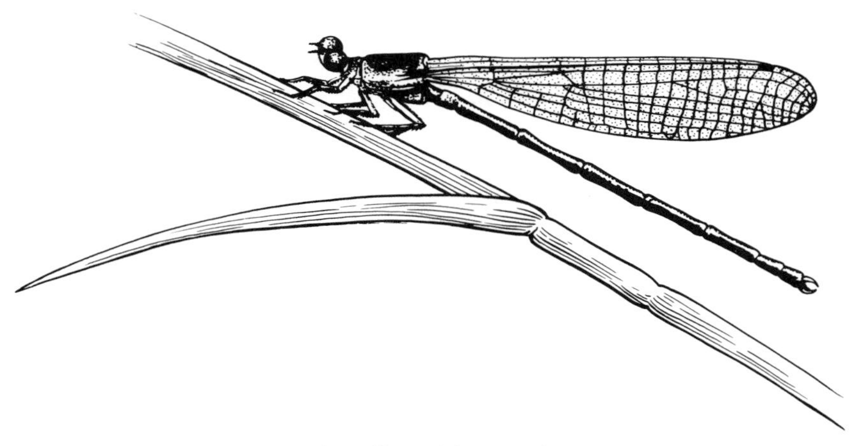

A damselfly, *Archilestes grandis*.

way to the Poudre, but now the way is blocked by Soldier Canyon Dam. For much of the year, the streambed carries no more than a trickle, and in its lower sections nothing at all. There is not even a good foot trail up the canyon. But there are few square feet of earth that do not hold treasures, and since we once lived not far from Soldier Canyon, we came to know it well. It is a particularly fine winter hike, when higher canyons are clogged with deep snow. Oozing from the hills at about 7,000 feet elevation, it drops about 1,500 feet to the picnic area in Lory State Park, the starting point for most hikers.

The origins of the canyon's name are obscure. Presumably it dates from the time when Camp Collins was a military post. One story is that soldiers from the camp used the canyon for access to the foothills, another that the skeleton of a soldier was found there. No matter; perhaps a more poetic name would be wasted on so minor a canyon.

Just above the picnic area, the canyon is barred by a rock wall too high and steep for easy climbing so that most hikers detour around it. During most seasons a little water trickles over the rocks and into quiet pools below, shaded by cottonwoods and box elders. This is the haunt in late summer of a damselfly called *Archilestes grandis* (*Archilestes* is Greek for "ancient pirate," *grandis* Latin for "big"). The name tells a good deal; these are relatively large as damselflies go, about two inches in length, and like others of their kind they capture small insects on the wing. They are ancient in the sense that entomologists feel that they are kin to damselflies and dragonflies that roamed the swamps millions of years ago. But none of this describes the thrill of seeing these elegant insects, with their dark bodies and translucent wings, flitting elusively through the shadows, as if mistaking this mundane little stream for some primeval forest.

Above the falls the canyon forms a broad and remarkably deep trough for so tiny a stream. But of course it is a much more presentable stream when snows are melting or after a summer cloudburst — and it has had more time available than we in our minuscule life spans can really grasp. The north-facing valley slopes, as we proceed up the canyon, become covered with ponderosa pines and Douglas-firs, while south-facing slopes are meadowed with grasses, yuccas, and low bushes.

One of the most abundant of these bushes is squawbush or skunkbrush, growing two to four feet high and bearing leaflets in groups of three, suggesting poison ivy or poison oak. Indeed this is a relative of poison ivy and oak, though perfectly harmless in spite of the somewhat unpleasant odor that gives the plant one of its names. In September the bushes are adorned with clumps of fuzzy red berries that can be eaten raw but are better used with sugar to make a "pink lemonade." The Indians used the berries for making a similar drink and also made the berries into cakes for winter use. In his book on edible native wild plants, H. D. Harrington provides directions for making a "fairly good" beverage and also gives a Navajo recipe for stewed skunkbrush. He did not succeed in whetting our appetites.

On high, south-facing cliffs, canyon wrens can be heard — and less often seen — at any time of year. In the winter they can be identified by their distinctive "chink" and sometimes even a few snatches of their song, which when full blown in the spring is one of the most wonderful of all birdsongs — a burst of notes descending the scale, like a dripping of water from the cliffs, like the history of the canyon itself, down, down, down. How wrong if the canyon wren's song ascended the scale! And how different it might sound somewhere else, without the canyon walls to provide a resonating chamber for so small a bird.

Not far up the canyon, there is a second waterfall, perhaps twelve feet high, in summer dribbling over mossy rocks, in winter covered with several layers of ice. One winter day, after we had made our way up the canyon through deep snow and were admiring the frozen falls, we watched a long-tailed weasel dashing about, doubtless in pursuit of some small rodent. Weasels seem remarkably unmindful of humans and will sometimes approach within a few feet of a person who remains still.

We find them extremely attractive animals, with dark eyes, small, rounded ears, a slender body, and a long, black-tipped tail. In winter all but the tip of the tail is white, but in summer the fur is golden-brown. Weasels require as many as four mice a day, so they are forever on the prowl. We once saw a weasel that had killed a rabbit but was carrying still another small mammal in its jaws.

Weasels mate in late summer, but as the embryos do not begin to develop immediately, the young are not born until the next spring. They are born blind but are weaned at about six weeks and by summer's end may be as large as their parents. Weasels are known to raid poultry yards, so, like many predators that occasionally intrude on human endeavors, they are not greatly beloved. But they do a great deal to keep small rodents under control, as well as adding a touch of wildness in a world now so thoroughly tamed.

Soldier Canyon, however meager the credentials of its stream, is one of only a very few places where a remarkable, remotely shrimp-like crustacean has been found. This is a blind, opaque white amphipod, or "scud," less than a quarter of an inch long, that belongs to a group associated with caves or subterranean habitats. The word amphipod is based on Greek meaning "feet all around," with reference to the many pairs of appendages which are diverse in form and function — some are used as feelers, others for grasping, chewing, moving about, and probably other activities. Waldo Schmitt, for many years the crustacean expert at the Smithsonian Institution, once remarked that "they seem to carry about with them almost as many tools as the proverbial plumber." Like other animals adapted for living in dark places, these amphipods have no use for eyes or for body coloration, and they have been lost. J. V. Ward, a professor of biology at Colorado State University, first discovered and named this particular amphipod species found among pine needles and cow dung in a small seepage on the slopes of the hogback along the east side of Horsetooth Reservoir. It is near the site where students have painted a large "A" on the rocks, for "Aggies" (the former name of the football team) — or was it for Amphipod? Later other individuals of the same species were found beneath rubble and gravel in wet places in Soldier Canyon. These obscure animals are known from only a few sites in Colorado, chiefly because only a few specialists have looked carefully for them. They add a note of distinction to an otherwise rather ordinary little streamlet.

Above the second falls, the valley is narrow and heavily wooded,

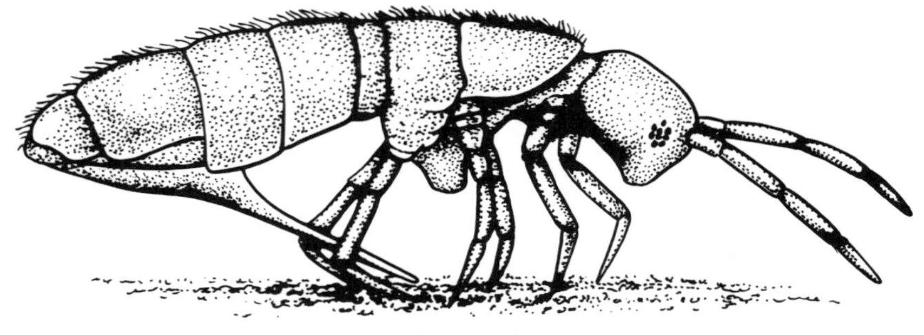

A springtail.

and there are brambles and fallen trees that impede progress. But a woodsman takes these in stride. Early one spring we spotted a great flock of red crossbills in these woods. These birds are so unpredictable in their occurrence that it is always a surprise to meet them. Their twisted bills appear awkward, but they are uniquely suited for opening cones and picking out the seeds.

It was in this part of the canyon — perhaps that same spring — that we came upon a swarm of snowfleas. The snows were melting, but in protected places there were still drifts, and on one of them thousands of these minute, black creatures were hopping about. Snowfleas are not by any means true fleas. They belong to a primitive group of insect-like animals that have a peculiar terminal appendage that enables them to hop about readily; hence they are also called springtails. These are enormously abundant organisms in most soils. A British entomologist once calculated 248,375,000 springtails in one acre of rather ordinary pasture. We know from experience how abundant they can be in the Rocky Mountains, as we were involved in censusing the soil fauna in areas devastated by the Lawn Lake flood of 1982 in Rocky Mountain National Park. Even though we were sampling soil gouged by the Roaring River and spread in a fan of rocks and sand, where virtually no plants had taken hold, in places there were hundreds of springtails in no more than a cupful of soil. However, persons other than entomologists or soil scientists are aware of springtails only when certain kinds emerge in great numbers onto the surface of snow, where they blacken the surface like coal dust. Why they emerge onto snow is anybody's guess.

The mating behavior of these small creatures stretches one's credulity. The males produce their sperm in a ball and place it on the end of a stalk. The female must pass over this blob and pick it up in her genitals. Sometimes the male surrounds the female with a ring of stalked blobs of sperm, rather like a picket fence. In some cases the male plasters the earth with so many of these stalked droplets that they resemble a growth of mold. The female can scarcely move about without losing her virginity. This behavior has been seen only by specialists using a microscope and special rearing chambers. It is just as well; we humans are sufficiently obsessed with our own sexual inventiveness.

A persistent hiker eventually reaches the source of the stream and passes on to the broad meadows on the crest of the hills. Here, in season, are fields of lupine, wallflowers, larkspurs, and many other flowers. This is privately owned pastureland, and the larkspur is doubtless little appreciated by the rancher who runs his cattle here. Although poisonous to livestock, larkspur has its uses, aside from adding a touch of blue to spring landscapes. There are many species throughout the world, and tincture of larkspur has long been a standard folk remedy for controlling head, body, and pubic lice. It has also been used for delousing cats and dogs. Probably it is the same alkaloid that poisons cattle that is lethal to the lice.

Once at the top, the hiker may return the way he or she came or look for the top of one of several other canyons that dissect these hills. Several contain the tumbled remains of log cabins, and it is fun to stop and examine these, wondering about the lives of their long-gone inhabitants. Were they trappers, miners, or simply hermits who had little use for towns? Did children once build dams on the stream and swing on the trees?

Returning via Empire Gulch, one can study the rocks in the tailings of long-extinct Empire Mine. Copper was discovered here in 1865, and in the late 1890s the mine was sold to the Boston and Colorado Mining Company for $10,000. Like so many mines in the Front Range, it never produced in quantities sufficient to justify its continuance for more than a few years.

Or one may return via Well Gulch, where there are long-abandoned waterworks, or via Arthur's Rock, affording a magnificent view of Horsetooth Reservoir, the hogbacks, and the plains beyond. There is no better place to reflect on how precious a gift the Poudre and its tributaries have been to all that lives in these mountains and plains.

9

SOME PEOPLE OF THE POUDRE

To those of us who grew up in the East, the newness of the West is a continual surprise. Almost anything over sixty years old seems to be an antique, and there are still people around who, if not homesteaders as children with their parents, had grandparents who helped open the frontier. The cowboy ethic, though perhaps no longer as romantic as once painted, is still here. Cowboys still drive cattle, and some even still do so while riding horses. Ruts made by stagecoaches still crease the prairie in places, and wounds made in hillsides by prospectors still have not healed.

The Indians

The West is new in one sense but old in another. The history of the white man in this part of the country is not old, but the Indian and pre-Indian occupation of this region has a long history, not fully appreciated for many years until an archeological discovery that was made here in northern Colorado. It had long been known that early man had entered this continent from Asia by crossing the land bridge to Alaska. This probably occurred during the time of the last Ice Age, some 18,000 to 20,000 years ago — the same time that glaciers were forming the high valleys of the upper Poudre in what was to be part of Rocky Mountain National Park. These early humans, over the centuries, worked their way south, fanning out across the North American continent, on through Central America, and into and down through South America. The details of these migrations and the reasons for them are still not entirely known or understood, but nevertheless the story is intriguing, particularly from the perspective provided by the local archeological findings.

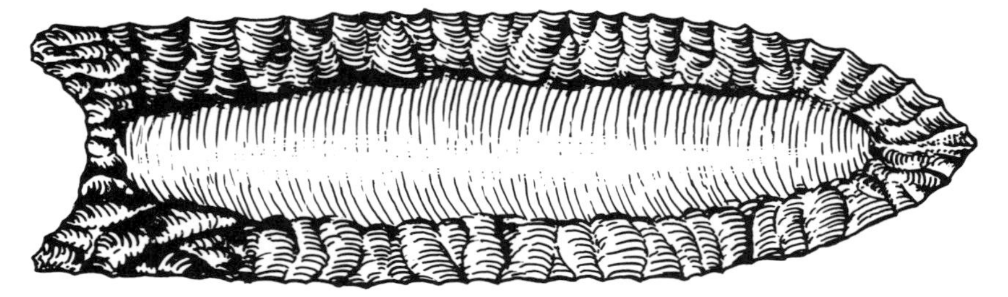

A Folsom point.

The presence of early man in the high, dry plains and the mountains was doubted until the discovery of Folsom points at the Lindenmeier Ranch north of Fort Collins, not far south of the Wyoming border. These were delicate, fluted projectile points and were found at this former campsite with other relics, including bones of such animals as pronghorn, rabbit, fox, wolf, coyote, turtle, and bison. Presumably these animals had been killed somewhere else and brought back to the camp for the people waiting there to prepare for use then, or later, as needed. The Lindenmeier site was discovered in 1924, and since then many other Folsom points have been found — all up and down the base of the Front Range. But few sites have produced as much information as was gathered from the Lindenmeier location.

According to radiocarbon dates made on materials from Lindenmeier, Folsom man lived about 9000 B.C. (give or take a 1,000 years). Slightly outside of the Poudre drainage area, upstream from the mouth of the Poudre River on the South Platte River, another site was found with evidence of an even older Paleo-Indian, Clovis man. At the Dent site, not only were there slightly larger fluted projectile points, but one was found in a bone from a mammoth. These huge animals are known to have died out at the end of the last Ice Age, before Folsom man came on the scene. At the other sites in Colorado, camel, horse, and large bison bones were also found. One wonders if perhaps the mammoths were helped into extinction by this new predator.

Gordon Creek, in the hills above Hewlett Gulch, also contains an important archaeological find known as the "Gordon Creek Burial." In 1963 some U.S. Forest Service personnel were engaged in watershed improvement activities when they noticed what appeared to be human bones along the bank of a small tributary of Gordon Creek. They reported their findings to the proper authorities, who salvaged them immediately. The grave proved to be that of a young woman whose body was flexed and covered with red ocre, a pigment often used in burial ceremonies. Also found were some stone tools that were thought to be grave offerings. The carbon date for this skeleton was determined to be about 7700 B.C. Thus, she was a Paleo-Indian who lived not long after the people who made Folsom points, and her grave is one of only a very few Paleo-Indian graves ever found in the Americas.

The people who came after the Paleo-Indians apparently wandered around the plains and into the mountains looking for game as well as suitable plants to eat. But they left little evidence of their presence, aside from a few projectile points (some found not far from the older site at Lindenmeier) estimated to be about 4,000 years old. Most of this Colorado Indian activity, so far as we know, occurred farther south, on the Western Slope, and especially in the Four Corners area. It was not until about A.D. 100 that there was a large migration into Colorado's plains from the east. These Indians spread up the rivers and came into this area via the Platte River. They brought pottery, made more permanent shelters, developed bows and arrows (as different from spears with projectile points), and cooperated in hunts. They often drove game over large cliffs and then shared the kill. One of these large jumps is on the north fork of the Poudre near Livermore; at the base of a massive sixty-foot cliff is a bed of bison bones plus associated camp debris. This site, because it has been disturbed, has been difficult to date, but it might have been used for a thousand years or more — up into the time of modern Indians.

The prehistory of the Ute tribe is not clear, but the Utes are considered to be the historic Indians of Colorado, although perhaps not so much of the eastern plains as of the Colorado Plateau to the west. The first written records of their presence in the western part of the state were made by early Spanish explorers in the 1600s, and an early history of New Mexico noted that the Utes were on the plains with Apaches. The Apaches were pushed south when the Comanches moved into the plains, and when the plains Indians acquired horses from the Spanish (by trading or stealing), the Ute-Comanche raids on other tribes, and later white settlers, became notorious. But by the early 1800s, this alliance had been broken, the Comanches had moved south of the Arkansas River, and the Utes had gone back up into the mountains. The new tenants of the northeastern plains were the Arapahoes and their allies, the Cheyennes, both of whom had migrated

Indian petroglyphs in the Boxelder drainage. *After* E. A. *Morris, 1979.*

in from the north and northeast. There they remained until forced to move to reservations by 1870.

The plains, the foothills, and many mountain valleys and stream banks over the years have yielded arrowheads, pieces of pottery, grinding stones, and many other artifacts left by the various tribal people who were living here or passing through in hunting parties. But perhaps the most intriguing remnants of Indian life left for us to ponder are the stone "tepee" rings. It is widely believed that these circles of stones once held down the outer, or perhaps the inner, skin coverings of tepees. But dating these rings has been difficult. They may have been made by prehistoric Indians or by any of the tribal people coming through the area. Even the specific use of these rings has not been determined with certainty. The general consensus is that they were made in winter camps when it was difficult to pound stakes into frozen soil. Summer camps, such as some investigated near today's Joe Wright Reservoir at an altitude of almost 10,000 feet, do not have any evidence of such rings.

Another intriguing matter has to do with the scarcity of rock art, so common in some areas of the West. In the Poudre drainage, only one cliff of drawings has been found; it is in the Boxelder Creek area out on the plains. The main drawing has been somewhat damaged by time and vandals, but seems to be a horseback rider with a shield — a rather sophisticated piece of art similar to some in Kansas and probably drawn around A.D. 1800. Another much simpler picture is unique: a stick figure (human) hanging by an arm and a leg between two posts. One is tempted to think, though with no authority, that hungry, nomadic people had little time for art.

There are many sad stories relating to the treatment by the U.S. government of the Indians in the West — and in the East, too, of course. Stories of broken treaties, of forced movement of tribes from their own lands to the reservations in another area, unequal treatment under the law, and so on — an endless list of mistreatments of Indians by the white man. And Colorado has its share. When we first arrived to live near the Poudre and were trying to steep ourselves in local lore, we were greatly surprised to find that there was, in the hills near the North Fork, a section called Cherokee Park. The story, as might be expected, is not a happy one.

In 1829 President Andrew Jackson asked Congress to remove the Indians from the southeastern part of the country to some more "useless" land further west. Thus in 1838 most of the Cherokees, living in the southern Appalachians, were rounded up at gunpoint and herded to Indian Territory, now part of Oklahoma. Some time later a party of Cherokees decided to look for a better place to live. Perhaps also lured by the California gold rush, they went all the way to the Pacific Coast. On their return (or the return of most of them) in 1859, they camped briefly in what is now called Cherokee Park. A war party of Utes, so the story goes, attacked them, and although the Cherokees won, there were casualties on both sides. Some of the graves were found later by white settlers, and in 1908 a small settlement nearby was named Cherokee Park. Today there is no such specific settlement, but the whole area is called by this name. It seems a strange quirk of history that a large tract of western land should be named for a small group of southeastern Indians that spent only a few days there.

Another local Indian story concerns an Arapahoe, Chief Friday, who, with a small band of his people, wanted a reservation established on the Poudre so they, who loved the area, could continue to live there. Friday had been found as a child by a white trader and was educated in a white man's school in St. Louis. Although he was sympathetic to many causes of early white settlers (he spoke English well and often acted as interpreter), his peacemaking efforts were unappreciated, and in 1879 he and his band were forced, along with other Arapahoes, to go to the Wind River Reservation in Wyoming.

Arrival of the Europeans

The first white people entering the Poudre area were probably trappers looking mainly for beaver. Many of them were French-Canadians — hence the many French names found in Colorado. The traders, who followed the trappers, generally came up the rivers from St. Louis and thus tended to be other than Canadian. The trappers may have reached the main stem of the Poudre (we have no records), but probably traders did not because the canyon was too narrow and it was easier to continue north along the foothills. Also there were probably few people in the upper Poudre with whom one might trade — perhaps only a few unfriendly Utes.

The fur trappers were usually called mountain men and were the first to enter lands previously unknown to whites. Many were illiterate and consequently left no written accounts of the countryside through which they traveled, of the Indians they met, or of their adventures in general. The same was true, more or less, of the traders who came a little later. But the early explorers who began to come into the area in the mid-1800s provided us with the first maps, descriptions of geological formations, notes on rainfall, and scientific notes. Their parties often included artists to make permanent pictures of the scenery, the Indian tribes and their ceremonies, and plants and animals encountered.

The first white settlers, those who came and stayed, did not do so in any numbers until after the Civil War, and primarily not until the stagecoaches and railroads made traveling west easier. Neither the Oregon Trail to the north nor the discovery of gold to the south brought people to the Poudre, at least not directly.

The village of Laporte seems to have been officially organized in 1860, but it never was much until Ben Holladay made it a stage stop in 1862. When so many of the forts were depleted as the men were pulled out to fight in the war, local Indians increased their attacks on stagecoaches and stage stations. Consequently, Holladay moved the routes south from Wyoming. The coaches came up along the Platte River to the mouth of the Poudre, where Holladay built a station called

The original Weld County courthouse is preserved in Greeley's Centennial Village.

Latham. From there he sent a spur down to Denver, but the main part of the Overland Trail went due west to Laporte and then north along the base of the foothills back to Wyoming. At about the same time, a Lt. Col. William O. Collins reached Fort Laramie with a battalion of soldiers from Ohio. Some of these he sent south to Laporte to set up a new post to guard the stage line from Indian attack. The soldiers named the post Camp Collins. While it lasted, Camp Collins brought some prosperity to Laporte, but the soldiers there saw little battle with Indians. In the spring of 1864, there was a tremendous cloudburst in the upper part of the Poudre, and Camp Collins, along with most of Laporte, was washed away. Camp Collins was rebuilt on a new site a little further downstream (still on a floodplain) and was closed down in early 1867. Presumably Fort Collins came into existence in the latter years of the military post, but it did not officially do so until about 1872 — a couple of years after the founding of Greeley, its sister city on the Poudre.

Greeley, named for its patron Horace Greeley, was founded in 1870 by Nathan C. Meeker, who had worked as the agricultural reporter on the *New York Tribune* and had long been interested in utopian communities. He had also had at least some experience farming. In the fall of

1869, he was sent west by his paper so that he could write some articles about the Mormon settlements in Utah. He traveled by train as far west as Cheyenne, Wyoming, where snowdrifts blocked his train, so he turned south and studied the high plains of Colorado. He liked what he saw and thought the area had great potential for agricultural communities. His editor, Horace Greeley, encouraged him in this, advertised the proposal to found a settlement to be called Union Colony, and apparently even helped financially, as he was listed briefly as treasurer. The colony succeeded, though not without setbacks, one being the cost of getting water to the crops (apparently these easterners had not realized how much irrigation water would be needed) and how expensive it would be to deliver it (dig the proper ditches). Another problem faced by the colonists was a belief by the local ranchers that these lands were for cattle grazing and should remain unfenced. When the colonists defied this belief by building a forty-five-mile fence completely around the colony in order to protect the crops, mainly from the roving livestock, the colony was greatly resented by the ranchers. The greatest disappointment to Meeker himself seemed to be the establishment of the land grant agricultural college in Fort Collins instead of in Greeley, which he considered the heart of the agricultural belt.

There were many who remained skeptical, not only about the need for an agricultural college, but about agriculture per se in Colorado. Nevertheless, in 1870 the territorial legislature authorized the establishment of a college, and it was confirmed by the state general assembly in 1877. This took place in spite of comments such as the following (quoted by A. T. Steinel in his *History of Agriculture in Colorado, 1858 to 1926*):

> When the State Agricultural College [was located] at Fort Collins, representatives from other localities did not consider their loss irreparable or Fort Collins' emolument beyond compare. . . . A school for the promotion of agricultural science and mechanic arts, located in the Great American Desert, with nothing in sight more suggestive of enlightened civilization than dry prairies, dotted with cactus patches, bestrewn with bleaching bones of departed buffalo, and inhabited by prairie dogs, coyotes and buzzards, with only here and there a little oasis along the creek bottoms, was an enterprise that was considered both amusing and pathetic.

Meeker left the Union Colony (Greeley) in 1877 to become the government agent at the White River Indian Agency in the western part of the state. He was supposed to restrict himself to distributing supplies to the local Utes, but he wanted to "better" their lives by teaching them how to grow crops and by educating their children. His youngest daughter, Josephine, did the teaching, which seemed successful, perhaps because she was young and enthusiastic. But the Utes did not like growing crops, wishing instead the agent would give them their supplies and otherwise leave them alone to live as they liked, without plowing up their sacred lands. Discontent increased, and on September 29, 1879, they attacked the agency, killed all the men, and took the women captive. Captivity lasted less than a month, and it was the last Indian massacre because soon all the Indians were subdued on the reservations. Chief Ouray, who had been to Washington and sensed that the old Indian life was doomed, made the White River Utes, for their own protection, return the white women unharmed and promise to shoot no more white men.

Stagecoaches continued to bring people west, but today little remains to show that the Overland Stage Line came through Poudre country except for a few old wheel ruts across a few meadows, the tiny grave of Eddie Hale, nineteen months, April 17, 1864, at Bonner Springs north of Laporte, and most notably the old stage station at Virginia Dale. One of the most famous, or infamous, characters of the region was the first agent of this station — Jack Slade. He built the station house in a beautiful setting among granite outcroppings and named it for his wife. The structure has had additions and subtractions over the years, and there is a photograph of it made by William H. Jackson, whose early photographs of the West, especially Colorado's Mountain of the Holy Cross, are so valued. The building deteriorated for years, but recently local people interested in saving it have been slowly replacing rotting timbers and shoring up the foundation.

But to return to Jack Slade. He had been an agent at Julesburg, Colorado, and was apparently very competent in overseeing the route between northeastern Colorado and Casper, Wyoming. When Holladay moved his lines south, he asked Slade to move west to the Cherokee Park section. Slade's competency seemed to be inversely proportional to the amount of alcohol he consumed and grew worse during his four months in the area. When drunk he was ugly and domineering and, according to one legend, was in league with local desperadoes, who

The Virginia Dale stage station still stands in the village Jack Slade named for his wife.

seemed somehow to know when the approaching stage carried large amounts of gold and was worth robbing.

Mark Twain in *Roughing It*, published in 1871, described his meeting with Slade. Twain was traveling to Nevada on the Overland Trail stage, and his description of this encounter at Virginia Dale is preceded by several pages relating the terrible stories of "a man whose heart and hands and soul were steeped in the blood of offenders against his dignity." But when the two met at the stage stop, Slade was "so friendly and so gentle-spoken that I warmed to him in spite of his awful history. It was hardly possible to realize that this pleasant person was the pitiless scourge of the outlaws, the raw-head-and-bloody-bones the nursing mothers of the mountains terrified their children with."

And then a typical Mark Twain anecdote: Only one cup of coffee remained, and Slade was about to take it when he noticed Mark Twain's empty cup, and so he offered it to him. Twain refused, he said, because he was afraid that if he did accept it, Slade, who had not killed anyone that morning, might decide he wanted a diversion. Slade insisted, and then Twain was afraid not to accept it for the same reason. A good story!

Ben Holladay sold his line in 1866 to the Wells Fargo Company shortly before the advance of the railroads. Thus disappeared the Overland Stages, which had brought so many famous and not-so-famous men through this countryside briefly on their way to the California goldfields and other West Coast localities. Small companies did continue to run for a while, mainly to serve the mining camps in the mountains. Some came through Livermore, branched west up the road to Log Cabin and Manhattan, and down the hill to the Poudre and up across the divide to the various silver mining camps, such as Lulu City and Teller City. In 1975, to help celebrate Colorado's centennial, the then owners of the Livermore Forks Cafe (built before Colorado was a state) had a replica of one of the old stagecoaches built and offered rides to tourists for a small fare. We rode on it one day, enjoyed the experience, but were thankful we did not go far. How passengers of the previous century survived those jolting, dusty rides "overland" is a mystery to us.

The First Railroads

The railroad era in Colorado began in late 1867, more or less, by the laying of track into the northeast corner of the state. The tracks generally followed the old stage route up the Platte, going through Latham and on to Denver. This had little effect on Poudre Valley except for its contribution of ties. In the winter of 1868–69, trees were cut and skidded down to Chambers Lake using horses. Then in June the log dam at the outlet was opened and the flotilla of ties sent downstream to Greeley or Laporte where booms caught them. As more and more ties were needed, new tie camps were established — on the South Fork, at Rustic, at Deadman, and elsewhere. Lumbering continued through the railroad-building years until 1885, when the hillsides of the Poudre and many other mountain areas were almost treeless. Then tie cutting was finally stopped.

Before leaving the subject of logging, we cannot resist quoting from an 1875 newspaper article from a scrapbook in the historical archives of the Greeley Museum. The article (no author given) is titled "The Cache la Poudre" and tells many delightful stories, one of which has to do with logging and log jams.

Hikers in the back country often come across the ruins of cabins, built perhaps by miners or tie cutters.

> In the canyon these jams are sometimes frightful to see. From the rocky cliffs hundreds of feet above the stream one can look down at such a time on one of the grandest sights imaginable. The jams in the canyon sometimes pile up logs forty feet high, and the water dashes over the dam with a frightful velocity, thundering like Niagara, and throwing its spray into the air so thick as to completely shut out observation. Suddenly there will be a mighty upheaval of the entire mass; followed by a roar and a crash as of a tremendous explosion, and with a mighty surge the vast volume of water and the mountain of timber goes leaping down the stream with the force and fury of ten thousand demons.

Most of the early trains in northern Colorado, at least those coming through the Poudre area, were more smoke than steel. In 1880 the Denver, Salt Lake and Western, a subsidiary of the Chicago, Burlington and Quincy, made a survey up the canyon, and the surveyor's profile was posted in the county courthouse. When the Union Pacific discovered this work of a competitor, it formed the Greeley, Salt Lake and

Pacific and in turn began to survey the Poudre. Two railroads up the Poudre? And was there room? So wondered the excited local citizenry. Meanwhile, the Cache la Poudre and North Park Toll Road Company, directed by Samuel B. Stewart, had opted for some of the right-of-way and built a toll road from Rustic tie camp up over Cameron Pass down into Teller. A regular stage line, as we have mentioned previously, brought mail and supplies.

As if all this was not exciting enough, especially to speculators, yet another railroad company, the Greeley, Bear River and Pacific, proposed to send a line from Greeley to Fort Collins to Livermore, west to Red Feather Lakes (known then as Westlake), south along Green Ridge and down to Chambers Lake, then up over Cameron Pass and into and across North Park, up through Buffalo Pass and down to the Bear (Yampa) River, and finally to Utah. The survey was made up Lone Pine Creek, over Green Ridge, and on to Chambers Lake, but apparently there hopes died. The Denver, Salt Lake and Western's plans had also faded, but the Union Pacific did persist for a while. Many residents of Fort Collins, and perhaps Greeley, too, who had hoped to see their city become a great railroad center, accused the company of not living up to its promises and of only wanting to take sandstone out of the hogbacks. True or not, grading went on from Bellvue to the mouth of the canyon and then for about six miles in the canyon. A private contractor, Robert Walsh, did some of the last work for the Union Pacific, and he had a few personnel problems, which were left in the records. One worker tapped dynamite with steel instead of wood and blew himself up; another, "Tiger Jim" Wilson, was fired and came back with a gun to shoot Walsh, missed, but killed another worker by mistake. He ended up in the Fort Collins jail, though he denied any evil intent.

In 1882 the Union Pacific decided not to continue its work in the canyon, and whether it had ever intended to build a line up the Poudre is a moot point. It is known from abstracts of landowners that the company had secured a right-of-way over the pass. In 1911 there was a renewed interest in the route by the Union Pacific, and it was resurveyed. At that time it was determined that a 3,800-foot-long tunnel would need to be built near Cameron Pass at 9,000 feet altitude. Again the idea of a railroad along the Poudre was dropped. But when convicts built the highway a few years later, many of the graded sections were incorporated into it.

The 1911 renewal of interest by the Union Pacific was brought about, some say, by the appearance of yet another competitor in the area, the Denver, Laramie and Northwestern, which hoped to provide service between Denver and Seattle by way of Laramie. It did not intend to go up Poudre Canyon but up some of the northern tributaries. These were Boxelder Creek, Dale Creek, and Fish Creek, the latter being a tributary of Dale Creek. Although no locomotive ever got beyond Greeley, some grading was done north of Virginia Dale through the small but rugged canyon of Fish Creek. The route had been inspected and received approval from J. R. P. Taylor, former chief engineer of the Panama Canal, so the story goes. Work took place during 1910 and 1911 on the sections considered most difficult. One of the more interesting remains of this is a tunnel, once called the Butte Royal by the railroad company. It was made by boring through solid granite and is approximately 350 feet long and about 19 feet high. No doubt it will be there as long as Fish Creek Canyon remains.

Over the decades since the first white men came up the Poudre, there have been many who have contributed to the local lore of the country, and some, of course, who are still doing so. But Fort Collins, Greeley, and many of the smaller towns along the river have grown to the point that personal anecdotes tend to be lost in the crowds. And history, even our own, seems to belong to someone else or at least not have much meaning in our modern lives. That we can still find a Wild and Scenic river is a thread that connects us with those who preceded us into this valley.

People and Places

So who were some of the people of the Poudre who made a difference? We have already mentioned a few, and there are others we would like to include but could not even if we knew more about them. Often their names are preserved only in the landmarks where they lived or worked. Fortunately for us, however, there are several little books of reminiscences written by old-timers, along with some informal histories of the area that do provide help in sorting out the things we would like to tell. One of the best is *Cache la Poudre* by Norman Fry (1872–1954), which is mainly about early life on the upper Poudre. Fry said that there were tie camps in the 1870s up every gulch on the Poudre and that the pay was not bad, each man getting about ten cents a tie and cutting about forty a day. One tie foreman was Samuel B. Stewart, whom we have already mentioned in connection with the toll road. Stewart homesteaded Rustic, one of his tie camps.

Cameron Pass was named for General Robert A. Cameron (1828–94) by the Union Pacific surveyors. Although General Cameron did not settle permanently in Poudre Valley, he was important to it. He helped Nathan C. Meeker found the Union Colony then moved upstream to help organize the agricultural colony of Fort Collins. Sometime in the early 1870s, he must have explored the upper Poudre and, according to some accounts, "discovered" the pass. General Cameron also helped found Fountain Colony (now Colorado Springs) and later moved to Canon City to be the first warden of the Colorado State Penitentiary. During the Civil War, he had been a brigadier general.

John McNabb (1859–1935), a Scotch-Canadian, was another early settler on the Poudre. Described by his friend Fry as "a man to match the mountains," he helped deliver mail for Samuel B. Stewart — even snowshoeing it to Teller City when the snow was too deep for horses. In 1892 he supervised the rebuilding of the toll road after the dam at Chambers Lake had broken and washed it out. He was involved with, and often in charge of, the building of various irrigation projects in the high country, such as the Skyline Ditch from the Laramie River, the Michigan Ditch over Cameron Pass, Joe Wright Reservoir, and even the Grand Ditch. And when it came to hewing logs, said Fry, he was probably the finest axe man on the river. "It was a pleasure to see the way he could roll up a log cabin while other men were thinking about it!"

John McNabb had come to the Poudre with John Zimmerman and his family from Minnesota in 1880. After some rugged winters at Cameron Pass, the Zimmermans moved back down the canyon, where John Zimmerman had established a homesteading claim. Zimmerman, McNabb, and others made mining claims there, too, and eventually they built a stamp mill to refine their ore. In 1890 Zimmerman thought he had found a rich gold strike in his Elkhorn Mine. Prospectors poured into the area. But when he sent the refined ore to St. Louis to be tested, he was told that it was mostly copper. He always claimed that he had been swindled, but could not prove it.

The Zimmermans found their rewards elsewhere, however, by building and operating a very successful tourist resort. Zimmerman

The Keystone Hotel was for many years a major resort in upper Poudre Canyon. Few evidences remain today. *Courtesy of Fort Collins Public Library.*

bought a sawmill, moved it to his ranch, and powered it with water. He and his family also made bricks, and with these and their own lumber eventually built the Keystone Hotel in the late 1890s. It was three stories tall, had forty rooms, enough beds to sleep a hundred people, and hot and cold water and other "modern conveniences." The Zimmermans promised their guests inspiring scenery, fine trout fishing, musical evenings, and good food. Rates at the hotel ranged from eight to fourteen dollars per week. The trip of fifty-five miles from Fort Collins on the Zimmerman Stage Line via Livermore cost three dollars. John Zimmerman's son Ed often drove the stage that brought visitors to the hotel, regaling them with stories. When one lady asked him how the rocks of the hogbacks got so red, he reputedly replied, "Well, madam, a long time ago they had an Indian war here and they killed so many Indians that the blood stained the stone red."

In 1946 the Colorado Fish and Game Department bought the old hotel and surrounding land, and much to the consternation of many local people, tore the hotel building down. Now a trailer park is located near the site, just downstream from the fish hatchery and ponds. But the Zimmermans are not forgotten, because near Cameron Pass is

Agnes Zimmerman painted the wildflowers of Poudre Canyon in loving and accurate detail. On this plate she included wood lilies and (in the lower left) swamp pyrola.

Zimmerman Lake, and over on the west side of the pass is Lake Agnes, named for Zimmerman's youngest daughter. Agnes was a talented artist who "painted all the wildflowers in the canyon." Her paintings are still treasured by members of the Zimmerman family.

Life on the upper reaches of the Poudre was rugged, and stories of the pioneers there are exciting and endless. However, life at the lower altitudes was often no easier. The land in the Poudre drainage has not produced many, if any, millionaires (as did the area around the famous mines to the south), but these lands are important as pasture and crop land. As we have pointed out, Greeley and Fort Collins began as agricultural colonies. Crops of vegetables and fruit orchards abounded, and for a time sugar beet fields seemed to be everywhere. There still are many farms around Greeley producing truck crops, but dryland wheat farming and irrigated cornfields now seem to dominate the landscape, except, of course, where the land has remained in grass and serves the livestock industry as pasture.

Cattle and sheep came into the area shortly after the Civil War. Early pioneers had noted the large herds of buffalo grazing on the hardy, perennial grasses of the high plains, and they surmised that cattle would do well here, too, even though early explorers had called the high plains the "great American desert." Cattlemen and sheepmen resented each other's presence, and although those who owned the largest ranches might have been involved in the cattle-sheep "wars" in Wyoming, trouble never erupted, at least to the same degree, around the Poudre. Also, it should be noted that most, if not all, of the local ranches were not as large, especially those close to or in the foothills. Presumably the area was well-watered (compared to that further east) and summer range in the mountains more easily reached.

Today many of the old ranch families are gone from Larimer and Weld Counties. When cattle were first run in the region, there were no fences. So, at roundup time, cowboys from all the ranches worked together to separate out the branded cattle, to brand their calves, and to drive all home — some from as far east as the Pawnee Buttes, far beyond Poudre grass. There are still cattle drives today, but they are mainly for moving cattle over well-traveled roads up to the high country for summer pasture (usually in the national forest), and back down again in the fall. And what patience it takes to get a car past a herd! Fortunately larger moves, generally to market, are made by truck.

Cattle drives today share the roads with recreation vehicles.

Life on the pioneer ranches, both on the Poudre and elsewhere in the West, is difficult for us to comprehend, even after hearing or reading stories about the early ranches and the people who established them. One of the most charming accounts is that of Carrie Williams Darnell, who wrote stories from her childhood recollections for her daughters. These stories are called *Three Ranch Children* and tell of her life with her family on Lone Pine Creek, a tributary of the North Fork. Carrie was born in 1888, the second "ranch child." She talks about the building of their "large" house with the help of neighbors; her mother's flower beds; their horses, cats, and dogs for companionship; and the beauty of the setting. Nevertheless, even as a child, she was aware of her mother's loneliness. The men, as they rode around their lands or went after mail and supplies, often saw other ranchers, but the women sometimes went for weeks or months without seeing other women. In this book, as in most others, much is made of the dances held on special occasions. These often went on all night, while the children slept in the wagons or back rooms. Rural schools could be a problem, too, as they often were at some distance from the ranch, perhaps even unreachable through the snowdrifts in winter, and often were taught by inexperienced teachers. To attend school the children, especially when older, had to board in town away from their families. But through all the hardships and inconveniences, many families not only persisted, but loved their life. Carrie Darnell wrote:

> Wild roses grew abundantly and were most beautiful along the path by the South Pine where shade gave them the lovely deep rose color. Here, too, beneath the edges of great rocks grew delicate little ferns, always one of Carrie's delights. Columbines grew just one place on the ranch, that was in Columbine Gulch. At a little higher elevation they grew in great masses among the aspen trees. Mariposa lilies and the dainty blue of the dwarf iris graced the meadowlands. There were shooting stars as the children knew them, and wild candy tuft growing near the creek. There were many shrubs growing upon the mountainside, a wild currant bush whose bright red berries were attractive but tasteless; the foliage having a pungent odor gave the name of skunk bush to this particular shrub. The service berries, sometimes called sarvice berries, were a bit tasteless but with lemon juice or vinegar added made a good pie. Thimble berry bushes were so beautiful with their fragrant white blossoms; their berries, too, were rather insipid, but the children ate them. Chokeberries made the jam which was a favorite spread for the school lunch sandwiches. In autumn the hills were a blaze of color from the aspens adding their glorious colors to the scene.

Many of the early ranches, especially the larger ones, were owned by English companies and operated by a manager, who was often English, too, but not always. Many of the men who worked the ranches were called remittance men. They tended to be second or third sons of English nobility (the ones who would not inherit the family title or estates), who received money periodically from their families so that they could stay in this country and away from home. The remittances apparently were sufficiently generous so that many such men could soon buy their own ranches. In the small book giving the history of the Larimer County Stockgrowers Association, acknowledgement is given as follows: "The story of the Livestock industry in Larimer County would not be complete without mention of the contribution made by the Englishmen who came here in the infancy of the cattle business. They brought with them the love of good cattle and horses as well as the knack of gracious living."

Some years ago, while making some biological observations in an area just beyond Boulder Ridge, not far out of the north Poudre country, we found a quotation carved in Greek into a sandstone cliff. From the cliff, the view northeast across a little brook and then the distant high country ranches is serene. We copied the quotation as best we could (there had been some erosion, so it had been there a while) and took it to a classical scholar who told us it came from Sappho and said, in essence: "therein cold water babbles through apple-branches, . . . and from the shimmering leaves the sleep of enchantment comes down. . . ." We do not know who did the carving in the sandstone, but we like to think it was one of the well-educated English remittance men. We wish he, whoever he was, had finished the poem, which mentions a meadow where horses graze, spring flowers blossom, and winds blow gently.

One of the "Poudre Englishmen" was Lord Cecil Moon, whose wife Kate "gave us a lot to talk about," according to Norman Fry. Lady Moon, born Catherine Lawder in Ireland, came to Colorado in 1883 when she was eighteen. She worked as a maid and waitress at the Elkhorn Hotel, not far from Manhattan, and soon married Frank Gartman, who was working at one of the gold mines there. Then along came Cecil Moon to stay with friends on a nearby ranch. "It soon became known," wrote Fry, "that Cecil Moon was the oldest son and direct heir . . . not only [to] a Baronet title, but also a considerable entailed estate.

" 'Kate' too heard the 'good news,' and although Cecil's father at this time stood between Cecil and the Title, she decided to take a shot at a romance. So she made love to the young Englishman — not such a hard job as she was a handsome and well developed Irish lass — divorced her husband, Frank Gartman, and was married to Cecil." After they inherited the title, they made trips back to England, but Kate did not behave like a lady, thus incurring the great dislike of Cecil's family. To continue with Fry's account:

"To get rid of her, the Moon family must have made arrangements to 'pension her off,' and back she came to the United States. 'Sir Cecil' for some time vainly sought a divorce. 'Kate' was not quite ready to 'kill the goose that laid the golden egg.' Eventually, however, terms were generously made, Cecil got his divorce, and returned to England." According to another account, when Cecil sued for divorce, Kate countersued, and when the divorce was settled, she received most of the ranch properties, but had to give up the title (she wept over that!) and also had to pay alimony to Cecil — unusual in those years, to say the least.

" 'Lady Moon' and her affairs degenerated rather quickly after her divorce from Cecil," continued Fry. "Among the rumors were those that she and one of her foreman were involved in cattle stealing to add to her revenues, and that they had burned down her home in order to collect insurance on it. . . . Eventually, 'Lady Moon' sold her property — though for some time keeping 160 acres on the head of the 'Pine' [on Lone Pine Creek, the old Gartman place]. There her men manufactured bootleg whiskey which she disposed of in town. She died — of alcoholic poisoning, I imagine — in the 1920s." Actually she died of cancer in 1926.

A novel based on Catherine Moon's life, *The Lady from Colorado*, was written by Homer Croy and published in 1957. In 1964 the Central City Opera Company gave a production with the same name, which was about "an early Colorado personality." For a time Ethel Merman apparently considered bringing the musical to Broadway, but these plans never materialized. We cannot vouch for the authenticity of many of the Lady Moon stories, but we do know that when we first came to Fort Collins in the early 1970s, we met people who assured us that they remembered Lady Moon's trips to the city in her chauffeur-driven limousine and how she looked in her large, plumed hats as she majestically paraded through town.

In the 1970s Wesley Swan published a book, *Memoirs of an Old Timer*, and in it he devoted over ten pages to the exploits of Catherine Moon, whom he, as a child, had known. Wes and his wife Jessie were living on the old Gartman place, where we visited them. One of our treasured keepsakes is a painting we made of the "Lady Moon" barn, as it is called, but which was built by Frank Gartman, who obviously was a good carpenter. As for Lady Moon, as Wes said, she was "perhaps the best known and [most] spectacular individual to live in this vicinity [in] the last hundred years."

The livestock industry had its blackguards, too, for thieves operated in the early days and certainly on the black markets during the world wars. In the 1860s the Musgrove Gang had a hideout on the North Fork at Ingleside, near Bonner Peak. Most of the early thieves would steal, usually horses, in one area, take them elsewhere to sell, and then bring back other stolen animals to sell locally. "Three-fingered" Musgrove was hanged in Denver in 1868 as a horse thief, but his legend lives on in a small novel called *The Bride of Bonner Peak*, written by Charles E. Roberts, a member of the prominent ranching family on the North Fork mentioned earlier. The story tells about an innocent young woman, orphaned during an Indian raid while coming west with her parents. She met and married John Musgrove, not knowing his trade. In the story, Calamity Jane (generally associated with General George Custer, Buffalo Bill Cody, and Wild Bill Hickok) "saves" her — an interesting idea, as Calamity Jane was known to be in and out of Colorado from time to time, though perhaps not in the vicinity of the Cache la Poudre River.

Bonner Peak was also the hideout for a gang of outlaws in a much more recent novel, the late Louis L'Amour's *The Cherokee Trail*. The setting of this story of the early days of the West — one of a hundred or so from the author's pen — is the old Cherokee Stage Station on the Overland Trail. (This station was just north of Livermore, near Steamboat Rock.) Scant Luther, one of the villains of this traditional western tale of good guys versus bad guys, may have been modeled on Jack Slade, who as we have seen was actually associated with the Virginia Dale Station, a few miles to the north.

Still another story of outlaws — in this case a true story — is associated with Chicken Park, near Creedmore Lakes, which we have already mentioned as a source of commercial diamonds. Chicken Park received its name when William Calloway, while running cattle in the area in 1874, took time out to carve a peacock into the trunk of a huge pine tree, along with his initials and the date. Local cowboys jokingly referred to his art work as a chicken and soon began to apply the name to the park. Around the turn of the century, Chicken Park became the hideout for horse thieves. According to a 1956 booklet published by the Larimer County Stockgrowers Association:

> The tumbled down shack, almost completely hidden among the aspen trees, proved to be a haven from law and order. The dugout, scarcely high enough for a man to stand upright, was built low so that it would be concealed. Port holes in the walls of the cabin provided a means of protection for the thieves. Operating at night and turning their herds loose in this isolated and thickly wooded area, thieves gathered between 200 and 300 head of horses before starting to the

> western slope, around Meeker, to sell them. Working that area, another herd of horses would be accumulated and brought back to be sold in this country.

Some of the local ranchers evidently made ends meet by serving meals to the outlaws and warning them when there was danger from the law. They did this by flying a flag from the top of an especially tall tree, but only when "the coast was clear." Both the "chicken tree" and the "flag tree" have succumbed to age, but local history aficionados have rescued parts of the tree bearing the peacock and part of the apparatus used for raising the flag to the top of the tree.

We have mentioned that sheep ranches were also present in the Poudre area, although perhaps not to the same extent as were cattle ranches. But they prospered, especially after sugar beets were grown locally and could be used to fatten lambs for the market. In 1909 Fort Collins, "the largest lamb-fattening district in America," barbecued 200 lambs in the center of town, and for the free meal an estimated crowd of eight to ten thousand people came from miles around. The feast was held again the next year, but after that the city fathers proclaimed they had had enough. The lamb-feeding industry was so profitable it did not need any extra publicity, and Fort Collins did not need a traffic jam.

Sugar beets were an important crop in Colorado for seventy years or so. Now sugar beet fields are fewer in number, and the processing plants plus the little trains serving them are mostly a thing of the past. The idea of processing beets for commercial sugar came from France and was present in surrounding states, especially Utah, but it did not materialize along the Front Range, including the Poudre area, until after the turn of the century. Two factors seem to have been important: the studies of the Colorado Agricultural College in Fort Collins to improve the beets and increase sugar content and the migration into the area of the German-Russian people to do the needed hand labor. Also helpful, of course, was the high government tariff against imported sugar.

The story of the German-Russians is interesting and important to this area, and probably without those people the sugar beet industry would never have been such a success. They originally were Germans who migrated in the 1760s to Russia, when Catherine the Great enticed them with promises of rich agricultural land along the Volga and assurances that they would not be subject to military service. But Catherine died, promises were forgotten, and the unhappy Volga-Germans again moved — this time to America. At first they came mainly to Kansas and Nebraska, but as the need for beet field labor increased, many came on to northeastern Colorado. The work was backbreaking, low paying, and involved the whole family, adults and children, regardless of age and health. They hoed and thinned by hand day after day in the summer heat.

In 1935 a novel was published by a woman who had taught in the public school where many of the German-Russian children went when they were not in the fields. She was Hope Williams Sykes and the book was called *Second Hoeing*. It portrayed the life of a German-Russian family in its own little community on the edge of Fort Collins (although the town had a different name in the story), and it was done so well, showing both the good and the bad, that not only did the old families of Fort Collins resent the implications of snobbery, but the German-Russians, most of whom had not read it, bitterly denounced it as offensive. And the story goes that the city library kept mysteriously losing its copies. Fortunately at least one copy survived, and in 1982 the book was reissued. In that time span of almost fifty years, not only had tempers cooled, the old way of life for the German-Russian-Americans had vanished, and the child labor laws had stopped the exploitation of the children. (Perhaps, said some, this story helped to strengthen those laws.)

The sugar beet industry also attracted Hispanics to this area. They worked in the fields, and as the German-Russians dispersed, they more or less replaced them. At first they congregated in Denver and came as temporary workers to Larimer and Weld counties, but gradually many moved permanently to the area. Their culture seems to have had much more impact locally, and although we will not go into this large subject, we do want to mention Lee Martinez Park. It is named for Librado "Lee" Martinez, who came to Fort Collins with his parents in 1906, when he was seventeen. His father had been a "boss" in the sugar beet fields. Lee served in the U. S. forces in France during World War I, lost a son in World War II, and was a political activist in the 1960s, trying to improve conditions for the Spanish-speaking families in Fort Collins. The park named for him along the river is a part of the city park system and is not far from the Hispanic community.

Because we are interested primarily in the natural history of the Poudre, we have limited our survey of its social history. But we cannot leave the subject without one more story of a colorful man, Frank C. Miller, Jr.

Frank was a city boy, born in Fort Collins in 1886 and educated there. His father, an immigrant from Denmark, was a successful businessman and member of the city council but best remembered for the Miller Block, a handsome, two-story, red sandstone building he erected in 1888 to serve local businesses. It was complete with a two-story outhouse behind it to serve both floors of the block. Frank presumably was expected to go into his father's business, and at first he did, working in the department store that his father had started. He also converted a livery into a garage, which he ran more or less, but he developed other interests, which tended to distract him from his businesses. He loved Wild West Shows, rodeos, pioneer day parades, and all the hoopla where he could display his skill as a crack shot. He traveled with the Buffalo Bill Cody Wild West Show, according to some, and knew the Irwins, who ran the Cheyenne Frontier Days for so many years. Frank was also an artist, painting in oil, and preferred landscapes, some of which he painted to portray historical events. His views of Fort Collins are interesting to historians, but one has to make allowances, we understand, for artistic license.

His greatest venture, however, was his dude ranch, Trail's End. Here he hoped to combine all his interests and establish, at last, a successful and enjoyable business. He and his wife, Peggy, who had been in show business, too, bought the ranch in 1920. It was in a beautiful location on the North Fork of the Poudre in Cherokee Park, near the mouth of Trail Creek, with Turkey Roost Mountain as a backdrop. The Millers invested considerable money in the ranch to fix it up for guests, and it seemed to be a great success, at least at first. Evadene Swanson, in her history of Fort Collins, wrote, "The Union Pacific advertised 'Trail's End' in a special pamphlet and noted that Frank and his wife could be coaxed to give performances for guests on weekends. He really loved wild animals and arranged cages and pastures for mule and Siberian deer, buffalo, bears, owls, eagles, hawks, skunks, wolves, coyotes, and porcupines. There were ponds for ducks and geese. The trout in the north fork of the Poudre responded to the feeding. He charged $25.00 a week."

In the historical museum in Fort Collins is one of Frank Miller's paintings, showing the view from the porch of the ranch house looking out across the flower gardens toward the mountains. It is impressive. The Millers entertained many people there over the years, including Will Rogers and other famous dignitaries, it is said. But perhaps because a guest ranch requires a lot of hard work to maintain, Trail's End, after twenty years or so, became a financial failure. Today the ranch is privately owned. Frank Miller's days there are still remembered by his former friends and neighbors, but the things most talked about seem to be the cages of animals that he kept. Frank Miller died in 1953 while living alone in the Linden Hotel in Fort Collins near his father's imposing Miller Block.

Fort Collins is no longer a small country town, as its population has reached 90,000 and Greeley, too, touches on 60,000. Colorado Agricultural College has become Colorado State University, with 20,000 students. Greeley's teachers' college, founded in 1890, is now the University of Northern Colorado, but it does still train many of the state's teachers. The smaller towns along the river continue pretty much as they were, mainly agricultural communities, except for Windsor, which has acquired a branch of the Eastman Kodak Company. The river has acquired a few small dams and many diversions, but still attracts tourists to its canyons. The road over Cameron Pass is now completely paved. And life goes on!

10

THE CACHE LA POUDRE TODAY

By a mountain stream, "it is impossible to believe that one will ever be tired or old. Every sense applauds it." So wrote Wallace Stegner in *The Sound of Mountain Water*. Yet the mountain-born streams of the West are precisely what have made human endeavors possible in this semiarid land. Hence a common alternate view, that any water flowing downstream is "water wasted." This is a constant dilemma of the West, one that pits environmentalists against developers; those who opt for clean air and water against those that press for more industry and jobs; those who treasure the serenity of forests and streamsides against those who delight in roaring cross-country in off-road vehicles; those who respect the integrity of the plants, animals, and soil of natural communities against those who see these as resources to be developed. The waters of the Cache la Poudre were diverted soon after the first white settlers arrived, and they remain vital to agriculture, industry, and family life in the area. Yet the basin remains well forested, reasonably rich in wildlife, and drained by a stream that still retains, at least in the canyon, enough of its original character to justify its designation as Wild and Scenic. To a degree, those of us who live in the Poudre basin have the best of both worlds. Retaining a balance may not be easy as the human population along the Front Range continues to grow.

In this chapter we shall first consider the Poudre's waters and the ways they have been stored and diverted for human use. Thus we shall be talking about ditches, dams, reservoirs, irrigation, water law, and similar matters. We shall not include a discussion of groundwater, although this is really part of the overall picture of water use. In a later section of this chapter, we shall consider some of the less tangible values of the Poudre watershed, with special reference to plant and animal species that occur in diminished numbers. These require special attention if we hope to maintain the diversity of life that makes the Poudre basin the very special place that it is.

The Poudre as a Source of Water for Human Use

The earliest activity by whites on the river was probably that of beaver trappers in the early 1800s, but these hardy men left no record of their presence except perhaps for the river's name. Before that time various Indians, mainly Utes and Arapahoes, and still earlier Paleo-Indians, used the valleys and canyon rims as routes through the country on their hunting expeditions, leaving evidence in projectile points and other artifacts at scattered sites. In the late 1860s and the 1870s, river use increased dramatically when loggers in the high country floated logs downstream to be used as ties by the railroads.

During these same decades, settlers on the plains began to divert water into gardens and pastures as well as to the cities of Greeley (Union Colony) and Fort Collins (Agricultural Colony). That these people could not foresee the enormous problems they would be facing in trying to irrigate this arid country becomes more and more obvious when one reads such items as the following from the *New York Tribune* of April 12, 1870: "The Cache-a-la-Poudre comes down from the Rocky Mountains clear as crystal, and with little labor ice-cold water can be brought into the house of every family, for there is sufficient head to force it up the highest building. The cost of irrigation will be much less than anticipated. There is abundance of water for all mechanical purposes."

The first ditchdiggers had had little, if any, experience, and many mistakes were made. Sometimes they started at the river with a horse-drawn plow and kept just ahead of the water that followed behind. Often the ditches were narrow and had too steep a gradient, so that the flow was too swift. Initially, ditch owners took water as they pleased, causing other ditches on the river to dry up. This resulted in meetings "which could have led to bloodshed," according to William R. Kelly. Eventually the quarrels led to the formation of Colorado's water laws.

Over time, lessons were learned and ditch building became a more exact technology. Some of the early developers of irrigation systems were colorful characters. One of them, R. Q. Tenney, would often appear in water court, according to Kelly, "in boots, flannel shirt and with tousled hair [giving] him the look of a mountain man." Tenney was the first surveyor of the Laramie-Poudre Tunnel. Construction of the tunnel was to be supervised by an engineer, Wellington Hibbard, who was brought in from St. Louis, but Hibbard was killed in 1910 when his automobile ran out of control on one of the steep curves on Pingree Hill.

Irrigation canals soon were provided with decrees, "upon proper evidence." The oldest decreed one still on record is the Yeager Ditch west of Fort Collins in Bellvue, which dates from June 1, 1860. The 1870s saw the chartering of many canals in Poudre Valley, and by 1882 the basin between Laporte and the confluence with the South Platte was declared to be "one vast network of irrigating canals." One of the largest was the Larimer and Weld Canal, which was owned by a British investment company and contained three of the early plains reservoirs; in 1881 it watered 60,000 acres.

Another canal, named for someone who must have been interesting or at least notable, was built in 1861 near Windsor. It took water from the north side of the Poudre near the "old Pinkerton trading place and sod fort," and was called the Whitney (Dead Beat) Ditch.

The story of how Fort Collins acquired its waterworks is well told in a booklet, *"From Bucket to Basin": 100 Years of Water Service*, written by Molly Nortier and Michael Smith and published in 1982. Before the waterworks were built, the local citizens dipped water directly from ditches or the Poudre. Some had it delivered, first by a barrel strapped to a travois drawn by a mule, later by a horse-drawn water wagon. A bucket of water cost a nickel. But in the early 1880s, Fort Collins experienced a typhoid scare as well as several devastating fires, and the need for a waterworks intensified. A municipal election was held on April 4, 1882, the issue approved, bonds issued, and a Denver firm hired to build it. The pump house had brick walls a foot thick, and the water was taken from a ditch by one or perhaps two waterwheels. Water was pumped several miles east into town through wooden pipes, the last wooden pipe in Fort Collins not being replaced until 1982. Everything went so smoothly and quickly that barely a year after it was approved it was ready for use. On June 14, 1883, the system was tested by combining pressures from several hoses and shooting water over 140 feet up in the air. The old waterworks buildings were neglected for many years, but the city has recently stabilized the walls of the old pump house, reshingled the roof, and painted the trim close to the original color. No one seems to know about the fate of the waterwheel or wheels

— surprising in this dry country where waterwheels are certainly not common.

As for Greeley, the Union Colony members, when they first arrived, started digging ditches to water their gardens and trees. The first one to be operational was Number Three, and it took water from the south side of the river about six miles west of Greeley. Ditch Number Two was also built early by the community, took water from the north side about six miles southeast of Fort Collins, and was much larger in order to provide water for more extensive areas of benchland to the north. Number Two proved to be too small and was consequently enlarged, becoming thirty-six miles long and thirty-two feet wide on the bottom. In 1872 it was bought from Union Colony by the farmers using it and renamed the Cache la Poudre Canal, the basis for the Cache la Poudre Irrigation Company.

As the need for water grew, more ditches were built to divert the water, mainly for the benefit of agriculture, but also for the growing towns and cities. As it was purer when taken from higher up the stream, more and more "mountain reservoirs" and ditches were established. The Poudre River was overappropriated even before the turn of the century, according to some. It became obvious that still more water was needed, so simple and then more complex schemes were devised to divert "foreign" water (water from outside of the basin) into the Poudre. Most of the people of Colorado, as well as the state's most valuable agricultural lands, were (and still are) on the wrong side of the Continental Divide, since rainfall and snowfall on the eastern side are much less than on the western side. Consequently, increasing amounts of water were taken from the Western Slope, culminating in the Colorado-Big Thompson Project. For this project, begun in 1938, water was collected from tributaries of the Colorado River into the Granby and Shadow Mountain reservoirs, shunted through a tunnel under Rocky Mountain National Park, and down the canyon of the Big Thompson River, which runs parallel to, but about ten miles to the south of, the Poudre Canyon. Part of this water was then diverted into the Poudre basin by a canal and stored in Horsetooth Reservoir until needed.

The judicial and civil systems which control the distribution of water across the arid western states are complicated at best, at least to those of us who are trained neither as water lawyers nor as water engineers. In the eastern United States, where there is water in quantity

TRANSMOUNTAIN DIVERSIONS INTO THE CACHE LA POUDRE

Source	Via	Average Acre-Feet (1976–1985)
COLORADO RIVER DRAINAGE		
Colo. River Headwaters	Grand Ditch	17,429
Grand Lake, Shadow Mt. Reservoir	Adams Tunnel, Big Thompson, Horsetooth Reservoir	231,750[1]
NORTH PLATTE DRAINAGE		
Michigan River	Michigan Ditch	862
Laramie River	Skyline Ditch	1,844
Laramie River	Laramie-Poudre Tunnel	16,453
Deadman Creek (Laramie River)	Columbine Ditch	1,377
Sheep Creek (Laramie River)	Wilson Supply Ditch	1,325

Source: League of Women Voters of Colorado, 1988. Two minor ditches are omitted.
[1]But not all of this enters the Poudre system.

Joe Wright Reservoir, at 9,900 feet altitude, is the highest of the eleven mountain reservoirs in the Poudre drainage.

(if not necessarily quality), most users are served by what are called riparian rights. These, generally defined although modified for modern use, allow a landowner to use the water which is within or beside his or her property. In the West, where much property has no surface water, all water is subject to state regulation and can be taken, when properly appropriated, across great distances to a designated user or users. In Colorado, unlike most other western states, permits for water use are granted through the courts rather than the state engineer's office. As one wag has said, if you want to mine western gold these days, become a water lawyer!

Colorado is unique in other ways regarding its water law and policies. It has the highest mean elevation of any of the lower forty-eight states, and seven major river systems begin here. In fact, Coloradoans tend to regard their rivers, and the water in them, as personal property — not to be allowed to leave "home" without an argument. Over the years many of Colorado's neighboring states have taken Colorado to court to try to make the state give up more of the water from the rivers which arise in its mountains. Locally the Colorado River, the Laramie River, and the Big Thompson River all begin in the same general area of the Rockies as the Poudre. Of these the Colorado River, on the west side of the Continental Divide, is the biggest and is also the most notorious because not a drop of its water reaches the river's mouth in the Gulf of California, having been fully diverted and used. That story is nowhere better told than in *A River No More* by Philip L. Fradkin, who said that he wrote his book because, "[F]or too long, a narrow group of men has distributed the ultimate source of wealth in the West with diminishing wisdom."

In the early days of settlement, most western water, including the Poudre, was diverted into agricultural uses — "to make the desert bloom." Even today, with the tremendous growth of the population, and especially with urban growth, over 90 percent of appropriated water is still used to irrigate crops and pasture land, although perhaps less Poudre water than that (70 to 80 percent) goes into irrigation for agriculture.

The appropriation system originated "in custom" — a right to use water for a specific, beneficial purpose that could be claimed against others who later wanted to use the same limited supply. Thus the earliest proven claims (permits or decrees) are the most valuable, and when there is insufficient water to meet all needs, "senior" appropriators' rights ("first in time, first in right") are fulfilled before "junior" appropriators'. If a senior appropriator fails to divert (a requirement) and beneficially use his full complement of water, or if he changes its use, he may be challenged by juniors and may lose his rights. Needless to say, this system does not encourage water conservation.

Water rights do not go with property and may be sold separately. As water left in a stream had for so long been considered to be wasted, instream flow needs to maintain fish and other wildlife, for recreation, and for groundwater recharge were long ignored. In the last ten to twenty years, most states, including Colorado, have tried to create laws to insure instream flows by removing the requirement that water must be diverted. Water users have opposed this because they have perceived it as a threat to their "prior" water rights. In 1975 the Colorado Supreme Court ruled in favor of maintaining instream flows "to preserve the natural environment to a reasonable degree." The Colorado legislature modified the ruling in several ways, one of which was to subordinate the instream flow rights to all other rights established before the ruling. Consequently, if any state, county, or private entity wishes to maintain a flowing stream, it has to obtain (usually buy) water rights, and if they are "junior" rights, as they often are, the stream could still dry up, especially during a drought. In 1974 there was a large trout kill in the Poudre near Laporte because there was no water in the riverbed. In 1987 the city of Fort Collins requested instream flow rights for recreation, fish and wildlife habitat, and sewage dilution. To the best of our knowledge, this has not been resolved.

Today approximately $4.5 billion per year are poured into Colorado's economy by recreationists, and the tourist industry depends on the maintenance of "natural waters." This, plus the current litigation between water users and the U.S. Forest Service concerning instream flow rights through the federal lands, has caused much rethinking on how the state handles such rights.

The amount of water delivered to appropriators is determined, at least in the Poudre basin, by the depth of snowpack measured each year in early April. The amount of water that will be available is then calculated and may vary from 60 to 100 percent. If the forecast is low, the mountain reservoirs are filled first to conserve water by reducing evaporation; but if it is high, the plains reservoirs are filled first. There are approximately two hundred reservoirs within the Poudre drainage, eleven of which are in the mountains. Their capacities vary from about 90 to 18,000 acre-feet, totaling over 200,000 acre-feet. An acre-foot (the amount of water required to cover an acre of land to a depth of one foot) is equivalent to approximately 326,000 gallons, which is considered to be enough water to supply an average family of four for a year.

The Northern Colorado Water Conservancy District, which includes the Poudre basin, was established in 1937 during the era of New Deal largesse and following the dust bowl years. Because of the need to repay the U. S. Bureau of Reclamation for the costs of the Colorado-Big Thompson Project, it was given the power to tax property within its borders. It was further permitted to condemn or purchase property and water rights and to fix water rates. It was put in charge of all water delivery, including that for irrigation as well as for municipal use, and of the delivery of the hydroelectric power generated by the system.

The "Northern" was the state's first water conservancy district and created a precedent for others. Its board of directors is not elected but

The Cache la Poudre, as it flows through Fort Collins, is little more than a trickle for two-thirds of the year and a convenient dumping place.

appointed by a judge. Although appointments are made for four-year periods, they are usually renewed, such that the current trustees have served an average of 17.8 years. Efforts by environmentalists to have at least one person of their persuasion appointed have been constantly thwarted.

The power of the conservancies (this one and others around the state) has not gone unchallenged. On April 15, 1989, Friends of the Poudre, a nonprofit organization dedicated to the protection and recreational use of the river, demonstrated at one of the dams on Horsetooth Reservoir by holding a "tea party." The peaceful demonstration, like various similar ones held around the state, was named, of course, for the famous Boston Tea Party to protest "taxation without representation." There was one difference, however, as clippings of Kentucky bluegrass were dumped instead of tea. A statewide group called Taxpayers for Responsible Water Projects is working to persuade the state legislature to require all forty-six of the water conservancy districts to have their boards elected.

The Northern Colorado Water Conservancy District, representing the various ditch and water companies, is also considered today to be an influential lobbying force for water users. Since the decline of federal funding for large water projects, the conservancy district has become the organization attempting to promote and finance the various water projects.

In the Poudre basin, there are over thirty ditch and reservoir companies that have decreed water rights. The person who has the physical responsibility to deliver the water correctly is the local river commissioner. He represents the State Engineer's Office and works with the conservancy district representing the users. His work involves constant monitoring and evaluating to make certain water is distributed as allocated according to each user's rights. He also arbitrates disputes. This is the academic description, but as all western water users know, the person most closely involved with the distribution of the West's most valuable asset is the "ditch rider" or "tender." He is out in all kinds of weather, opens and closes the water gates, checks the ditches, watches the water levels, notes the gauges, and keeps everyone legal. As Fradkin has said, "[He] is the unsung hero of the West, unfairly eclipsed by the more glamorous cowboy."

According to the most recent figures available to us, the annual measurements of water in the Poudre are as follows: 1,100,000 acre-feet of water enter the Poudre basin (water which is available for use), and 400,000 acre-feet flow out of the Poudre into the Platte River, which leaves 700,000 to be utilized. Through various measuring devices, we know that 3,000,000 acre-feet of water are used from the river, making the total 3,400,000 acre-feet. This is possible, of course, because water is used three times as a result of return flows from irrigation ditches and wastewater treatment facilities.

So why are we interested in all these numbers? We are interested because periodically there are attempts to increase the amount of water available for users. Historically these users have been in the Poudre basin, but recently the possibility has arisen of selling some of the Poudre's water to cities outside the area, mainly Denver suburbs. Water advocates claim that more water, as well as hydroelectric power, will be needed in the future as the population increases. Perhaps they are right, although the U.S. Census Bureau estimated that about 15,000 more people moved out of Colorado than moved in between mid-1988 and mid-1989.

Big water projects, especially huge dams, are expensive, and now that it is difficult to obtain federal funds to pay all or even part of the expense, local governments as well as the individual water users are finding their water too expensive — or, as they say, "not cost-effective." A good example is the Windy Gap project. In 1969, six Front Range cities, including Fort Collins and Greeley, went together to build a dam and pumping facility at the confluence of the Fraser and Colorado rivers near Granby on the Western Slope. This facility could provide 18 million gallons of water a year to the Front Range through the Colorado-Big Thompson system. This water proved to be so expensive that Fort Collins quickly sold its share, and Greeley has sold part of its share to a Denver suburb. Fort Collins said it really did not foresee a need for so much water (as Windy Gap would have provided), and it enlarged one of its mountain reservoirs (Joe Wright) to provide a lesser but adequate supply. Halligan Reservoir on the North Fork of the Poudre is under consideration for enlargement in the future.

Another story concerns a dam proposal on the Platte River slightly downstream from the mouth of the Poudre but still on the high plains of Colorado. It is told in great detail in *Cadillac Desert,* by Marc Reisner. Because of continued interest in more water by users and the constant argument between Colorado and its neighbors over rights ("don't allow a drop of Colorado water to reach Nebraska, or Kansas, or Wyoming"), the U.S. Bureau of Reclamation proposed in the mid-1970s to build a dam on the Platte just above Fort Morgan. This would keep more Colorado water in the state and increase irrigation water for local agriculture. Costs had not been estimated. At about this same time (1976), the Teton Dam, built by the bureau on the Snake River in Idaho, collapsed, resulting in many deaths and great loss of property. So a meeting was called in Denver to consider the safety of the proposed dam on the Platte. State Engineer Clarence J. Kuiper was included, of course, and was asked for his opinion. Kuiper, whose whole career had been in water development and who was greatly respected throughout the state for his expertise and fairness, was the state's top official regarding water matters. His opinion was important, as ultimately he would be the person responsible for the success (or failure) of the dam. He said that the alluvial bed under the river at the proposed site was huge, and without a lot of earth-moving there would be nothing to which a dam could be anchored. Seepage would be tremendous. "If they build the dam," he is reported to have said, "those Fort Morganites had better learn to swim." Federal and state officials were stunned, but the state engineer would not back down. The dam has never been built, but Kuiper, admitting he was tired of the constant hassle, retired early.

A well-known water engineering firm hired him according to Marc Reisner, but he has never been allowed to work in Colorado since, depriving Colorado of a very capable water engineer who is especially knowledgeable about the state and its water.

Today 400,000 acre-feet of water from the Poudre River basin still flow into the Platte and eventually into Nebraska. In an article in the *New York Times,* the U.S. Bureau of Reclamation stated that a new (1989) policy was being initiated whereby the bureau would "serve as a facilitator for water marketing proposals between willing buyers and sellers." Water problems, including those of the Poudre River, will be an ongoing concern in the arid West.

There are currently no dams on the main stem of the Poudre, all of the reservoirs being on tributaries or off channel. The possibilities of building dams in the canyon has long been debated. In 1982 the Colorado Water Conservation Board presented six alternatives for increasing water storage and producing hydroelectric power on the Poudre based on studies by the Tudor Engineering Company of Denver. One of these would have involved a dam just below Kinikinik, another dam at Indian Meadows, and a third dam in the area around Dutch George Flats; each would involve a lengthy conduit to a reservoir lower in the canyon. We attended several meetings in which CWCB members described the projects and listened to public responses. There was standing room only at each meeting, and many were eager to respond — almost all negatively. Local environmentalists formed a group called "Save Our Poudre" and sold T-shirts suitably emblazoned. "Dam meets wall of criticism" headlined the Fort Collins *Coloradoan* on February 24, 1983, and then on March 4, "Board rejects canyon dams." Lack of economic feasibility was the main reason given for setting aside these proposals.

Into the middle of these proposed increased uses of the Poudre and its water came the idea of making the river the first on the Front Range to be Wild and Scenic, to preserve at least the upper part from being changed from a pristine, or near pristine, state of beauty. As specified in the 1968 National Wild and Scenic River Systems Act, wild rivers should possess "outstandingly scenic, recreational, geologic, fish and wildlife, historic, cultural, or other similar values, [and] shall be preserved in free-flowing condition." Further, the act stated that such

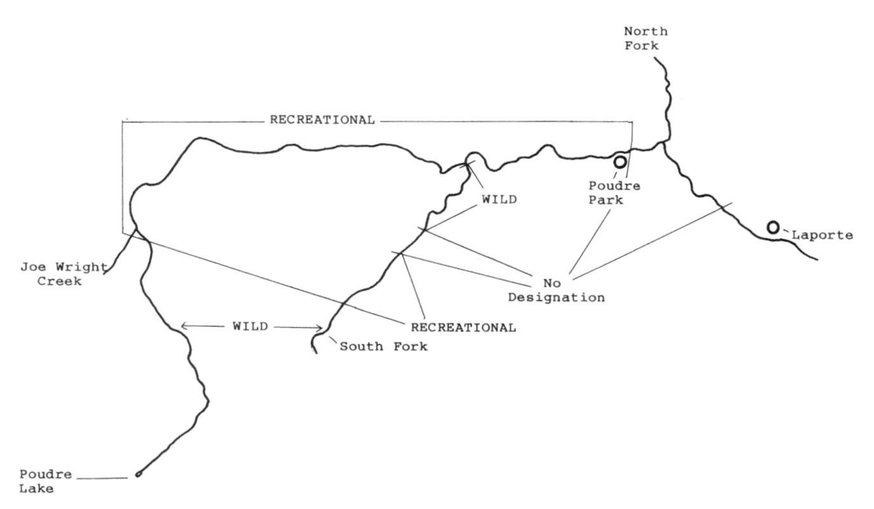

The Cache la Poudre as designated Wild and Scenic in 1986.

rivers and "their immediate environments shall be protected for the benefit and enjoyment of present and future generations."

And so, in October 1985, U.S. Representative Hank Brown from Greeley presented to the 99th Congress a bill to designate at least some of the Poudre as Wild and Scenic. The bill was approved first in the House and then the Senate and finally signed into law by the president on October 30, 1986. The law, which had been a compromise between developers and environmentalists, designated thirty miles as "wild" and forty-five as "recreational." The wild section begins at the source in Rocky Mountain National Park and continues eighteen miles down to Joe Wright Creek; it also includes parts of the South Fork. These areas are free of roads and other developments. The recreational designation applies to the section on the main stem which is paralleled by the highway and runs from Joe Wright Creek past innumerable small communities to just below the little settlement of Poudre Park, which is about eight miles upstream from the mouth of the canyon. Thus the Cache la Poudre River became not only the first river on the Front Range but the first river in Colorado to be added to the National Wild and Scenic River System. The legislation also called for a further study of the section of the river from the western edge of Fort Collins east to the Larimer/Weld county line to determine whether it could or should become a National Recreation Area.

While the Wild and Scenic designation will keep any further dams from being built on most of the river in the mountains, it does not keep the lower part from being further dammed or diverted. Currently the Northern Colorado Water Conservancy District is proposing a project that includes three new reservoirs. One, to be called Glade Reservoir, would not be in the canyon. The proposed location is in Hook and Moore Glade, which runs between hogbacks from a mile or so north of the mouth of the Poudre Canyon to the Owl Canyon highway cut. U.S. Highway 287, which now passes through there on its way from Fort Collins to Laramie, would have to be rerouted. That reservoir would be for water storage only and is projected to have a 350,000-acre-feet capacity. The second proposed dam, Grey Mountain, would be built in the canyon (about five miles above the mouth) and form a reservoir to hold 200,000 acre-feet. State Highway 14 would have to be moved out of that part of the canyon. The third reservoir would be formed west of Greyrock Mountain, which towers about 1,400 feet above the river. It would be used to hold water pumped up from Grey Mountain Reservoir during low electricity demand times, and then at high demand (peak) times, water would be released from it down through a 2,100-megawatt facility to generate electricity.

It is projected that if such dams are built, it will take ten to twenty years to complete the project. When finished, the Grey Mountain Reservoir would submerge the lower canyon of the main stem for about seven and a half miles, and the North Fork, including Seaman Reservoir, up to an elevation of 5,600 feet. Meanwhile, a dam and two dikes in Greyrock Meadow would flood about two hundred acres of the meadow to a level of approximately 7,000 feet. Greyrock Mountain (altitude 7,613 feet) would be surrounded by a large industrial complex, including a power station, switchyard, surge chamber, conduits, and tunnels. Since this proposal was first presented, there have been a few changes made, mainly to try to reduce probable costs. There had been hopes that electricity sales would pay for the project, but at present this seems unlikely. As we have mentioned, earlier plans to dam the Poudre were abandoned because of expense. Because Colorado's economy is slow, the same fate may befall these dam proposals, at least in the near future. But we are biologists and not economists!

The Poudre Basin as Habitat for People and for Plants and Animals

For people who live by or who visit the Cache la Poudre, these are the best of times in the best of places. No longer must they endure the hardships of the pioneers; the wildlife is no longer a threat, but something to cherish. There is water for everyone. Roads and trails make most parts of the basin easily accessible, yet great sections are preserved in seminatural condition by being part of Rocky Mountain National Park or Roosevelt National Forest, the latter including four wilderness areas. A major part of the Poudre and its South Fork have been designated Wild and Scenic, and The Nature Conservancy has preserved Phantom Canyon on the North Fork

No matter that the Poudre is very different than it was before whites arrived. Seven transmountain diversions add "foreign" water during the warmer months; there are eleven mountain reservoirs, innumerable plains reservoirs, and a network of irrigation ditches that defy comprehension. Some of these ditches and reservoirs actually increase diversity of species by providing wetlands not previously available. And wilderness, as we all know, is a relative term. As Wallace Stegner has said, "the conservationists who created our national wilderness system knew from the beginning that by this date [1964], wilderness in America is an approximation only."

Early settlers and tie cutters found the streams to be filled with native greenback cutthroat trout and the forests sometimes too abundantly filled with game. "The lumbermen of the Upper Poudre lead a wild and adventurous life," reported *The Denver News* on July 28, 1875. "When the winter snows drive game down from the range, their cabins are actually surrounded by night and by day. Then every cabin is an arsenal, and guns are loaded for protection as well as for game. Mountain lions roar around them."

When ranchers began to run cattle in the upper Poudre valleys, they became sufficiently alarmed to press the state legislature for protection from predators. In 1889 a law was passed providing a bounty of one dollar for each wolf or coyote killed and a bounty of ten dollars for each bear or mountain lion. The law attracted professional hunters, and within a few years the threat of predators was gone. Populations of deer, elk, bighorn sheep, turkeys, and other game birds and mammals were also greatly decimated over the next few decades.

River otters are playful animals that do not often pose for a photograph. Those in the Poudre are doing well, though small in numbers and not often seen. *Photo by David Leatherman.*

Some of the larger mammals of the Poudre are now extinct (though still surviving elsewhere). Bison now occur only in fenced pastures, and gray wolves, grizzly bears, and wolverines are gone. Many would agree that this is for the best. These animals are potentially dangerous to humans, and most of us would prefer not to confront a grizzly on a trail near our homes. Too bad we cannot get rid of a few other, lesser nuisances, such as wood ticks, mountain pine beetles, and mistletoe. However, the elimination of any species has ecological consequences, however subtle, so it is dangerous to draft a list of species we could do without.

More profitable is a listing of animals and plants that seem to be tottering on the verge of local or of total extinction, or at least occurring in numbers so small that we need to be concerned that they may soon be lost. We have mentioned several of these in earlier chapters and present here a partial list of species that deserve special consideration in the Poudre basin.

Mammals

- River otter (listed by the state as endangered)

- Pygmy shrew (a subarctic species known from a few sites in the Poudre basin)

Birds

- Peregrine falcon (listed federally as endangered)
- Bald eagle (listed federally as endangered)
- Boreal owl (a subarctic species with limited populations in the Poudre basin)

Amphibians

- Wood frog (listed by the state as threatened)
- Boreal toad (western toad) (declining in numbers)
- Northern leopard frog (numbers greatly reduced)

Fish

- Greenback cutthroat trout (listed by the state and federally as threatened)
- Johnny darter (state "special concern")
- Iowa darter (few Colorado records)

Smoky-eyed brown butterfly.

Insects

- Steven's tortricid moth (*Decodes stevensii*) (known only from the Owl Canyon pinyon grove; under federal review for listing)
- Smoky eyed brown butterfly (*Satyrodes eurydice fumosa*) (listed in the Federal Register of Wildlife under review for listing as endangered or threatened)

- Two-spotted skipper butterfly (*Euphyes bimacula*) (an eastern species with an isolated population in the lower Poudre basin; state "special concern")

Plants

- Larimer aletes (*Aletes humilis)* (occurs in a few small populations in the Poudre basin, at one site in Boulder County, and one site in Albany County, Wyoming; under federal review; state "special concern")
- Bells' twinpod (*Physaria bellii*) (very limited range; under federal review; state "special concern")
- Purple-stem cliff-brake (*Pellaea atropurpurea*) (listed as rare in Colorado)
- Rock-cliff cinquefoil (*Potentilla rupincola*) (listed by state as threatened; occurs on a few rocky cliffs in the North Fork drainage, rarely elsewhere in the state)
- Golden-fruit hawthorn (*Crataegus chrysocarpa*) (listed as rare in Colorado)

This list could easily be expanded. The Colorado Native Plant Society has recently published a beautifully illustrated book that covers nearly one hundred rare plants of Colorado. Included are several species that occur (or once occurred) in the Poudre basin but are not listed above: wood lily, tulip gentian, twayblade orchid, and Colorado butterfly weed. The Colorado Native Plant Society includes both amateur and professional members who are dedicated to preserving as much of the state's floral diversity as possible. Their book fittingly concludes with the words of Harvard biologist E. O. Wilson: "the loss of genetic and species diversity by the destruction of natural habitats . . . is the folly our descendants are least likely to forgive us."

With respect to insects, the fauna has by no means been fully explored. In earlier chapters we mentioned mayflies and caddisflies yet to be named, as well as a stonefly just recently named. We ourselves have recently discovered and named a spider-hunting wasp that occupied an artificial wooden boring attached to the deck of our house. We called it *Dipogon lignicolus* (meaning two-beard that lives in wood, "two-beard" because the female has a pair of mouth brushes that help her carry particles used in nest construction). Among the prey of a predatory fly we have been studying, we found a tiny bagworm moth that belongs to an undescribed genus with its closest relatives in Eurasia.

Concerning larger and more familiar animals, it must be remembered that in many cases populations result from reintroductions of species that had once been eliminated from the Poudre basin, or nearly so: elk, moose, bighorn sheep, wild turkeys, and trout. Those of us who enjoy the outdoors often feel frustrated during hunting seasons, when the woods seem full of people bent on killing animals we admire. But it is the Colorado Division of Wildlife, which receives nearly all its funding from hunting and fishing licenses (over half from out-of-state hunting licenses), that is responsible for the management of game, and its efforts over the years have resulted in the enhancement of wildlife for everyone. It is reported that in the early 1900s, there were in the state only about 5,600 elk, 8,000 deer, and 1,000 pronghorns. The numbers are now more like 200,000 elk, 600,000 deer, and 60,000 pronghorns. And we would have no bighorns, turkeys, moose, or river otters in the Poudre basin without reintroduction by the Colorado Division of Wildlife.

It is true that hunting practices could be improved. Shooting from vehicles is reprehensible, and it is regrettable that unsportsmanlike behavior such as baiting for black bears and mountain lions remains legal. And there is far too much illegal hunting. Budgets for the Colorado Division of Wildlife are scarcely adequate to patrol the woods and fields for poachers. In Colorado as a whole, loss of habitat resulting from human population growth and the desire of many to escape to the hills or to enjoy forms of recreation that are destructive to the environment (such as the use of off-road vehicles) is a factor that cannot be reasoned away. In an average year in the 1980s, 117,000 Colorado acres were lost to building and highway construction and to ski developments, to say nothing of the loss of pure and free-flowing streams as a result of pollution and damming.

The Poudre basin would appear to be immune to habitat loss, since so much of it is ostensibly protected. But it is not the time for environmentalists to relax their vigil. The U.S. Forest Service has been known to exchange parcels of land with little fanfare, as well as to engage in practices deleterious to watersheds and to wildlife. Designation of the river as Wild and Scenic is reassuring, but we well remember efforts to place dams in Dinosaur National Monument and Grand Canyon National Park, when only uproars by the Sierra Club and similar organizations prevented them from becoming a reality. Even so, the Colorado River as it flows through Grand Canyon has become "the ultimate ditch in the effort to transport water from Lake Powell to Lake Mead," according to Philip L. Fradkin. As for planned dams on lower Poudre Canyon made possible by the compromise when the upper canyon was declared Wild and Scenic, perhaps someday an off-channel reservoir such as Glade may be justified. But it would be foolish to accept the statement by the general manager of the Northern Colorado Water Conservancy District that dams here are "inevitable."

What is good for the Northern Colorado Water Conservancy may or may not be good for you and for us and is not likely to be any good at all for wildlife and wildflowers, never forgetting that ecosystems, once destroyed, can never be restored. Nowadays we hear much talk of compensating for loss of habitat by "mitigation" (definition: the alleviation of pain). What is usually meant is that if a dam is built and a canyon flooded, an effort will be made to provide equally good hunting, fishing, and rafting elsewhere. That the *canyon* can be reproduced elsewhere is, of course, nonsense. Natural ecosystems contain innumerable subtle interdependencies that can never be duplicated by our crude machinations. We have built giant earthmovers but cannot build a pasque flower, to say nothing of a mountain meadow with its myriad of plants, insects, birds, and mammals, or a stream with its own diverse fauna and flora.

There is a danger of another sort, the danger that the Poudre basin will be loved to death. To designate a river as Wild and Scenic or a forest as wilderness is to invite people to come and see — which is fine up to a point. Rocky Mountain National Park's campgrounds are full throughout the summer, and camping in the back country requires standing in line for a permit. On summer weekends the demand for campsites in Poudre Canyon is almost twice the supply of developed campsites, resulting in much camping in undesignated sites that produces erosion and pollution along the river. Backcountry trails are often littered with trash and spotted with old fire rings. Use of the river for recreation has increased at a steady rate. The Poudre has the second highest fishing use in the state, averaging 43,000 user days per year. Over 9,000 people enjoyed guided rafting or kayaking from five commercial enterprises in 1989. Ironically, it is the recreational opportunities of the Poudre and other Rocky Mountain rivers that attract many people to the cities of the Front Range, increasing pressure to harness the water for the cities.

But there are causes for optimism. Upon the designation of the Poudre as Wild and Scenic, the U.S. Forest Service was required to prepare a management plan for the sixty-one miles within Roosevelt National Forest. The process is now under way, and efforts are being made to improve opportunities within the forty-five-mile, half-mile-wide corridor that has been declared "recreational" and to enhance the wilderness experience in the sixteen miles declared "wild" (another fourteen miles of wild river are in Rocky Mountain National Park). It is hoped to approximately double the campground capacity along State Highway 14 in the canyon by adding two new campgrounds and expanding others. Picnic areas, trails for hiking, biking, and horseback riding, and accesses to the river for boat launching will all be expanded. There will be nature trails and interpretive signs. Visitors in the future can look forward to more regulation and more user fees, but this is surely preferable to increased degradation of this precious environment.

The Colorado Division of Wildlife has recently become concerned with nonconsumptive uses of wildlife, that is, the use of the fields and forests by bird and mammal watchers, native plant enthusiasts, photographers, and persons simply out for a hike and hoping to glimpse an elk, a bighorn, or something as simple as an unusual display of lichens on a rock. In 1973 the Colorado legislature enacted the Nongame and Endangered Species Act, which permitted the Colorado Division of Wildlife to employ two specialists in this field. In 1977 a nongame state income tax checkoff was initiated, the first in the nation. Several million dollars have now been raised through the checkoff, some of it used to obtain federal matching funds. Understandably most programs on nongame wildlife have been directed toward visible and popular birds and mammals such as peregrine falcons and river otters, but there are ongoing surveys of reptiles, mollusks, and even algae.

In 1977 the Colorado legislature established the Natural Areas Program, designed to protect rare and threatened natural features in Colorado through cooperative agreements between landowners and the Colorado Division of Natural Resources. Some sixty-two areas have been included in the program as of 1987. Two of these are in the Poudre drainage: the Owl Canyon Pinyon Grove and the Specimen Mountain Natural Area. The program supplies listings of these areas as well as of plant and animal species of special concern.

In 1987 the governor of Colorado assembled the Executive Task Force on the Future of Wildlife in Colorado, called Wildlife 21, since

Workers from the Division of Wildlife sometimes make controlled burns to improve habitat for bighorn sheep and other wildlife. *Courtesy of the U.S. Forest Service.*

it addressed the future of wildlife into the twenty-first century. New sources of funding would clearly be needed, since hunters and anglers cannot be expected to support passive users such as bird watchers and wildflower fanciers. Suggested were taxes on noncommercial automobiles, including recreational vehicles, snowmobiles, and other off-road vehicles, as well as small excise taxes on binoculars, hiking boots, backpacks, and even birdseed. The key phrase in the new program will be "Watchable Wildlife," and the hope is to produce brochures and guidebooks to wildlife as well as interpretive trails, all of this to be funded by "those who most enjoy the benefits."

On a chilly April day, we were fortunate to be able to join a field trip sponsored by the Watchable Wildlife program of the Colorado Division of Wildlife. We traveled up Poudre Valley as far as Chambers Lake, then still deep in snow. We learned of some of the management practices being used to enhance wildlife, including controlled burns designed to improve grazing opportunities for bighorn sheep. Sheep were plentiful on several south-facing slopes along the canyon, and there were mule deer, hawks, mergansers, and other wildlife. Without a doubt the greatest pleasure was simply spending a day with a group of professionals and amateurs all of whom were wildlife enthusiasts.

The Watchable Wildlife Program concentrates on wildlife with little attempt to define what is meant by that word (surely a bumblebee or a yellow violet is both wild and watchable). Nor is there much consideration of the conditions that make for viable habitats for plants and animals — or for quality habitats for people. Predators such as eagles and mountain lions require smaller birds and mammals as food; deer and elk require bitterbrush and mountain-mahogany for winter browse; songbirds require seeds and insects; wildflowers require bees and flies for pollination. Plants are the primary producers both on land and in the water; insects and small birds and mammals are primary consumers, and so on up the food chain to the top predators. Implicit in the definition of an ecosystem is energy flow, beginning with the sun and passing through plants up the several levels of the food chain, all in a matrix of fertile soil and clear waters. Food chains contain both generalist feeders, such as many grasshoppers and insectivorous birds, and specialists, such as Townsend's solitaires, which require juniper berries as winter sustenance. All food chains contain detritivores — organisms that consume organic wastes and dead plants and animals. Thus there is a need for bacteria, fungi, dung beetles, and turkey vultures. Even the simplest ecosystem provides a bewildering array of interrelationships.

Environmental changes often foretell events that may influence our lives. In an earlier chapter, we spoke of lichens as indicators of air pollution. Currently there is much concern over the unexplained decline in populations of boreal toads and leopard frogs. "What are the toads telling us?" asks William Stolzenburg of the National Wildlife Federation in a recent issue of *Colorado Outdoors*. One explanation for their decline may be acid rain, perhaps concentrated in a spring surge when the snow melts. Others are toxins in the air which are absorbed in the moist and sensitive skin of these amphibians. Or perhaps these are simply normal, long-term population fluctuations; there are no long-range data that enable us to judge whether this might be so. As Stolzenburg points out, frogs and toads are to be cherished not just as possible indicators, but for the roles they play in nature. A frog eats many insects, and a pond full of frogs can consume most of the mosquito larvae; furthermore frogs and toads serve as food for snakes and for many birds and mammals.

There is much to be learned about what species occur in the Poudre basin and what roles they play in the complex webs of life. Researchers at universities along the Front Range, as well as those at the Colorado Division of Wildlife and the U. S. Forest Service, have been studying the fauna and flora of the area for many years. They will not soon run out of things to study. Entomologists by inclination and training, we have been studying wasps that prey on diverse insects and spiders. One of these proved to be an exclusive predator on western tent caterpillars that disfigure and sometimes kill bushes and trees in the foothills each spring — bushes that deer require for browse. Another preys on defoliating larvae such as those of spruce budworms that periodically cause the death of many Douglas-firs. These and others play little-appreciated roles in regulating populations of destructive insects that might, in their absence, do far more damage than they commonly do. Research of this nature is usually done as a labor of love, for there is little public support for solving problems not of obvious and immediate importance. Meaningful research must usually be conducted in places that are relatively undisturbed. Many of the wasps we study nest in the ground and cannot survive in places trampled by cattle, for example.

Why is it important to learn more about the fauna and flora of the Poudre basin — or anywhere else? Most basically it is because we humans have taken our place in a world containing tens of thousands of other creatures that evolved along with us and impinge on our lives in innumerable and often unexpected ways. Yet the natural world is inexorably slipping away as our numbers and our desires for luxuries-become-necessities expand. That we should let it disappear to the point that we live (or try to live) in a wholly artificial environment — without ever having fully inventoried and understood the world we have replaced — is to thinking people, well, unthinkable.

Of course one does not need to be an entomologist, an ornithologist, or even a biologist in the broadest sense to appreciate and enjoy the Cache la Poudre and the wonderful country it drains. To sensate persons, there are not only the pleasures of the seasons — the first spring beauties appearing where the snows have melted back; the return of the nighthawks in June; the turning of the aspens; the first fresh snows on the peaks — but there are always surprises — a wildflower never seen before, occasioning a rush to the field guides; a snowy egret on a plains reservoir; a glimpse of a marten in a subalpine forest. To persons who crave a less passive experience in the wild, there are trails for vigorous hiking and cross-country skiing, the river to be rafted or kayaked, and of course hunting and fishing. Nature is inex-

The Cache la Poudre is ideal for rafters with minimum experience — and parts of it for more experienced rafters and kayakers. *Courtesy of the U.S. Forest Service.*

haustibly rewarding. That this is so sometimes escapes the attention of those who live in the mushrooming cities that nestle beneath their canopies of carbon monoxide and particulates. All too often, nature is seen as merely a source of fuels, minerals, building materials, and space for shopping malls.

Nature does have other values, not only recreational but also aesthetic, scientific, symbolic, even religious, and should also be valued for its future resource potential — the genetic diversity we may someday need to enrich our food supplies; still to be discovered natural chemicals that may serve as drugs or natural pesticides; examples of living in harsh environments that may someday serve as models for us. That nature has intrinsic values — that species and ecosystems may have their own "right to life" — is a thought alien to most people, though being eloquently espoused by a few. Is it too much to hope that the majority may someday be convinced of the need for an ethic of the environment, a belief that we are part of a complex web of life that can be violated only so far before we find that we have irretrievably violated our own humanity?

Spring has come again to the Cache la Poudre. Mountain bluebirds flash on the hillsides and chipmunks scurry among the rocks. The aspens are hung with catkins, and on warm slopes pasque flowers and Easter daisies are in bloom. Once again free of ice, the river whispers quietly, as if saving its energies for the tumult soon to come, when the snows melt in the high country. Then the stream will speak more loudly, reminding us that it is the architect of this canyon, the wherewithal of everything that lives here. There will be rafters riding its currents, anglers probing its pools, hikers exploring its side canyons, a cohabitation of man and nature that is all too rare in a society that often seems to spin upon itself, forgetful of its heritage and its ultimate sustenance. Summer's exuberance will pass; autumn will bring gold to the aspen leaves, winter its arctic blasts; then another spring. Whatever new directions human history may by then have taken, the river will be there, the pines soughing in the wind, the birds singing the same songs, the wildflowers attracting bees and setting seed. And we shall need them.

REFERENCES

GENERAL

Arno, S. F., and R. P. Hammerly. 1984. *Timberline: Mountain and Arctic Forest Frontiers*. Seattle: The Mountaineers.

Arps, L. W., and E. E. Kingery. 1977. *High Country Names*. Estes Park, Colo.: Rocky Mountain Nature Association.

Austin, Mary. [1903] 1961. *The Land of Little Rain*. New York: Doubleday Anchor.

Burroughs, John. 1951. *John Burroughs' America*. F. A. Wiley, ed. New York: Doubleday Anchor.

Cassells, E. S. 1983. *The Archaeology of Colorado*. Boulder: Johnson Books.

Chronic, J., and H. Chronic. 1972. Prairie Peak and Plateau: A Guide to the Geology of Colorado. *Colorado Geological Survey Bulletin* 32. Denver: Colorado Geological Survey.

Cushman, R. C., and S. R. Jones. 1988. *The Shortgrass Prairie*. Boulder: Pruett Publishing Co.

Doig, Ivan. 1980. *Winter Brothers: A Season at the Edge of America*. San Diego: Harcourt Brace Jovanovich.

Eiseley, Loren. 1957. *The Immense Journey*. 2d printing. New York: Random House.

Fradkin, P. A. 1981. *A River No More*. New York: Knopf.

Gibbons, Euell. 1971. *Stalking the Good Life: My Love Affair with Nature*. New York: D. McKay Co.

Gray, J. S., S. A. Grillos, C. Tresner, J. Paulmeno, and F. Hall, eds. 1976. *The Poudre River*. Denver: The Gro-Pub Group.

Hagen, Mary. 1984. *Larimer County Place Names: A History of Names on County Maps*. Fort Collins: Fort Collins Corral of Westerners.

McPhee, John. 1986. *Rising from the Plains*. New York: Farrar, Straus, Giroux.

Marr, J. W. 1967. *Ecosystems of the East Slope of the Front Range in Colorado*. University of Colorado Studies, Series in Biology, no. 8. Boulder: University of Colorado Press.

Mills, E. A. 1911. *The Spell of the Rockies*. Boston: Houghton Mifflin.

Muir, John. [1894] 1961. *The Mountains of California*. New York: Doubleday Anchor.

Mutel, C. F., and J. C. Emerick. 1984. *From Grassland to Glacier: The Natural History of Colorado*. Boulder: Johnson Books.

Ramaley, Francis. 1927. *Colorado Plant Life*. Boulder: University of Colorado Press.

Reisner, Marc. 1986. *Cadillac Desert: The American West and Its Disappearing Water*. New York: Viking Penguin.

Rennicke, Jeff. 1985. *The Rivers of Colorado*. Billings and Helena, Mont.: Falcon Press.

Richmond, G. M. 1974. *Raising the Roof of the Rockies*. Estes Park, Colo.: Rocky Mountain Nature Association.

Seton, E.T. [1929] 1953. *Lives of Game Animals*. Boston: C. T. Branford.

Stegner, Wallace. [1969] 1985. *The Sound of Mountain Water*. Lincoln: University of Nebraska Press.

Thoreau, H. D. [1850] 1961. *The Heart of Thoreau's Journals*. Odell Shepard, ed. New York: Dover Publications, Inc.

———. [1864] 1940. *The Maine Woods*. From *The Works of Henry D. Thoreau*. New York: Thomas Y. Crowell.

United States Department of Agriculture, Forest Service, Arapaho and Roosevelt National Forests. 1982 and 1985. *Cache la Poudre Wild and Scenic River. Final Environmental Impact Statement and Study Report*. Washington, D.C.: U.S. Government Printing Office.

United States Department of Agriculture, Forest Service, Arapaho and Roosevelt National Forests, Estes-Poudre Ranger District. 1990. *Cache la Poudre Wild and Scenic River Final Management Plan*. Fort Collins, Colo.: U.S. Forest Service.

Whitney, Gleaves. 1983. *Colorado Front Range: A Landscape Divided*. Boulder: Johnson Books.
Zwinger, Ann. 1981. *Beyond the Aspen Grove*. New York: Harper and Row.
Zwinger, A. H., and B. E. Willard. 1972. *Land Above the Trees: A Guide to American Alpine Tundra*. New York: Harper and Row.

Field Guides and Aids to Identification

Armstrong, D. M. 1987. *Rocky Mountain Mammals: A Handbook of Mammals of Rocky Mountain National Park and Vicinity*. Boulder: Colorado Associated University Press.
Beckman, W. C. [1952] 1974. *Guide to the Fishes of Colorado*. Denver: Colorado Game and Fish Department. Reprint. Boulder: University of Colorado Museum.
Borror, D. J., and R. E. White. 1970. *A Field Guide to the Insects of America North of Mexico*. Boston: Houghton Mifflin.
Colorado Native Plant Society. 1989. *Rare Plants of Colorado*. Estes Park, Colo.: Colorado Native Plant Society and Rocky Mountain Nature Association.
Craighead, J. J., F. C. Craighead, and R. J. Davis. 1963. *A Field Guide to Rocky Mountain Wildflowers*. Boston: Houghton Mifflin.
Everhart, W. H., and W. R. Seaman. 1971. *Fishes of Colorado*. Denver: Colorado Game, Fish, and Parks Division.
Ferris, C. D., and F. M. Brown. 1980. *Butterflies of the Rocky Mountain States*. Norman: University of Oklahoma Press.
Hammerson, G. A. 1986. *Amphibians and Reptiles in Colorado*. Denver: Colorado Division of Wildlife.
Harrington, H. D. 1967. *Edible Native Plants of the Rocky Mountains*. Albuquerque: University of New Mexico Press.
Lechleitner, R. R. 1969. *Wild Mammals of Colorado*. Boulder: Pruett Publishing Co.
Moore, Michael. 1979. *Medicinal Plants of the Mountain West*. Santa Fe: Museum of New Mexico Press.
National Geographic Society. 1983. *Field Guide to the Birds of North America*. Washington, D.C.: National Geographic Society.
Nelson, R. A. 1970. *Plants of Rocky Mountain National Park*. Estes Park, Colo.: Rocky Mountain Nature Association.
Peattie, D. C. 1953. *A Natural History of Western Trees*. Cambridge, Mass.: The Riverside Press.
Pennak, R. W. 1978. *Fresh-water Invertebrates of the United States*. 2d ed. New York: Wiley.
Peterson, R. T. 1961. *A Field Guide to Western Birds*. 2d ed. Boston: Houghton Mifflin.
Tilden, J. W., and A. C. Smith. 1986. *A Field Guide to Western Butterflies*. Boston: Houghton Mifflin.
Ward, J. V. 1985. *An Illustrated Guide to the Mountain Stream Insects of Colorado*. Fort Collins: Self-published.
Weber, W. A. 1972. *Rocky Mountain Flora: A Field Guide for the Identification of the Ferns, Conifers, and Flowering Plants of the Southern Rocky Mountains*. 4th ed. Boulder: Colorado Associated University Press.
Woodling, John. 1985. *Colorado's Little Fish*. Denver: Colorado Division of Wildlife.

Historical

Ahlbrandt, A., and K. Stieben, eds. 1987. *The History of Larimer County, Colorado*. Vol. 2. Dallas: Curtis Media Corp.
Ashley, W. H. [1822–38] 1964. *The West of William H. Ashley*. D. L. Morgan, ed. Denver: Old West Publishing Co.
Borland, Hal. [1956] 1984. *High, Wide and Lonesome*. Boston: G. K. Hall and Co.

Boyd, David. 1890. *A History: Greeley and the Union Colony of Colorado*. Greeley: Greeley Tribune Press.

Buchholtz, C. W. 1983. *Rocky Mountain National Park: A History*. Boulder: Colorado Associated University Press.

Croy, Homer. 1957. *The Lady from Colorado*. New York: Duell, Sloan, and Pearce.

Cutright, P. R. 1969. *Lewis and Clark: Pioneering Naturalists*. Urbana: University of Illinois Press.

Darnell, C. W. 1966. *Three Ranch Children*. Mimeographed.

Edwards, W. H. 1868–97. *The Butterflies of North America*. 3 vols. Boston: Houghton Mifflin.

Evans, H. E. 1987. Remembering Pioneer Naturalists. In *On Nature*, edited by Daniel Halpern. San Francisco: North Point Press.

Ewan, Joseph. 1950. *Rocky Mountain Naturalists*. Denver: University of Denver Press.

Frémont, J. C. [1844] 1988. *The Exploring Expedition to the Rocky Mountains*. Reprint. Washington, D.C.: Smithsonian Institution Press.

Fry, N. W. 1954. *Cache la Poudre "The River" as Seen from 1889*. 2d printing. Privately published.

Hafen, L. R. 1965–1972. *The Mountain Men and the Fur Trade of the Far West*. 10 vols. Glendale, Calif.: Arthur H. Clark Co.

Irving, Washington. [1836] 1982. *Astoria, or Anecdotes of an Enterprise Beyond the Rocky Mountains*. 2 vols. Philadelphia: Carey, Lee, and Blanchard.

Jessen, Kenneth. 1982. *Railroads of Northern Colorado*. Boulder: Pruett Publishing Co.

Kelly, W. R. 1967. Engineers and Ditch Men Developed on the Cache la Poudre, 1870–1920. Mimeographed.

L'Amour, Louis. 1982. *The Cherokee Trail*. New York: Bantam.

Larimer County Stockgrowers Association. 1956. *Larimer County Stockgrowers Association, 1884–1956*. Privately printed.

Lewis, M., and W. Clark. 1904. *Original Journals of the Lewis and Clark Expedition*. R. G. Thwaites, ed. 8 vols. New York: Dodd, Mead and Co.

Madson, John. 1985. *Up on the River: An Upper Mississippi Chronicle*. New York: Nick Lyons Books.

Metropolitan Museum of Art. 1987. *American Paradise: The World of the Hudson River School*. New York: Abrams.

Michener, J. A. 1975. *Centennial*. Greenwich, Conn.: Fawcett Crest.

Morris, A. J. 1985. *The History of Larimer County, Colorado*. Dallas: Curtis Media Corp.

Morris. E. A. 1972–1979. *The Archeology of the Boxelder Project: A Water Control Project in Larimer County, North Central Colorado*. Prepared for Interagency Archeological Services, Denver; Heritage and Conservation and Recreation Service, U. S. Department of the Interior.

Pennock, I. O. 1982. *Happy Hardships: A Profile of Pioneer Growing Pains*. Fort Collins: Privately published.

Roberts, C. E. 1939. *The Bride of Bonner Peak*. Fort Collins: B and M Printing Co.

Rydberg, P. A. 1906. *Flora of Colorado. Colorado Agricultural Experiment Station Bulletin* 100. Fort Collins.

Steinel, A. T. 1926. *History of Agriculture in Colorado, 1858 to 1926*. Fort Collins: Colorado State Agricultural College.

Stejneger, L. H. 1936. *Georg Wilhelm Steller, the Pioneer of Alaskan Natural History*. Cambridge: Harvard University Press.

Swan, Wesley. 1972. *Memoirs of an Old Timer*. Privately published.

Swanson, E. B. 1971. *Red Feather Lakes: The First Hundred Years*. Fort Collins: Privately published.

———. 1975. *Fort Collins Yesterdays*. Fort Collins: Privately Published.

Sykes, H. W. [1935] 1982. *Second Hoeing*. Reprint. Lincoln: University of Nebraska Press.

Townsend, J. K. [1839] 1987. *Narrative of a Journey Across the Rocky Mountains to the Columbia River*. Lincoln: University of Nebraska Press.

Twain, Mark. 1871. *Roughing It*. Vol. 1. New York: Harper.

Watrous, Ansel. [1911] 1976. *History of Larimer County, Colorado*. Reprint. Fort Collins: M M Publications.

Wilson, Alexander. 1808–14. *American Ornithology*. 8 vols. Philadelphia: Abraham Rees.

TECHNICAL REPORTS AND LIFE HISTORY STUDIES

Allan, J. D., and A. S. Flecker. 1989. The Mating Biology of a Mass-swarming Mayfly. *Animal Behaviour* 37:361–71.

Baker, M. C., K. J. Spitler-Nabors, and D. G. Bradley. 1981. Early Experience Determines Song Dialect Responsiveness of Female Sparrows. *Science* 214: 819–20.

Beattie, A. J., D. E. Breedlove, and P. R. Ehrlich. 1973. The Ecology of the Pollinators and Predators of *Frasera speciosa*. *Ecology* 54:81–91.

Bent, A. C. 1940. *Life Histories of North American Cuckoos, Goatsuckers, Hummingbirds, and Their Allies. U.S. National Museum Bulletin* 176.

———. 1940. *Life Histories of North American Jays, Crows and Titmice*. Parts 1 and 2. New York: Dover.

Bent, A. C., et al. 1968. *Life Histories of North American Cardinals, Grosbeaks, Buntings, Towhees, Finches, Sparrows, and Allies. U.S. National Museum Bulletin* 237. Part 1.

Berenbaum, May. 1983. Coumarins and Caterpillars: A Case for Coevolution. *Evolution* 37:163–79.

Berg, Eric. 1987. Literature Review of Terrestrial Resources of the Cache la Poudre River, Colorado. Loveland: Northern Colorado Water Conservancy District. Mimeographed.

Black, P. E., E. C. Frank, R. H. Hawkins, R. C. Maloney, and J. R. Meiman. 1959. Watershed Analysis of the North Fork of the Cache la Poudre River. Fort Collins: Cooperative Watershed Management Unit, Colorado State University. Mimeographed.

Braun, C. E., R. W. Hoffman, and G. E. Rogers. 1976. Wintering Areas and Winter Ecology of White-tailed Ptarmigan in Colorado. *Special Report* 38. Denver: Colorado Division of Wildlife.

Colorado Division of Wildlife, Wildlife Management Section. 1978. Essential Habitat for Threatened and Endangered Wildlife in Colorado. Denver: Colorado Division of Wildlife.

Comstock, J. H., and A. B. Comstock. 1906. *A Manual for the Study of Insects*. Ithaca, N.Y.: Comstock Publishing Co.

Executive Task Force on the Future of Wildlife. 1987. Wildlife 21: A Report to the Governor, the Legislature, and the People of Colorado on the Future of Wildlife in the 21st Century. Denver: State of Colorado.

Getches, D. H. 1984. Water Law in a Nutshell. St. Paul, Minn.: West Publishing Co.

Grant, M. C., and J. B. Mitton. 1979. Elevational Gradients in Adult Sex Ratios and Sexual Differentiation in Vegetative Growth Rates of *Populus tremuloides* Michx. *Evolution* 33:914–18.

Gruchy, D. F. 1951. A Limnological Study of a Transect of the Cache la Poudre River. M. S. Thesis, Colorado State University.

Hartshorne, Charles. 1973. *Born to Sing: An Interpretation and World Survey of Bird Song*. Bloomington: Indiana University Press.

Haynes, C. M., and S. D. Aird. 1981. The Distribution and Habitat Requirements of the Wood Frog (Ranidae: *Rana sylvatica*) in Colorado. *Special Report* 50. Denver: Colorado Division of Wildlife.

Heinrich, Bernd. 1988. Why Do Ravens Fear Their Food? *The Condor* 90:950–52.

———. 1989. The Raven's Feast. *Natural History*. February.

Hocking, Brian. 1968. *Six-legged Science*. Cambridge, Mass: Schenkman Publishing Co.

Inouye, D. W., and O. R. Taylor, Jr. 1980. Variation in Generation Time in *Frasera speciosa* (Gentianaceae), a Longlived Perennial Monocarp. *Oecologica* 47:171–74.

Johnson, K. L., ed. 1962. Watershed Analysis of the Little South Fork of the Cache la Poudre River. Fort Collins: Cooperative Watershed Management Unit, Colorado State University. Mimeographed.

Jordan, D. S. 1907. *Fishes*. New York: Henry Holt and Co.

Klein, W. D. 1974. Special Regulations and Elimination of Stocking: Influence on Fishermen and the Trout Population at the Cache la Poudre River, Colorado. *Technical Publication* 30. Denver: Colorado Division of Wildlife.

League of Women Voters of Colorado. 1988. Colorado Water. Denver: League of Women Voters.

Linsdale, J. M. 1937. The Natural History of Magpies. *Pacific Coast Avifauna* 25.

Macior, L. W. 1974. Pollination Ecology of the Front Range of the Colorado Rocky Mountains. *Melanderia* 15:1–59.
Morrison, S. M. 1978. Surveillance Data. Plains Segment of the Cache la Poudre River Colorado 1970–1977. Colorado Water Resources Institute, Colorado State University, Information Series no. 25.
Nelson, C. R., and B. C. Kondratieff. 1988. A New Species of *Capnia* (Plecoptera: Capniidae) from the Rocky Mountains of Colorado. *Entomological News* 90:77–80.
Nortier, Molly, and Michael Smith. 1983. *"From Bucket to Basin": 100 Years of Water Service*. Fort Collins: City of Fort Collins.
Palmer, D. A. 1986. Habitat Selection, Movements and Activity of Boreal and Saw-whet Owls. M. S. Thesis, Colorado State University.
Pettus, David, and G. M. Angleton. 1967. Comparative Reproductive Biology of Montane and Piedmont Chorus Frogs. *Evolution* 21:500–507.
Probst, D. L. 1982. Warmwater Fishes of the Platte River Basin, Colorado; Distribution, Ecology, and Community Dynamics. Ph. D. Dissertation, Colorado State University.
Roberts, L. D. 1983. Riparian Habitat in the Proposed Grey Rocks Reservoir. M. S. Thesis, Colorado State University.
Schmitt, W. L. 1965. *Crustaceans*. Ann Arbor: University of Michigan Press.
Scott, Jim. 1988. "Rattles in their Tayles." *Colorado Outdoors* 37:2–5.
Short, R. A., S. P. Canton, and J. V. Ward. 1980. Detrital Processing and Associated Macroinvertebrates in a Colorado Mountain Stream. *Ecology* 61:727–32.
Short, R. A., and J. V. Ward. 1981. Trophic Ecology of Three Winter Stoneflies (Plecoptera). *American Midland Naturalist* 105:341–47.
Stolzenburg, William. 1989. What Are the Toads Telling Us? *Colorado Outdoors* 38:24–27.
Swisher, Douglas, and Carl Richards. 1971. *Selective Trout*. New York: Crown Publishers, Inc.
Tordoff, Walter, III, David Pettus, and T. C. Matthews. 1976. Microgeographic Variation in Gene Frequencies in *Pseudacris triseriata* (Amphibia, Anura, Hylidae). *Journal of Herpetology* 10:35–40.
Ward, J. V. 1986. Altitudinal Zonation in a Rocky Mountain Stream. *Archiv für Hydrobiologie*, Suppl. 74, pp. 133–99.
Weber, D. J., T. D. Davis, E. D. McArthur, and N. Sankhla. 1985. *Chrysothamnus nauseosus* (Rubber Rabbitbrush): Multiple-Use Shrub of the Desert. *Desert Plants* 7: 172–208.
Wentz, D. A. 1974. Environment of the Middle Segment, Cache la Poudre River, Colorado. Denver: Colorado Division of Wildlife.
Winternitz, B. L., and D. W. Crumpacker, eds. 1985. Colorado Wildlife Workshop. Species of Special Concern. Denver: Colorado Division of Wildlife.

Index